University Press

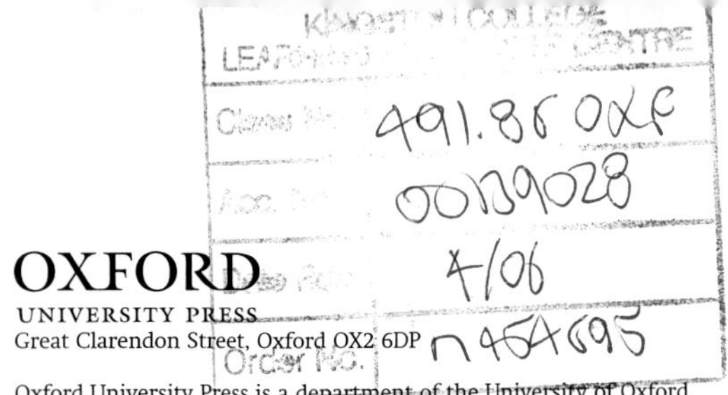

OXFORD
UNIVERSITY PRESS
Great Clarendon Street, Oxford OX2 6DP

Oxford University Press is a department of the University of Oxford. It furthers the University's objective of excellence in research, scholarship, and education by publishing worldwide in

Oxford New York

Auckland Bangkok Buenos Aires Cape Town Chennai Dar es Salaam Delhi Hong Kong Istanbul Karachi Kolkata Kuala Lumpur Madrid Melbourne Mexico City Mumbai Nairobi São Paulo Shanghai Taipei Tokyo Toronto

Oxford and Oxford English are registered trademarks of Oxford University Press in the UK and in certain other countries

First published 1992
Sixth impression 2005
Database right Oxford University Press (maker)

ISBN 0 19 431376 X

Editor: Jane Taylor

Printed in China

Acknowledgements

Location and studio photography by: Graham Alder, Chris Andrews, Martyn Chillmaid, Nigel Cull, Nick Fogden, Paul Freestone, Gareth Jones, Mark Mason.

The publishers would like to thank the following for permission to reproduce photographs: ABI Caravans Ltd; Allsport (UK) Ltd/B Asset, S Bruty, R Cheyne, T Duffy, S Dunn, J Gichigi, J Hayt, B Hazelton, H Heiderman, J Loubat, A Murrell, J Nicholson, M Powell, P Rondeau, H Stein; Animal Photography/S Thompson, R Willbie; Ardea London Ltd/D Avon, I Beames, L Beames, J Clegg, E Dragesco, M England, J Ferrero, K Fink, D Greenslade, A Lindau, J Mason, E Mickleburgh, P Morris, S Roberts, R & V Taylor, A Weaving, W Weisser; Art Directors Photo Library/S Grant; Associated Sports Photography; Clive Barda; Barnaby's Picture Library; J Allan Cash Ltd; Bruce Coleman Ltd/J Anthony, E & B Bauer, J Burton, M Dohrn, J Foot, N Fox-Davies, M Kahl, G Langsbury, W Layer, G McCarthy, M Price, A Purcell, H Reinhard, K Taylor, N Tomalin, R Wilmshurst; Colorsport/Compoint; Cotswold Wildlife Park; Cunard Line Ltd; Mary Evans Picture Library; Fiat Fork Lift Trucks; Michael Fogden; Ford Motor Company Ltd; Robert Harding Picture Library/Griffiths, G Renner; Eric Hoskin/W Pitt; Hovertravel Ltd; Libby Howells; The Hutchison Library/M Scorer; Rob Judges; Landscape Only; Frank Lane Picture Agency/A Albinger, R Jones, Silvestris, M Thomas, L West; Leyland Daf; London Tourist Board; Mazda Cars (UK) Ltd; Metropolitan Police; National Motor Museum, Beaulieu; Oxford Scientific Films Stills/S Dalton, L Lauber, M Leach, Partridge Films Ltd, Presstige Pictures, R Redfern, F Skibbe, G Wren; Planet Earth Pictures/Seaphot/M Clay, W Deas, D George, J George, K Lucas, J Lythgoe, N Middleton, J Scott, J Watt; Renault UK Ltd; Rex Features Ltd/N Jorgensen, J Tarrant; Rover Cars; RSPB/G Downey, P Perfect, M Richards; Science Photo Library/T Beddow, M Bond, Dr J Burgess, D Campione, M Dohrn, T Fearon-Jones, V Fleming, NASA, S Patel, R Royer, St Bartholomew's Hospital, J Sanford, S Stammers, J Stevenson, S Terry; Shell UK Ltd; Spectrum Colour Library; Swift Picture Library/T Dressler, M Mockler; Toleman Automotive Ltd; Trust House Forte; Wedgewood; World Pictures; Zefa/D Cattani, Damm, D Davies, Goebel, C Krebs, R Maylander, K Oster, J Pfaff, A Roberts, Rosenfeld, Selitsch.

The publishers would like to thank the following for their help and assistance: Abingdon Hospital; Abingdon Surgery; Russell Acott Ltd; Apollo Theatre; B & L Mechanical Services, Eynsham; Douglas Bader Sports Centre, St Edward's School; Barclays Bank; BBC Radio Oxford; The Bear & Ragged Staff, Cumnor; H C Biggers, Eynsham; Boswells of Oxford; Bournemouth International Airport; British Rail; Cassington Builders Ltd; Cheney School; Cherwell School; City Camera Exchange, Brighton; Comet; Daisies, Oxford; Early Learning Centre; Education & Sci Products Ltd; Elmer Cotton Sports, Oxford; Eynsham Car Repairs; Faulkner & Sons Ltd; For Eyes; Phylis Goodman Ltd, Eynsham; Habitat Designs Ltd; W R Hammond & Son Ltd, Eynsham; Hartford Motors Ltd; Headington Sports; Heather's Delicatessen, Hove; Hove Delicatessen; Inshape Body Studios Ltd; Johnsons of Oxford; Littlewoods PLC; London Underground Ltd; Malin Farms, Eynsham; P J Meagher, Eynsham; John Menzies Ltd; North Kidlington Primary School; Ocean Village Marina, Marina Developments PLC; Nigel Olesen BDS; Options Hair Studio, Eynsham; Oxford Despatch; Oxford Royal Mail & Post Office Counters; Paramount Sewing Machines; Parkwood Veterinary Group; Payless DIY; Phoenix One & Two; Qualifruit; Red Funnel Isle of Wight Ferries; SS Mary & John School; Southampton Eastleigh Airport; Stanhope Wilkinson Associates, Eynsham; Summertown Travel; Texas Homecare, Oxford; Paul Thomas; Richard Walton, Eynsham; Warlands, Cycle Agents; Welsh National Opera; Western Newsagents, Hove; Chris Yapp Consultants Ltd.

Obsah

1 Příbuzenské vztahy
3 Lidské tělo
5 Fyzický vzhled
6 Co je jim?
7 Zdravotní péče
9 Barvy a vzory
10 Oděvy
12 Masky
13 Budovy
15 Jídelna
16 Obývací pokoj
17 Koupelna
18 Ložnice
19 Komora
20 Kuchyně
21 Nářadí
22 Zahrada
23 Na trhu
25 V květinářství
26 V trafice
27 V lahůdkářství
28 V restauraci
29 Ve Foto-Kinu
30 V prodejně elektroniky
31 Poštovní služby
33 Čísla/Datum
34 V bance
35 Americké peníze
36 Britské peníze
37 Čas
38 Pohotovostní služba
39 Zaměstnání
41 Denní režim
43 Slovesa z kancelářské praxe
44 Kancelář
45 Laboratoř
47 Tvary a čáry
48 Rozměry, váhy, + - ÷ x
49 Třída
50 Vesmír
51 Počasí
52 Teplota/Roční období
53 Svět
55 USA
56 Britské ostrovy
57 Předložky
59 Město
61 Silnice a dopravní značky
63 Vozidla
64 Automobil
65 Jízdní kolo a motocykl
66 Železnice
67 Na letišti
69 V přístavu
71 Dovolená
73 Životní prostředí
74 Záliby
75 Hudební nástroje
76 Hudba a divadlo
77 Sporty
82 Udržování kondice
83 Slovesa
87 Protikladná přídavná jména
89 Zvířata
91 Ryby a plazi
92 Hmyz a další živočichové
93 Ptáci
94 Fonetické symboly/Značení britských a amerických termínů
95 Rejstřík
126 Cvičení
141 Klíč ke cvičením

Family Relationships page 1

Johnova rodina	John's Family
babička	**1** grandmother
dědeček	**2** grandfather
teta	**3** aunt
strýc	**4** uncle
matka	**5** mother
otec	**6** father
tchán	**7** father-in-law
tchyně	**8** mother-in-law
sestřenice/bratranec	**9** cousin
švagr	**10** brother-in-law
sestra	**11** sister
manželka	**12** wife
švagrová	**13** sister-in-law
neteř	**14** niece
synovec	**15** nephew
syn	**16** son
dcera	**17** daughter

John je Annin **manžel**.	**18** John is Ann's **husband**.
Tom a Lisa jsou **děti** Johna a Anny.	**19** Tom and Lisa are John and Ann's **children**.
John a Anna jsou **rodiče** Toma a Lisy.	**20** John and Ann are Tom and Lisa's **parents**.
Mary a Bob Coxovi a Ian a Jane Hillovi jsou **prarodiče** Toma a Lisy.	**21** Mary and Bob Cox and Ian and Jane Hill are Tom and Lisa's **grandparents**.
Tom je jejich **vnuk**.	**22** Tom is their **grandson**.
Lisa je jejich **vnučka**.	**23** Lisa is their **granddaughter**.

Family Relationships

The Human Body 1

page 3

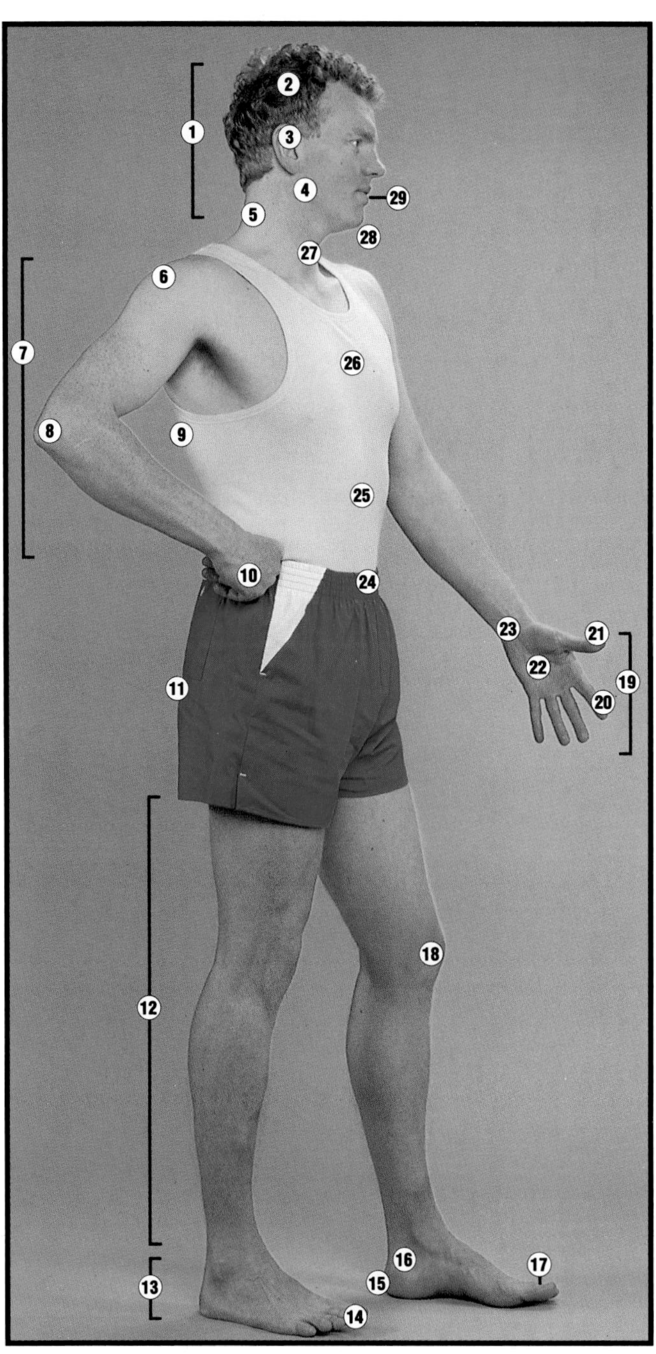

hlava **1** head
vlasy **2** hair
ucho **3** ear
čelist **4** jaw
krk **5** neck
rameno **6** shoulder
paže **7** arm
loket **8** elbow
záda **9** back
pěst **10** fist
hýždě/zadek **11** buttocks/bottom
noha **12** leg
chodidlo **13** foot
prst (u nohy) **14** toe
pata **15** heel
kotník **16** ankle
nehet **17** nail
koleno **18** knee
ruka **19** hand
prst **20** finger
palec **21** thumb
dlaň **22** palm
zápěstí **23** wrist
pás **24** waist
břicho **25** stomach
hruď **26** chest
hrdlo **27** throat
brada **28** chin
ústa **29** mouth

The Human Body 2

page 4

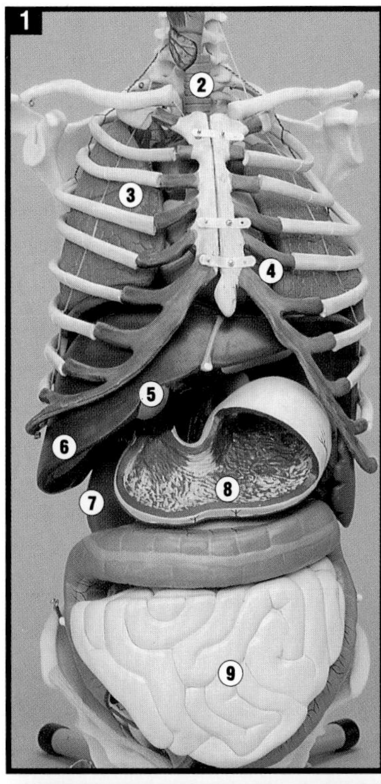

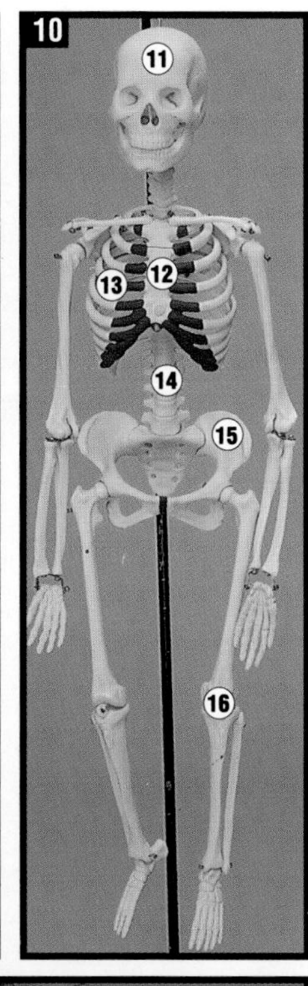

vnitřní orgány	**1** internal organs
průdušnice	**2** trachea/windpipe
plíce	**3** lung
srdce	**4** heart
žlučník	**5** gall-bladder
játra	**6** liver
ledvina	**7** kidney
žaludek	**8** stomach
střeva	**9** intestines
kostra	**10** skeleton
lebka	**11** skull
hrudní kost	**12** breastbone
žebro	**13** rib
páteř	**14** spine/backbone
pánev/kyčelní kost	**15** pelvis/hip-bone
čéška	**16** kneecap

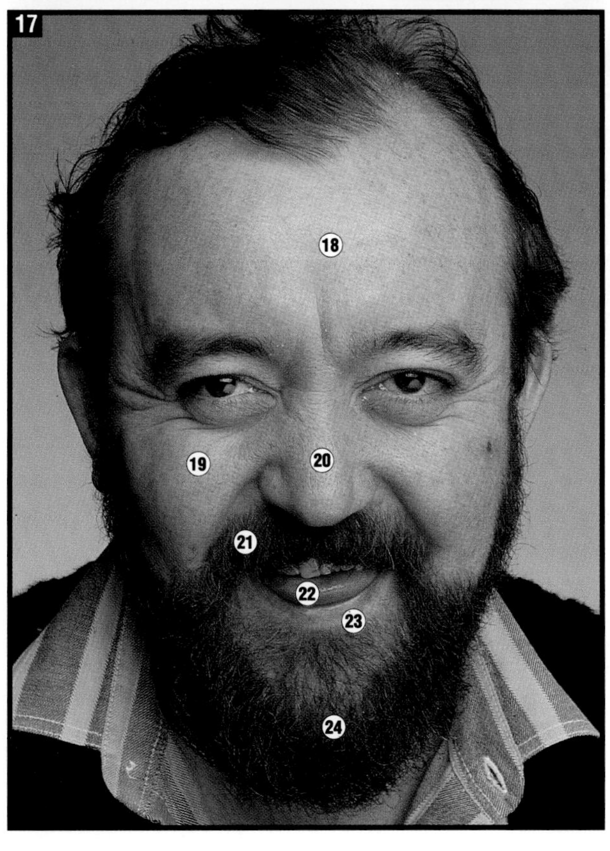

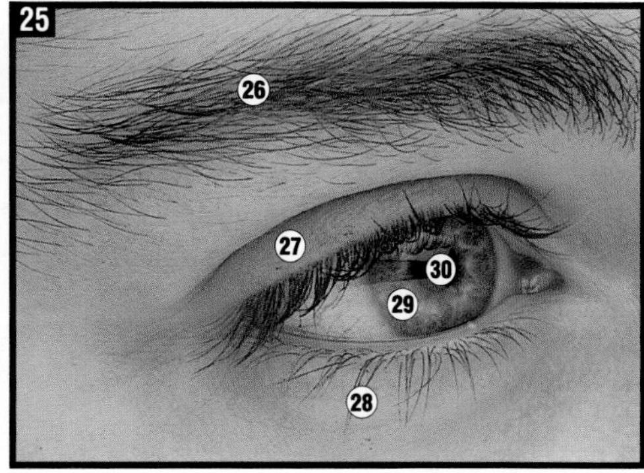

obličej	**17** face
čelo	**18** forehead
tvář	**19** cheek
nos	**20** nose
knír	**21** moustache
jazyk	**22** tongue
ret	**23** lip
plnovous	**24** beard
oko	**25** eye
obočí	**26** eyebrow
oční víčko	**27** eyelid
oční řasa	**28** eyelash
duhovka	**29** iris
zornice	**30** pupil

Physical Description

page 5

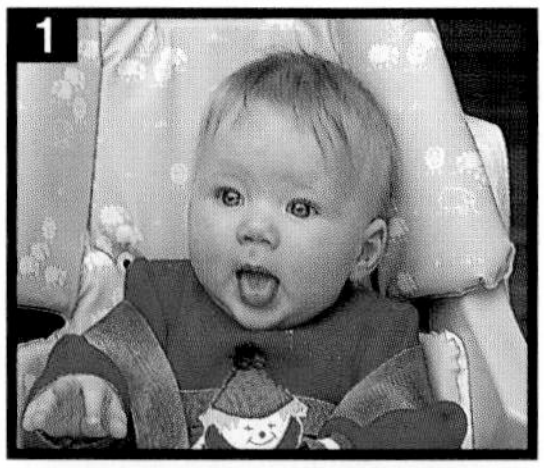

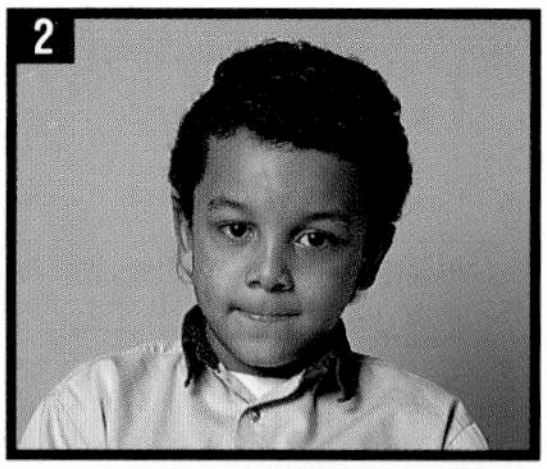

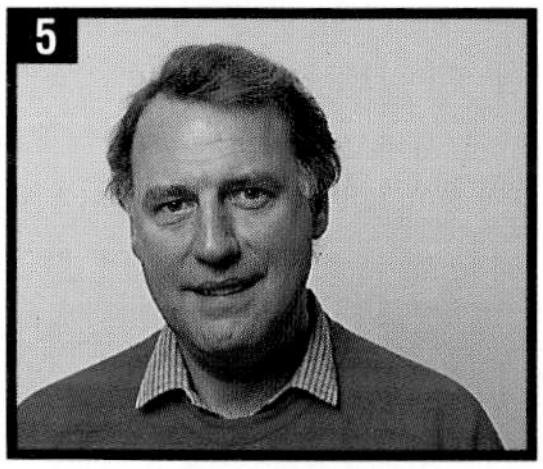

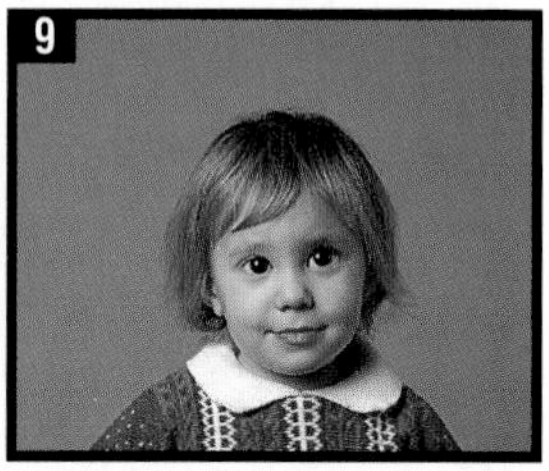

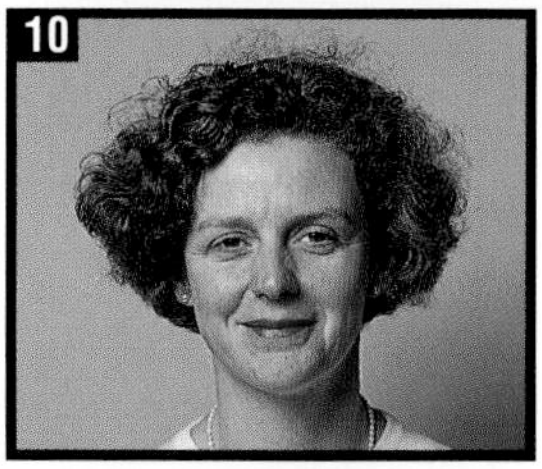

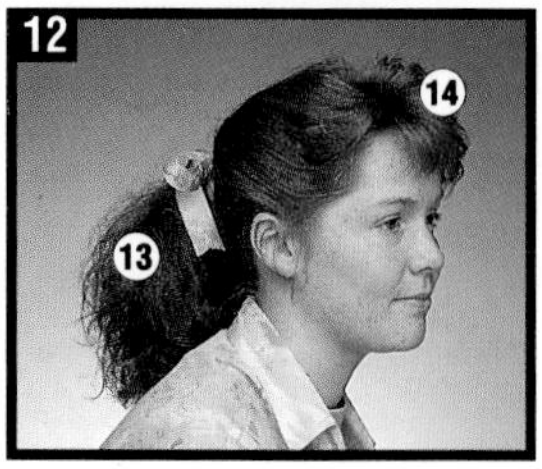

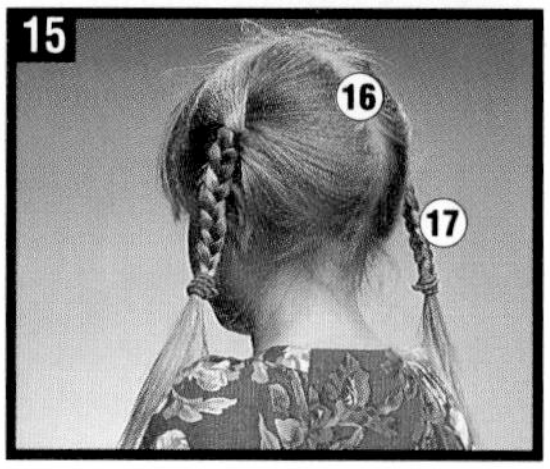

Věk	**Age**
mimino/malé dítě	**1** baby
dítě/chlapec	**2** child/(young) boy
teenager/dívka	**3** teenager/teenage girl
dospělá/žena	**4** adult/woman
dospělý/muž	**5** adult/man
starší (*nebo* starý) muž	**6** elderly (*or* old) man
Vlasy	**Hair**
pleš	**7** bald head
krátké rovné tmavé	**8** short straight dark
krátké rovné světlé	**9** short straight fair
krátké kudrnaté	**10** short curly
krátké vlnité	**11** short wavy
dlouhé ryšavé/zrzavé	**12** long red (*Brit also* ginger)
ohon	**13** pony tail
ofina	**14** fringe (*US* bangs)
dlouhé blond	**15** long blonde
pěšinka	**16** parting (*US* part)
cop	**17** plait (*US* braid)
vysoký/velký	**18** tall
malý	**19** short
hubený	**20** thin
tlustý	**21** fat

What's the matter?

page 6

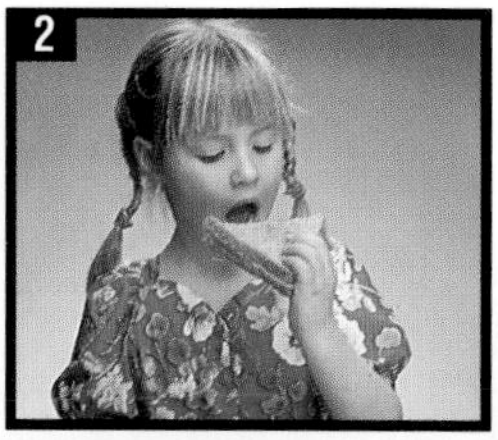

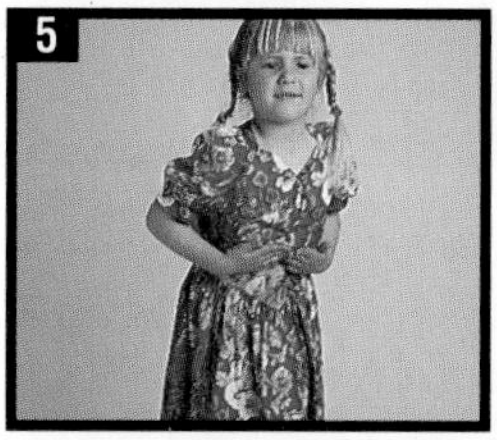

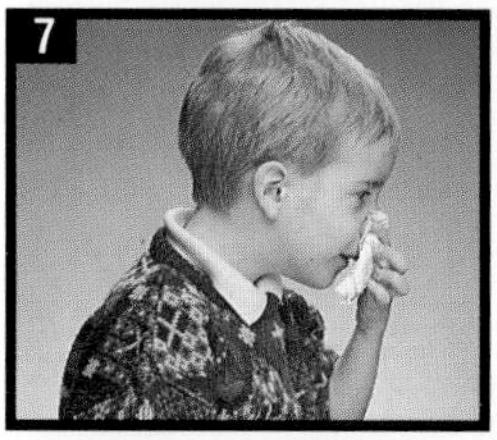

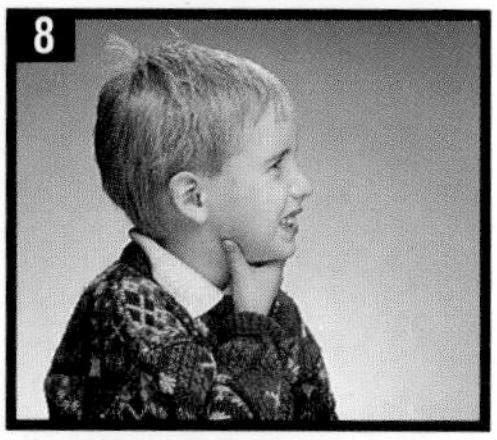

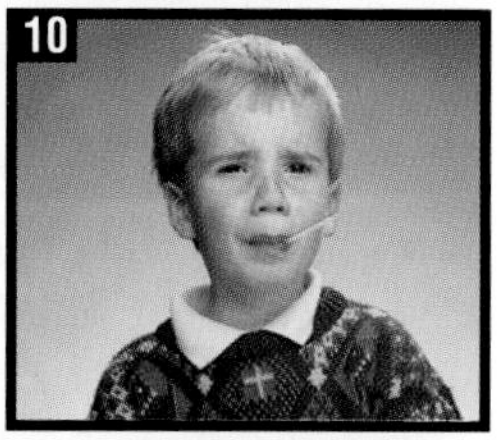

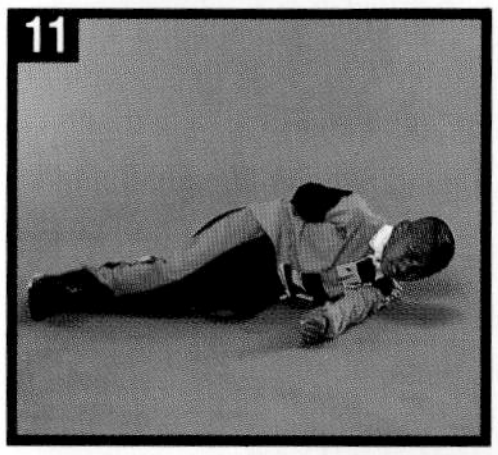

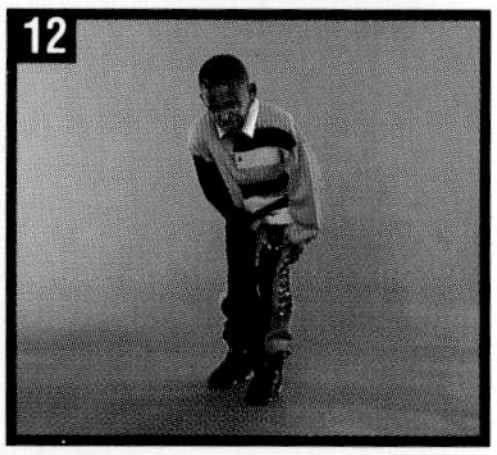

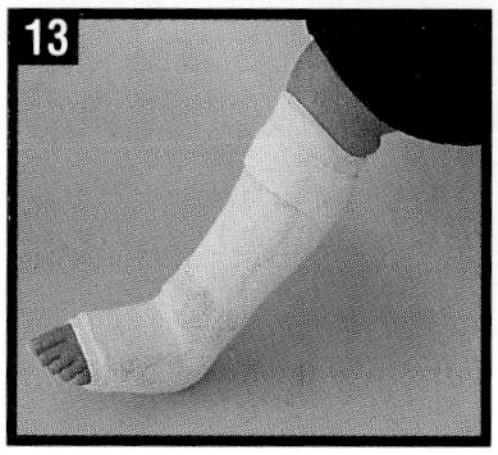

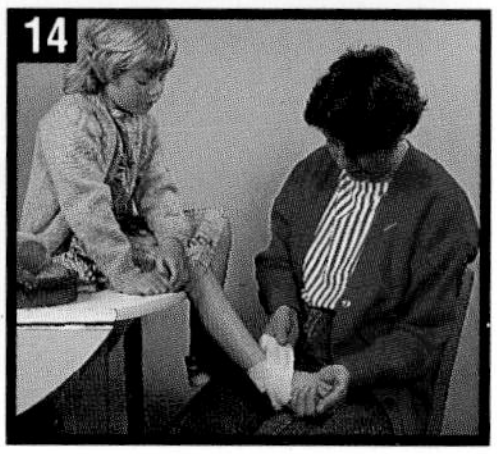

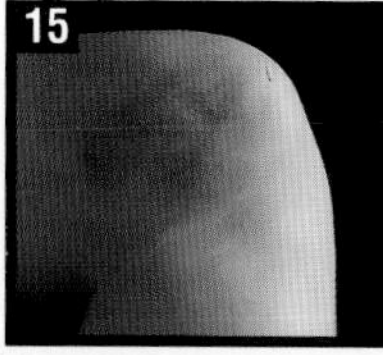

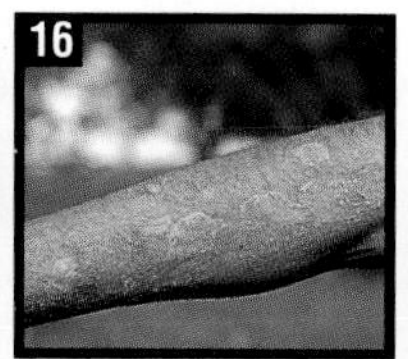

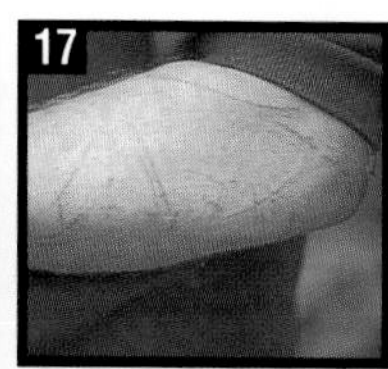

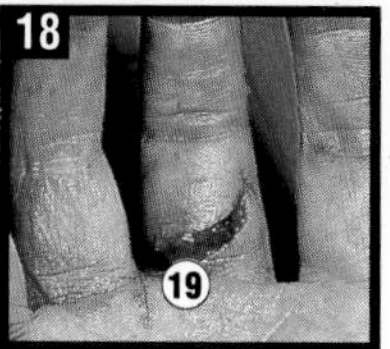

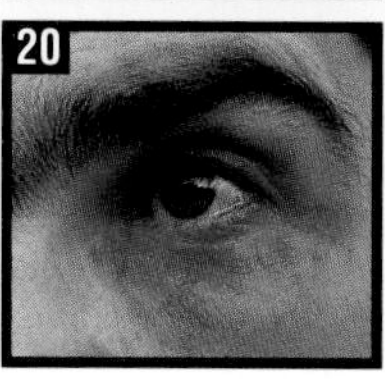

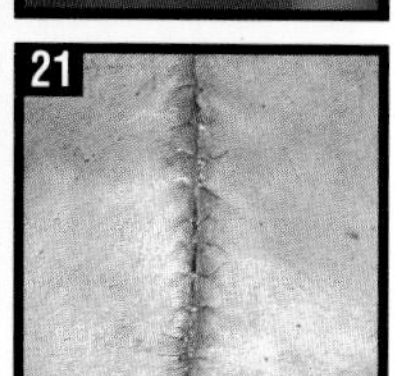

Má žízeň.	**1** She's thirsty.
Má hlad.	**2** She's hungry.
Je unavená.	**3** She's tired.
Bolí ji zub.	**4** She's got toothache. (*US* She has a toothache.)
Bolí ji břicho.	**5** She's got stomach-ache. (*US* She has a stomachache.)
Bolí ji hlava.	**6** She's got a headache. (*US* She has a headache.)
Je nachlazený.	**7** He's got a cold. (*US* He has a cold.)
Bolí ho v krku.	**8** He's got a sore throat. (*US* He has a sore throat.)
Má kašel.	**9** He's got a cough. (*US* He has a cough.)
Má teplotu.	**10** He's got a temperature. (*US* He has a temperature.)
Úrazy	**Accidents**
Upadl.	**11** He's fallen over. (*US* He fell over.)
Poranil si nohu.	**12** He's hurt his leg. (*US* He hurt his leg.)
Zlomila si nohu.	**13** She's broken her leg. (*US* She broke her leg.)
Vyvrtla si kotník.	**14** She's sprained her ankle. (*US* She sprained her ankle.)
modřina	**15** bruise
spálenina (ze slunce)	**16** sunburn
škrábanec	**17** scratch
říznutí	**18** cut
krev	**19** blood
monokl	**20** black eye
jizva	**21** scar

Health Care 1 page 7

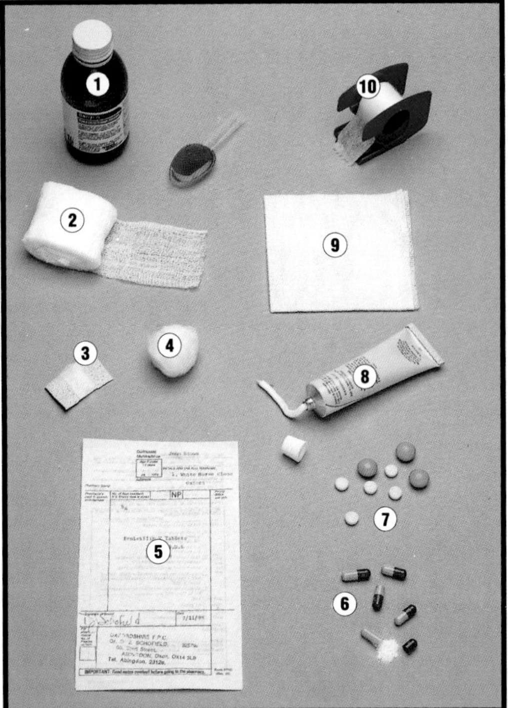

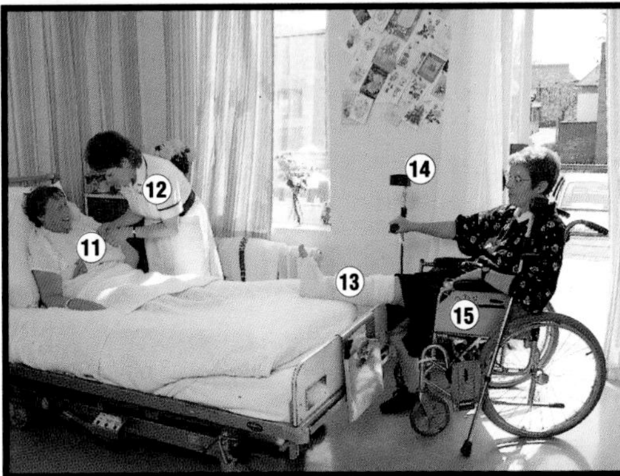

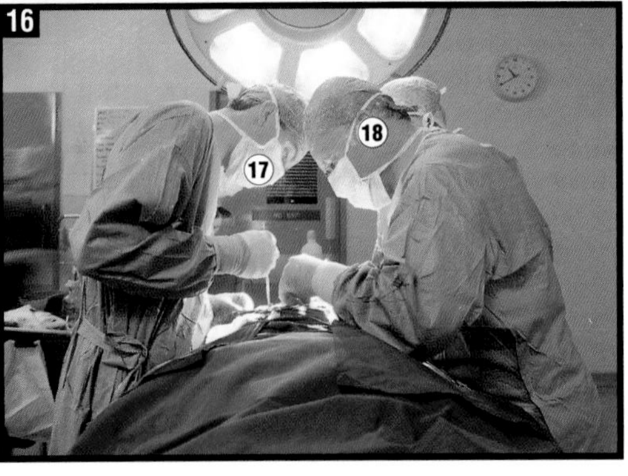

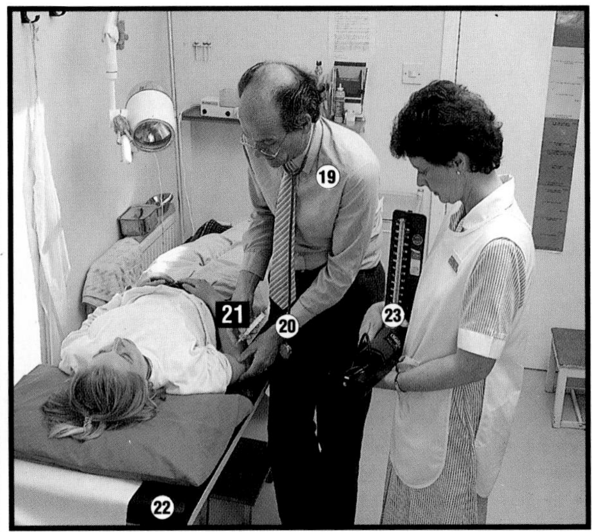

lék	**1** medicine
obvaz	**2** bandage
náplast	**3** (sticking-)plaster (*US* Band-Aid)
vata	**4** cotton wool (*US* cotton ball)
lékařský předpis	**5** prescription
kapsle	**6** capsule
tableta	**7** pill/tablet
mast	**8** ointment
gáza	**9** gauze pad
leukoplast	**10** adhesive tape
Nemocniční pokoj	**Hospital Ward (*US also* Hospital Room)**
páska	**11** sling
zdravotní sestra	**12** nurse
sádrový obvaz	**13** plaster cast (*US* cast)
berle	**14** crutch
invalidní vozík	**15** wheelchair
Operace	**Operation**
operační sál	**16** operating theatre (*US* operating room)
rouška	**17** mask
chirurg	**18** surgeon
Ordinace	**Doctor's Surgery (*US* Doctor's Office)**
lékař	**19** doctor
stetoskop	**20** stethoscope
injekce	**21** injection
vyšetřovací lůžko	**22** examination couch (*US* examining table/ examination table)
tonometr	**23** blood pressure gauge

Health Care 2

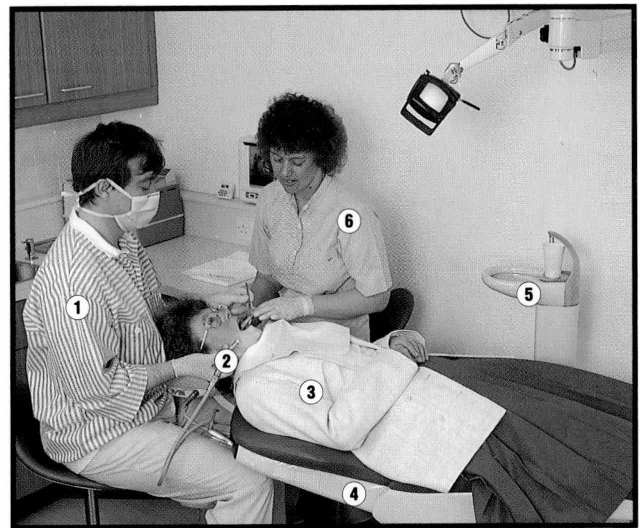

U zubaře	At the Dentist's
zubař	**1** dentist
zubní vrtačka	**2** drill
pacient	**3** patient
zubařské křeslo	**4** dentist's chair
plivátko	**5** basin
zubní sestra	**6** dental nurse (*US* dental assistant)
dáseň	**7** gum
zub	**8** tooth
plomba	**9** filling
rentgen	**10** X-ray (*also* x-ray)
přední zuby	**11** front teeth
stoličky	**12** back teeth

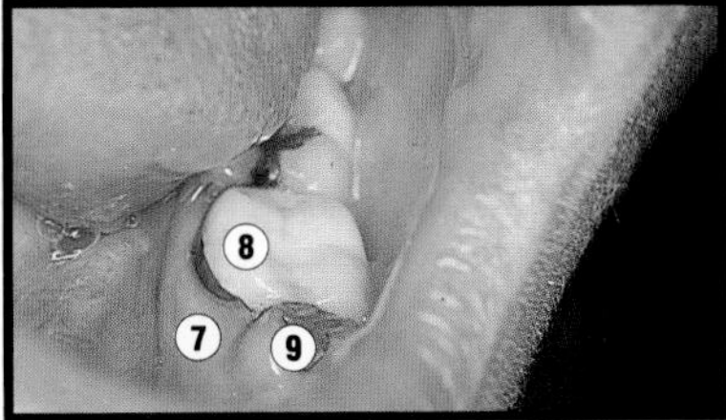

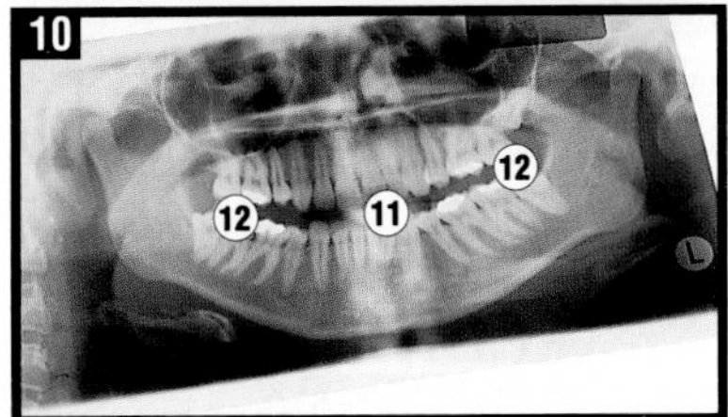

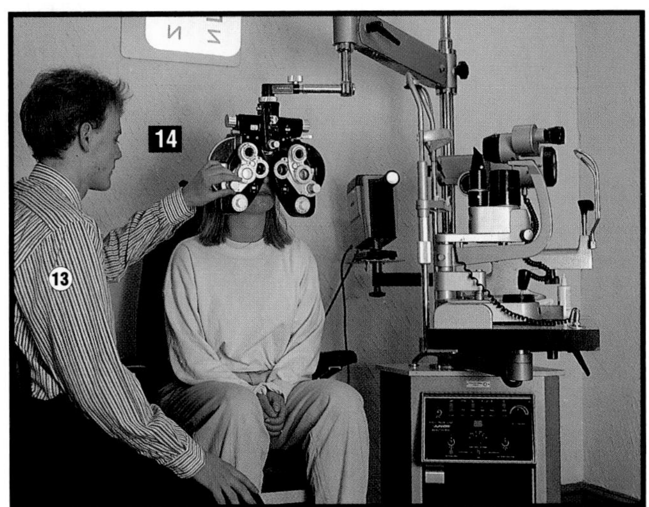

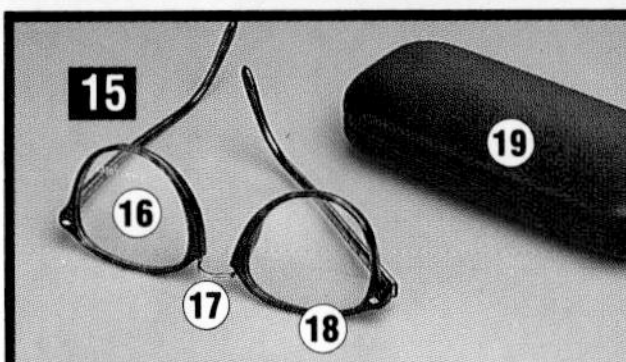

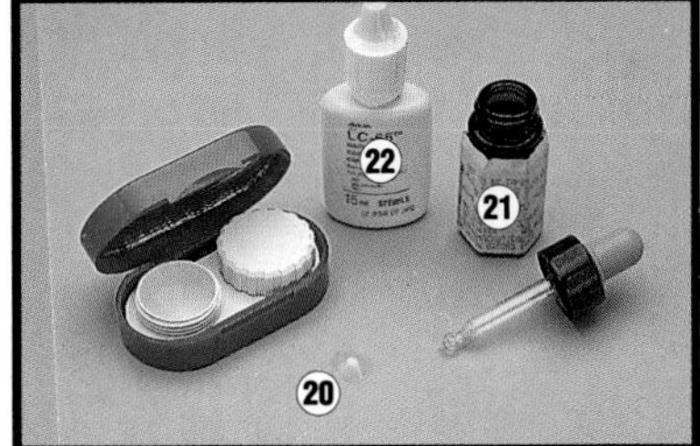

U optika	At the Optician's
optik	**13** optician
oční vyšetřeni	**14** eye test
brýle	**15** (pair of) glasses
čočka	**16** lens
nosník	**17** bridge
obroučky	**18** frame
pouzdro na brýle	**19** glasses case (*US also* eyeglass case)
kontaktní čočka	**20** contact lens
oční kapky	**21** eye drops
roztok na čištěni kontaktních čoček	**22** contact lens cleaner

Describing Clothes

page 9

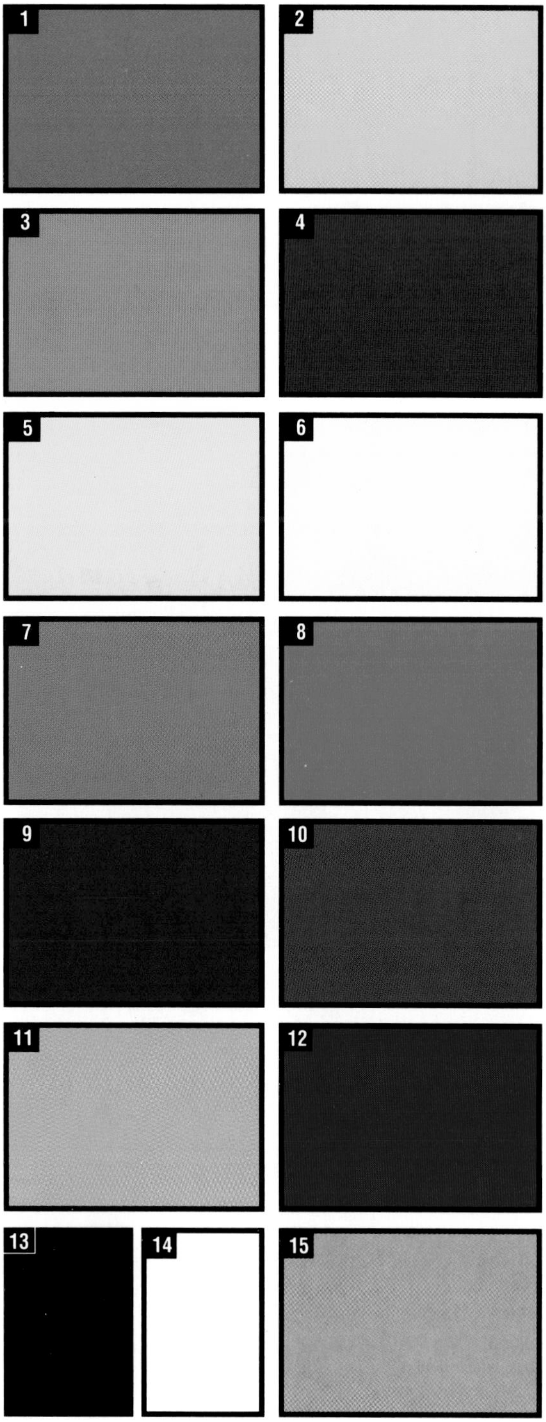

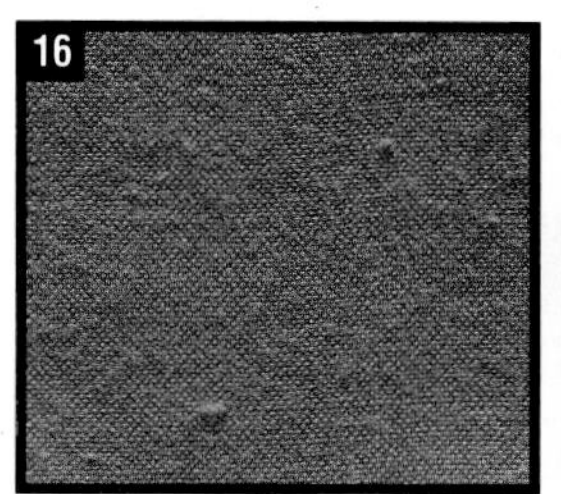

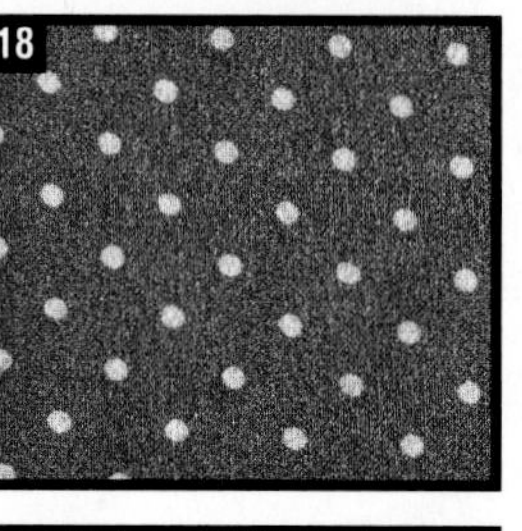

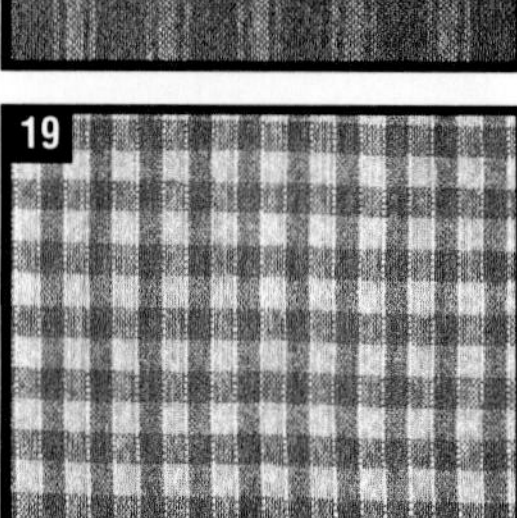

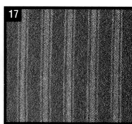

Barvy	Colours (*US* Colors)
červená	**1** red
růžová	**2** pink
oranžová	**3** orange
hnědá	**4** brown
žlutá	**5** yellow
krémová	**6** cream
modrá	**7** blue
tyrkysová	**8** turquoise
tmavomodrá	**9** navy
fialová	**10** purple
světle zelená	**11** light green
tmavě zelená	**12** dark green
černá	**13** black
bílá	**14** white
šedá	**15** grey (*esp US* gray)

Vzory	Patterns
bez vzoru/jednobarevný	**16** plain (*US* solid)
proužkovaný	**17** striped
puntíkovaný	**18** polka-dot
kostkovaný	**19** check (*US* checked)
skotská kostka/tartanový	**20** tartan (*US* plaid)
se vzorem/vzorovaný	**21** patterned (*US* print)

page 10

Clothes 1

školní uniforma	**1**	school uniform
čepice	**2**	cap
blejzr	**3**	blazer
kalhoty	**4**	trousers (*US* pants)
tričko	**5**	T-shirt
svetr	**6**	sweater
džíny	**7**	jeans
sako	**8**	jacket
halenka	**9**	blouse
kabelka	**10**	handbag (*US also* purse)
sukně	**11**	skirt
aktovka	**12**	briefcase
bota (nad kotníky)	**13**	boot
šála	**14**	scarf
rukavice	**15**	glove
deštník	**16**	umbrella
kabát	**17**	coat
oblek	**18**	suit
košile	**19**	shirt
kravata	**20**	tie
kapesník	**21**	handkerchief
plášť do deště	**22**	raincoat
polobotka	**23**	shoe

Clothes 2 page 11

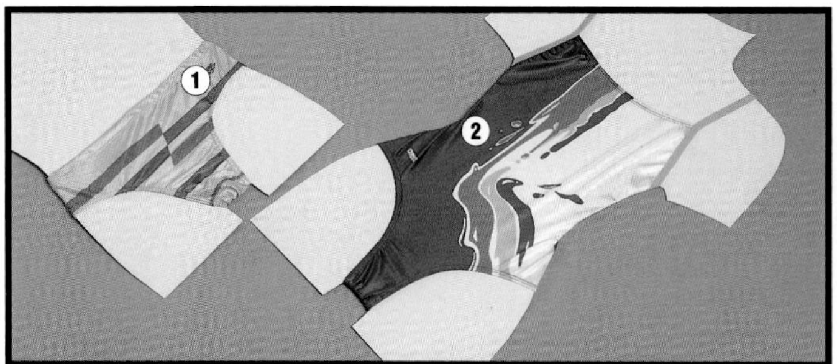

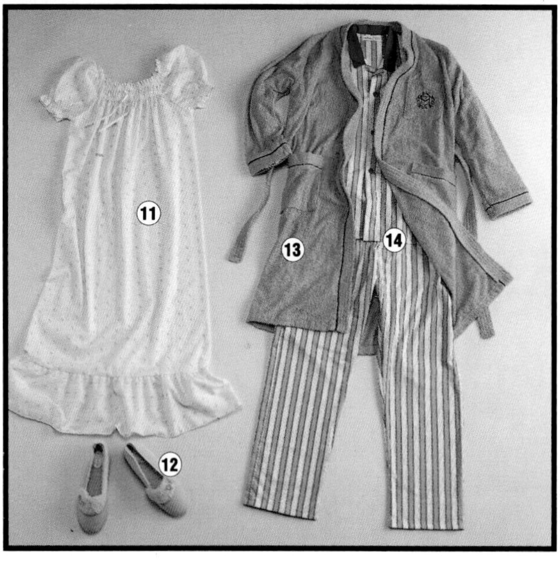

plavky (pánské)	**1** swimming-trunks (*US* bathing suit)
plavky (dámské)	**2** swimsuit (*US* bathing suit)
spodní prádlo	**3** underwear
ponožky	**4** socks
kombiné	**5** full slip
punčochy	**6** stockings
punčochové kalhoty	**7** tights (*US* pantyhose)
spodnička	**8** half slip
podprsenka	**9** bra
slipy/kalhotky	**10** pants (*US* underpants)
noční košile	**11** night-dress (*US* nightgown)
pantofel	**12** slipper
župan	**13** dressing gown (*US* robe)
pyžamo	**14** pyjamas (*US* pajamas)
límec	**15** collar
rukáv	**16** sleeve
manžeta	**17** cuff
kapsa	**18** pocket
spona	**19** buckle
podpatek	**20** heel
náprsní taška	**21** wallet
peněženka	**22** purse (*US* wallet)
tkanička	**23** shoelace

page 12

Dressing up

automobilový závodník	**1** racing driver (*US* race car driver)
přilba/helma	**2** helmet
tepláková souprava	**3** track suit (*US also* jogging suit)
teniska	**4** trainer (*US* sneaker)
cikánka	**5** gypsy
šátek	**6** scarf
propínací svetr	**7** cardigan
opánek/sandál	**8** sandal
boxer	**9** boxer
tílko	**10** vest (*US* tank top)
pásek	**11** belt
krátké kalhoty/šortky	**12** shorts
netvor	**13** monster
mikina	**14** sweatshirt
hodinky	**15** watch
čarodějnice	**16** witch
klobouk	**17** hat
sluneční brýle	**18** sun-glasses
šaty	**19** dress
líčidla	**20** make-up
rtěnka	**21** lipstick

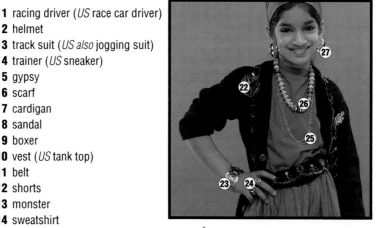

Šperky	**Jewellery (*esp US* Jewelry)**
brož	**22** brooch (*US* pin)
náramek	**23** bracelet
prsten	**24** ring
řetízek	**25** chain
náhrdelník	**26** necklace
náušnice	**27** earring

Buildings 1

page 13

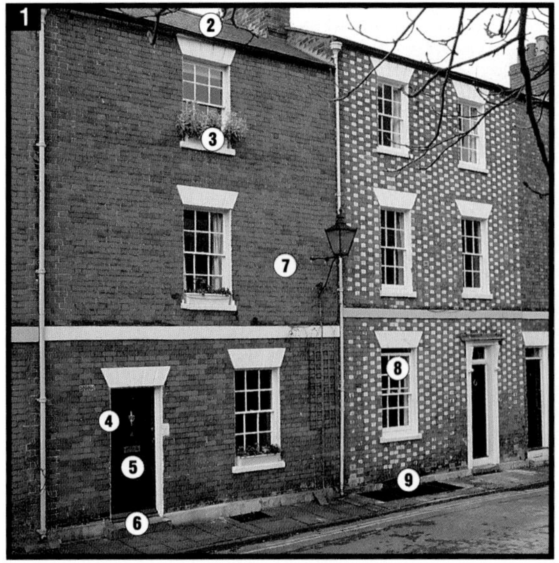

řadový dům	**1** terraced house (*US* town house)
břidlicová střecha	**2** slate roof
květinový truhlík	**3** window-box
klepadlo	**4** knocker
schránka na dopisy	**5** letter-box (*US* mailbox)
práh	**6** doorstep
cihlová zeď	**7** brick wall
vysunovací okno	**8** sash window
suterénní okno	**9** basement window
nájemní dům/činžovní dům	**10** block of flats (*US* apartment house)
nejvyšší patro	**11** top floor
balkon	**12** balcony
první patro	**13** first floor (*US* second floor)
přízemí	**14** ground floor (*US also* first floor)
parkoviště	**15** car-park (*US* parking lot)
Stavební materiál	**Building Materials**
cihla	**16** brick
kámen	**17** stone
beton	**18** concrete
taška	**19** tile
břidlice	**20** slate
došek	**21** thatch
dřevo	**22** wood
sklo	**23** glass

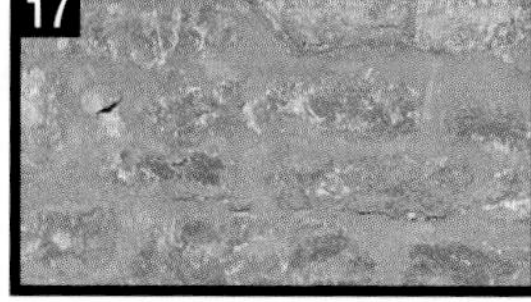

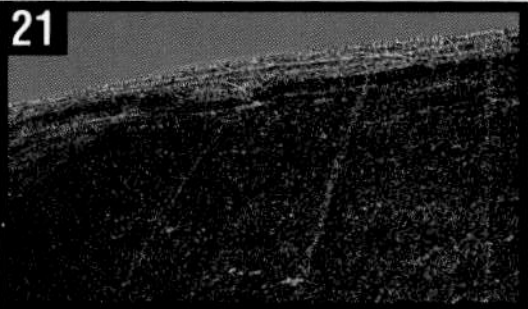

page 14

Buildings 2

rodinný domek	**1** detached house (*US* one-family house)
garáž	**2** garage
vchod	**3** front door
sloup	**4** pillar
okenice	**5** shutter
dvojdomek	**6** semi-detached house (*US* two-family house)
komín	**7** chimney
okno	**8** window
okenní římsa	**9** window-sill/window-ledge
klenba/oblouk	**10** arch
arkýřové okno	**11** bay window
betonová zeď	**12** concrete wall
chalupa	**13** cottage
došková střecha	**14** thatched roof
vikýř	**15** dormer
krytý vchod	**16** porch
dřevěná vrátka	**17** wooden gate
kamenná zeď	**18** stone wall
bungalov	**19** bungalow (*US* ranch house)
televizní anténa	**20** TV aerial (*US* antenna)
okapová roura	**21** drainpipe
okapový žlab	**22** gutter
tašková střecha	**23** tiled roof

The Dining-room page15

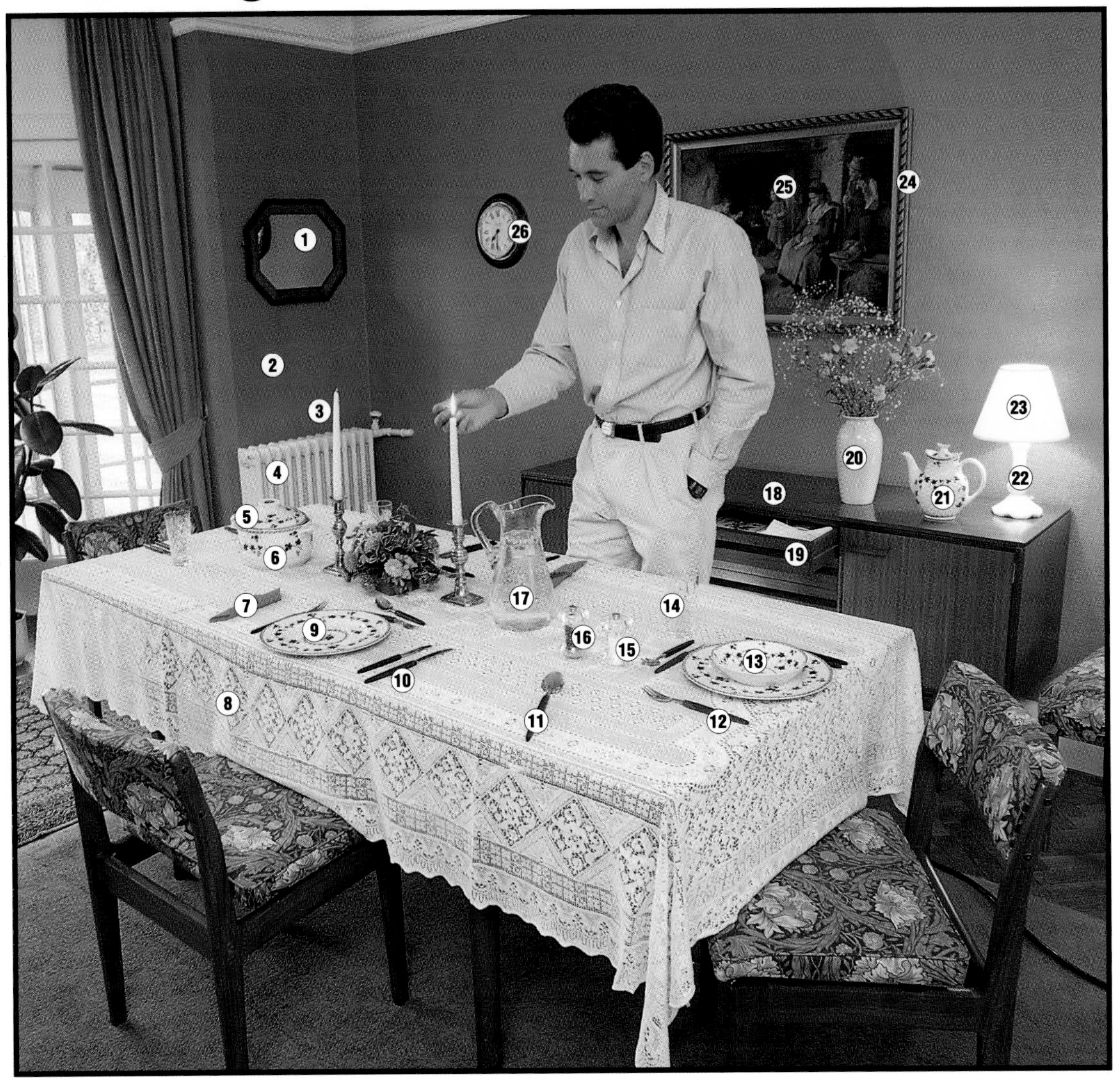

zrcadlo	**1** mirror
stěna	**2** wall
svíčka	**3** candle
radiátor	**4** radiator
poklička	**5** lid
mísa	**6** dish
ubrousek	**7** napkin
ubrus	**8** table-cloth
talíř	**9** plate
nůž	**10** knife
lžíce	**11** spoon
vidlička	**12** fork
miska	**13** bowl
sklenice	**14** glass
sůl	**15** salt
pepř	**16** pepper
džbán	**17** jug (*US* pitcher)
příborník	**18** sideboard (*US* buffet)
zásuvka	**19** drawer
váza	**20** vase
kávová konvice	**21** coffee-pot
lampa	**22** lamp
stínítko	**23** lampshade
rám	**24** frame
obraz	**25** painting
hodiny	**26** clock

The Living-room

strop	**1** ceiling
římsa nad krbem	**2** mantelpiece (*US* mantel)
krb	**3** fireplace
oheň	**4** fire
poleno	**5** log
předložka	**6** rug
koberec	**7** carpet
konferenční stolek	**8** coffee-table
dálkové ovládání	**9** remote control
krabice na sušenky	**10** biscuit tin (*US* cookie tin)
čajová konvice	**11** teapot
podnos/tác	**12** tray
podšálek	**13** saucer
šálek	**14** cup
lžička	**15** teaspoon
koš na papíry	**16** waste-paper basket
pohovka	**17** sofa (*esp US* couch)
polštář	**18** cushion
rostlina	**19** plant
závěsy	**20** curtains (*US* drapes)
sektorová stěna	**21** wall unit
křeslo	**22** armchair
televizor	**23** television/TV
videorekordér	**24** video cassette recorder/VCR

The Bathroom page 17

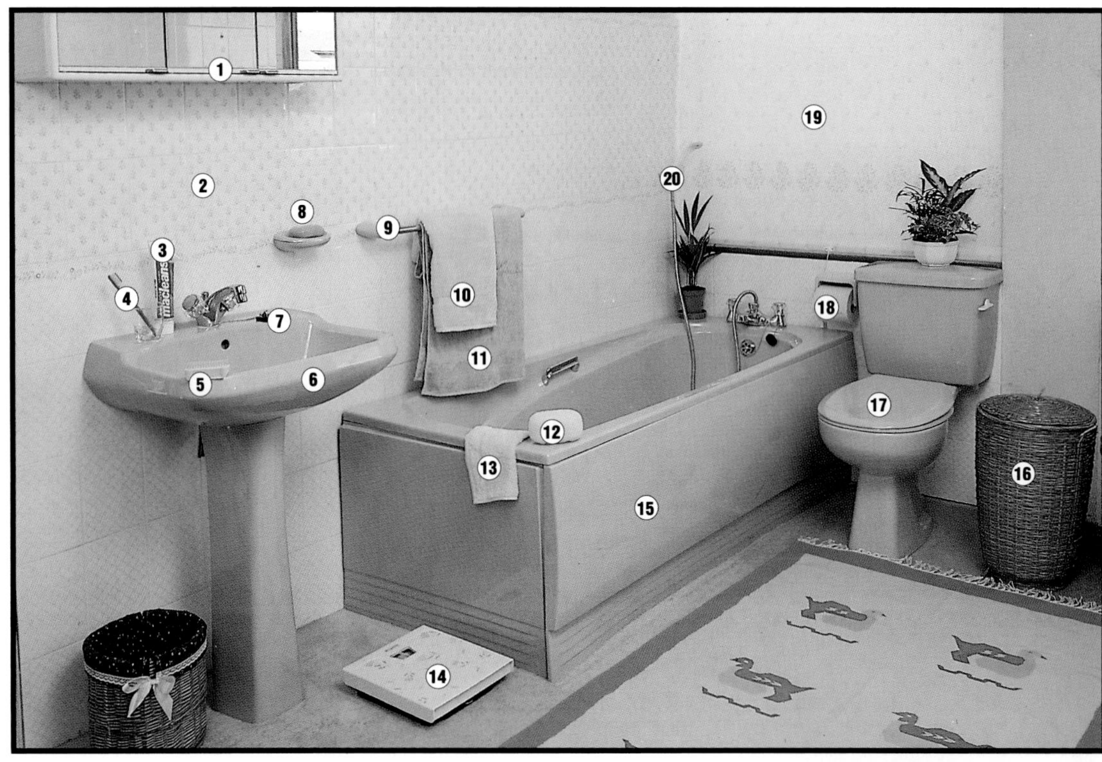

koupelnová skříňka	**1**	bathroom cabinet (*US* medicine chest/cabinet)
kachlík	**2**	tile
tuba zubní pasty	**3**	tube of toothpaste
zubní kartáček	**4**	toothbrush
kartáček na nehty	**5**	nail-brush
umyvadlo	**6**	wash-basin (*US* sink)
zátka	**7**	plug (*US* stopper)
kostka mýdla	**8**	bar of soap
věšák na ručníky	**9**	towel-rail (*US* towel rack)
ručník	**10**	hand-towel
osuška	**11**	bath-towel
(mycí) houba	**12**	sponge
žínka	**13**	flannel (*US* washcloth)
váha	**14**	(bathroom) scales (*US* scale)
vana	**15**	bath (*US* bathtub)
koš na prádlo	**16**	laundry basket (*US* hamper)
záchod	**17**	toilet
toaletní papír	**18**	toilet paper
roleta	**19**	blind (*US* shade)
sprcha	**20**	shower
voda po holení	**21**	aftershave (*US* after-shave lotion)
elektrický holicí strojek	**22**	electric razor
holicí strojek	**23**	razor
žiletka	**24**	razor-blade
pěna na holení	**25**	shaving-foam (*US* shaving cream)
šampon	**26**	shampoo
hřeben	**27**	comb
(talkový) pudr	**28**	talcum powder (*also* talc)

page 18

The Bedroom

toaletní stolek **1** dressing table (*US* dresser)
ložní prádlo **2** bed-linen
postel **3** bed
přehoz **4** bedspread
přikrývka/deka **5** blanket
prostěradlo **6** sheet
povlak na polštář **7** pillowcase
kartáč na vlasy **8** hairbrush
rabice papírových kapesníků **9** box of tissues
noční stolek **10** bedside cabinet (*US* night table)
matrace **11** mattress
polštář **12** pillow
záhlaví postele **13** headboard
budík **14** alarm clock
plakát **15** poster
světlo **16** light
šatník **17** wardrobe (*US* closet)
ramínko na šaty **18** coat-hanger (*esp US* hanger)
prádelník **19** chest of drawers (*US also* bureau)
vysoušeč vlasů **20** hair-drier (*or* hair-dryer)

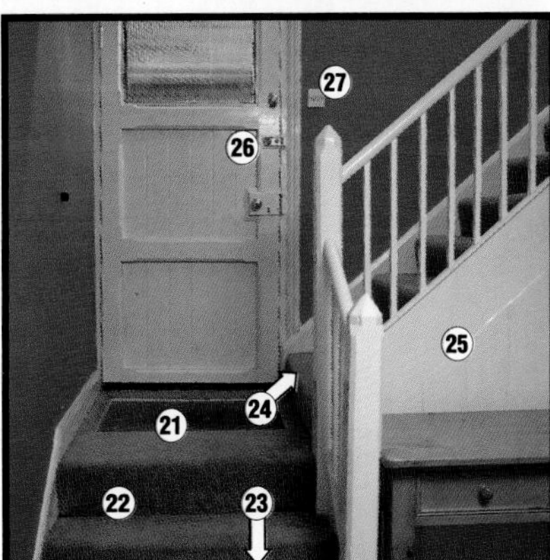

rohožka **21** doormat
schod **22** stair (*esp US* step)
dolů (ze schodů) **23** downstairs
nahoru (do schodů) **24** upstairs
schodiště **25** staircase
zámek **26** lock
vypínač (světla) **27** light switch

The Utility Room (*US also* Laundry Room)

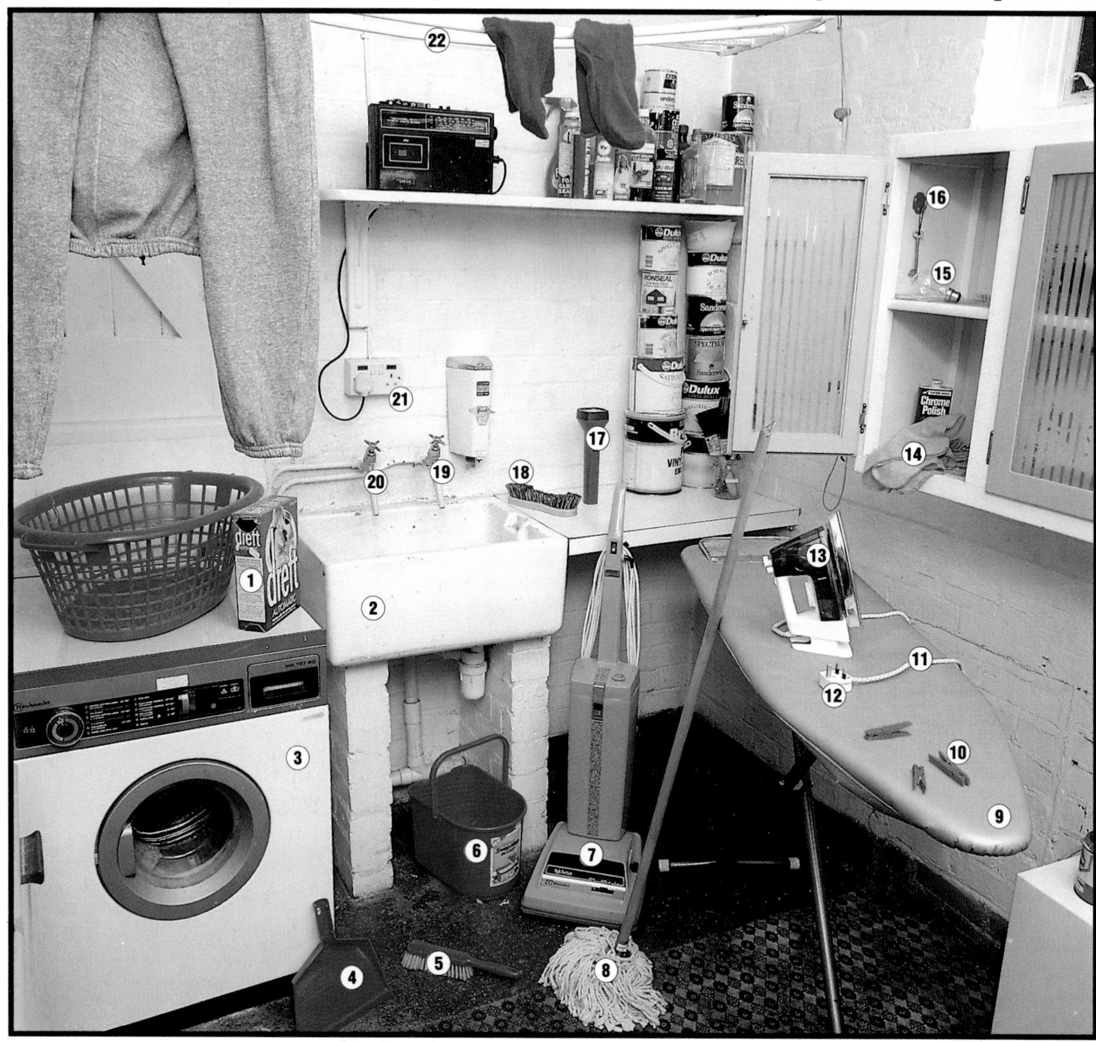

saponát	**1**	detergent
dřez	**2**	sink
pračka	**3**	washing-machine
lopatka na smetí	**4**	dustpan
smetáček	**5**	brush
kbelík	**6**	bucket (*esp US* pail)
vysavač	**7**	vacuum cleaner (*Brit also* Hoover)
mop	**8**	mop
žehlicí prkno	**9**	ironing-board
kolíček na prádlo	**10**	clothes-peg (*US* clothespin)
elektrická šňůra	**11**	flex (*esp US* cord)
zástrčka	**12**	plug
žehlička	**13**	iron
prachovka	**14**	duster (*US* dust cloth)
žárovka	**15**	light-bulb
háček/věšáček	**16**	hook
baterka	**17**	torch (*US* flashlight)
tvrdý kartáč/rýžák	**18**	scrubbing-brush (*US* scrub brush)
kohoutek na studenou vodu	**19**	cold(-water) tap (*US* cold water faucet)
kohoutek na teplou vodu	**20**	hot(-water) tap (*US* hot water faucet)
(elektrická) zásuvka	**21**	socket (*US also* outlet)
prádelní šňůra	**22**	clothes-line

page 20

The Kitchen

ohnivzdorný kastrol	**1**	casserole
síto	**2**	sieve (*esp US* strainer)
mísa na zadělávání	**3**	mixing bowl
kuchařská kniha/kuchařka	**4**	cookery book (*US* cookbook)
prostředek na mytí nádobí	**5**	washing-up liquid (*US* dishwashing liquid)
houba na mytí nádobí	**6**	scourer (*US* scouring pad)
utěrka	**7**	tea towel (*US* dish towel)
mixér	**8**	mixer
cedník	**9**	colander
otvírač na konzervy	**10**	tin-opener (*US* can opener)
naběračka	**11**	ladle
váleček (na těsto)	**12**	rolling-pin
pracovní plocha	**13**	work surface (*US* counter)
lednička	**14**	fridge (*esp US* refrigerator)
mrazák	**15**	freezer
hrnek	**16**	mug
opékač topinek	**17**	toaster
prkýnko na krájení	**18**	breadboard (*US* cutting board)
konvice	**19**	kettle (*US* electric teakettle)
skříňka	**20**	cupboard (*esp US* cabinet)
chňapka	**21**	oven glove (*US* pot holder)
trouba	**22**	oven
police	**23**	shelf
pánev	**24**	frying-pan
kuchyňský robot	**25**	food processor
rendlík	**26**	saucepan/pot
hořák	**27**	burner

Tools page 21

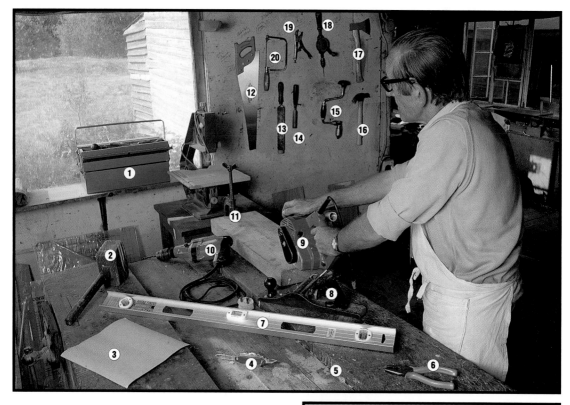

bedýnka na nářadí	**1** tool-box
palice	**2** mallet
skelný papír	**3** sandpaper
kapesní nůž	**4** penknife (*esp US* pocketknife)
pracovní stůl	**5** workbench
kleště/kombinačky	**6** pliers
vodováha	**7** spirit-level (*US* level)
hoblík	**8** plane
elektrická pila	**9** power saw
elektrická vrtačka	**10** electric drill
svěrák	**11** vice (*US* vise)
ruční pilka	**12** handsaw (*esp US* saw)
pilník	**13** file
dláto	**14** chisel
kolovrátek	**15** brace
kladivo	**16** hammer
sekera	**17** hatchet
ruční vrtačka	**18** hand drill
hasák	**19** wrench
lupenková pila	**20** coping saw

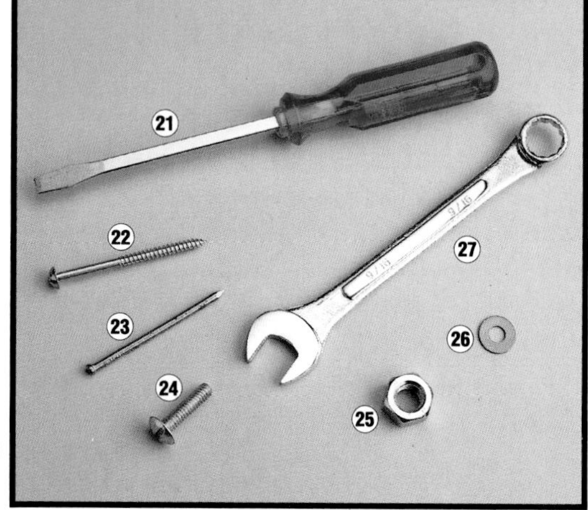

šroubovák	**21** screwdriver
vrut	**22** screw
hřebík	**23** nail
šroub	**24** bolt
matice	**25** nut
podložka	**26** washer
klíč (na matice)	**27** spanner (*US* wrench)

page 22

The Garden

zahrada za domem	**1** back garden (*US* backyard)
houpačka	**2** swing
trávník	**3** grass/lawn
strom(ek)	**4** tree
sekačka trávy	**5** lawnmower
kropicí konev	**6** watering-can
hrábě	**7** rake
nůžky	**8** shears
keř	**9** bush
květináč	**10** flowerpot
vydlážděná plocha za domem	**11** patio
lopatka (na sázení)	**12** trowel
koště	**13** broom
lavička	**14** bench
plot	**15** fence
rožeň	**16** barbecue
kolečko	**17** wheelbarrow
vidle	**18** fork
rýč	**19** spade
popelnice	**20** dustbin (*US* garbage can)

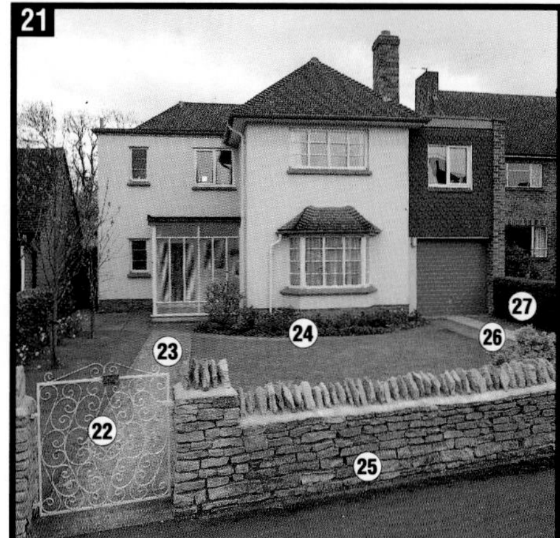

zahrada před domem	**21** front garden (*US* front yard)
vrátka	**22** gate
cestička	**23** path (*US* front walk)
květinový záhon	**24** flower-bed
zeď	**25** wall
vjezd/příjezdová cesta	**26** drive (*US* driveway)
živý plot	**27** hedge

In the Market 1 page 23

Zelenina	**Vegetables**
stánek na trhu	**1** market stall (*US* stand)
česnek	**2** garlic
zelená paprika	**3** green pepper
květák	**4** cauliflower
chřest	**5** asparagus
ředkvička	**6** radish
hlávkový salát	**7** lettuce
červená řepa	**8** beetroot (*US* beet)
brambor	**9** potato
okurka	**10** cucumber
cibule	**11** onion
cuketa	**12** courgette (*US* zucchini)
řeřicha	**13** watercress
mrkev	**14** carrot
růžičková kapusta	**15** Brussels sprout (*US* brussels sprout)
řapíkatý celer	**16** celery
brokolice	**17** broccoli
vodnice	**18** turnip
rajče	**19** tomato
lilek	**20** aubergine (*US* eggplant)
zelí	**21** cabbage
papírový sáček	**22** paper bag

page 24

In the Market 2

Ovoce	**Fruit**
meloun	**1** melon
košíček jahod	**2** punnet of strawberries (*US* basket of strawberries)
trs banánů	**3** bunch of bananas
jablko	**4** apple
burský ořech	**5** peanut
citron	**6** lemon
kokosový ořech	**7** coconut
ananas	**8** pineapple
pomeranč	**9** orange
hrozen vína	**10** bunch of grapes
broskev	**11** peach
sáček ořechů	**12** bag of nuts
avokádo	**13** avocado
papája	**14** pawpaw (*esp US* papaya)
liči	**15** lychee (*also* litchi)
hruška	**16** pear
limeta	**17** lime
kiwi	**18** kiwi fruit
mango	**19** mango
bluma	**20** plum
grapefruit/grep	**21** grapefruit
stoh košíků	**22** stack of baskets

At the Florist's page 25

jehličnatý strom(ek) (vánoční stromek)	**1** pine tree (*also* Christmas tree)
kmen	**2** trunk
kořeny	**3** roots
okvětní lístek	**4** petal
kapradí	**5** fern
košík	**6** basket
větev	**7** branch
kůra	**8** bark
svazek sušených květin	**9** bunch of dried flowers
naaranžované sušené květiny	**10** dried flower arrangement
list	**11** leaf
bonsaj	**12** bonsai
cibule	**13** bulb
narcis	**14** daffodil
chryzantéma	**15** chrysanthemum
palma	**16** palm
růže	**17** rose
orchidej	**18** orchid
lodyha/stonek	**19** stem
frézie	**20** freesia
kaktus	**21** cactus
borovicová šiška	**22** pine cone
kopretina	**23** daisy
karafiát	**24** carnation
tulipán	**25** tulip
lilie	**26** lily
poupě	**27** bud
iris	**28** iris

At the Newsagent's (*US* Newsstand)

Papírnické potřeby	**Stationery**
kotouček izolepy	**1** reel of Sellotape (*US* roll of Scotch tape)
klubko provázku	**2** ball of string
balíček obálek	**3** packet of envelopes (*US* pack of envelopes)
dopisní papír	**4** writing-paper
sada barevných fixů	**5** set of coloured pens (*US* set of colored pens)
role balicího papíru	**6** roll of wrapping paper
řada časopisů	**7** row of magazines
stoh novin	**8** pile of newspapers

Cukrovinky	**Confectionery (*US* Candy)**
bonboniéra	**9** box of chocolates (*US* box of chocolate)
sáček bonbonů	**10** bag of sweets (*US* bag of candy)
tabulka čokolády	**11** bar of chocolate
dvojité balení	**12** twin-pack
trojité balení	**13** triple-pack
pytlík bonbonů	**14** packet of sweets (*US* pack of candy)
rolička bonbonů	**15** packet of sweets (*US* roll of candy)
sáček bramborových lupínků	**16** packet of crisps (*US* bag of potato chips)
čokoláda	**17** chocolate
bonbony	**18** sweets (*US* candy)
bramborové lupínky	**19** crisps (*US* potato chips)

At the Delicatessen page 27

krabice obilných vloček **1** box of cereal
bochník chleba **2** loaf of bread
sendviče **3** sandwiches
houska **4** roll
sklenice džemu **5** jar of jam/pot of jam
tuňák v konzervě **6** tin of tuna (*US* can of tuna)
pečeně **7** joint of cooked meat (*US* roast)
plátek masa **8** slice of meat
pečené kuře **9** roast chicken
porce kuřete **10** chicken portion (*US* piece of chicken)
plněné pečivo **11** pie
kus plněného pečiva **12** piece of pie
tucet vajec **13** dozen eggs
půltucet vajec **14** half a dozen eggs
sušenka **15** biscuit (*US* cookie)
balíček sušenek **16** packet of biscuits (*US* package of cookies)
džem **17** jam
tuňák **18** tuna

kelímek jogurtu **19** pot of yoghurt (*US* container of yogurt)
krabička margarínu **20** tub of margarine
krabice pomerančového džusu **21** carton of orange juice
sýr **22** cheese
plněné olivy **23** stuffed olives
pinta mléka **24** pint of milk
láhev minerálky **25** bottle of mineral water
plechovka limonády **26** can of fizzy drink (*US* can of soda)
jogurt **27** yoghurt (*esp US* yogurt)
margarín **28** margarine
máslo **29** butter

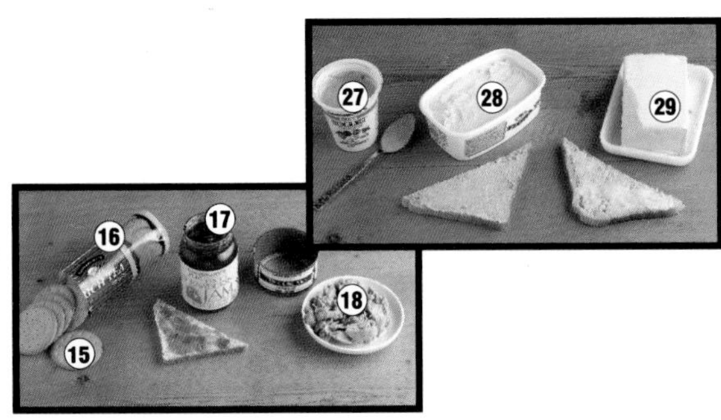

At the Restaurant

page 28

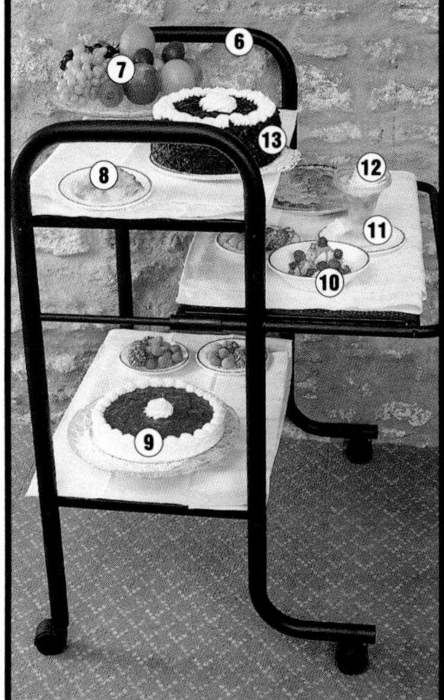

Předkrmy	**Starters (*US* Appetizers)**
třešně	**1** cherry
meloun	**2** melon
uzený losos	**3** smoked salmon
paštika s toasty	**4** pâté with toast
rajská polévka	**5** tomato soup
Zákusky	**Desserts**
servírovací stolek na zákusky	**6** dessert trolley (*US* dessert cart)
ovoce	**7** fruit
jablečný koláč	**8** apple pie
tvarohový dort	**9** cheesecake
malinová zmrzlina	**10** raspberry ice-cream
ovocný koktejl	**11** fruit cocktail
smetana/šlehačka	**12** cream
čokoládový dort	**13** chocolate gateau (*US* chocolate cake)
číšník	**14** waiter
jídelní lístek	**15** menu
Hlavní chody	**Main Courses**
rostbíf	**16** roast beef
pstruh na mandlích	**17** trout with almonds
biftek/steak	**18** steak
jehněčí kotlety	**19** lamb chops
Zelenina	**Vegetables**
kukuřice	**20** sweet corn (*US* corn)
houby	**21** mushrooms
salát	**22** salad
fazolové lusky	**23** runner beans (*US* string beans)
hrášek	**24** peas
brambor pečený ve slupce	**25** jacket potato (*esp US* baked potato)
vařené brambory	**26** boiled potatoes
hranolky	**27** chips (*US* French fries)

At the Camera Shop (*US* Camera Store) page 29

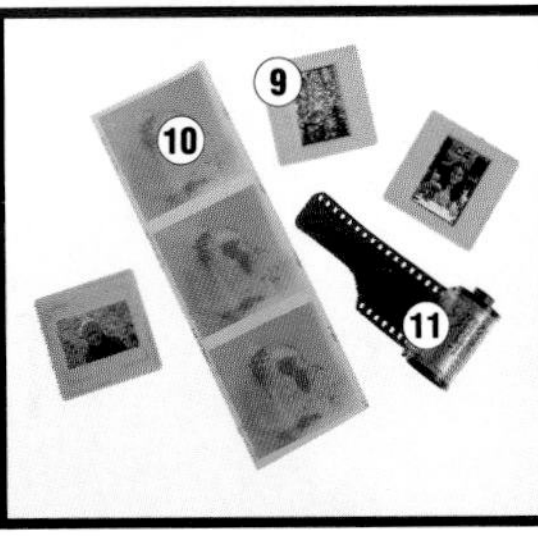

zákazník	**1**	customer
paragon	**2**	receipt
pokladna	**3**	cash register
stativ	**4**	tripod
dalekohled	**5**	telescope
prodavač	**6**	shop assistant (*US* salesperson)
triedr	**7**	binoculars
diaprojektor	**8**	slide projector
diapozitiv	**9**	slide
negativ	**10**	negative
cívka filmu	**11**	reel of film (*US* roll of film)
fotoalbum	**12**	photo album
barevná fotografie	**13**	colour print (*US* color print)
černobílá fotografie	**14**	black and white print
transfokátor/zoom	**15**	zoom lens
jednooká zrcadlovka	**16**	single lens reflex/SLR camera
objektiv	**17**	lens
blesk	**18**	flash (gun)
kompaktní fotoaparát 35mm	**19**	35 mm* compact camera
vestavěný blesk	**20**	built-in flash
brašna na fotoaparát	**21**	camera case
řemen	**22**	strap
polaroid	**23**	polaroid camera

milimetr — **mm = millimetre (US millimeter)*

At the Hi-fi Shop (*US* Electronics Store)

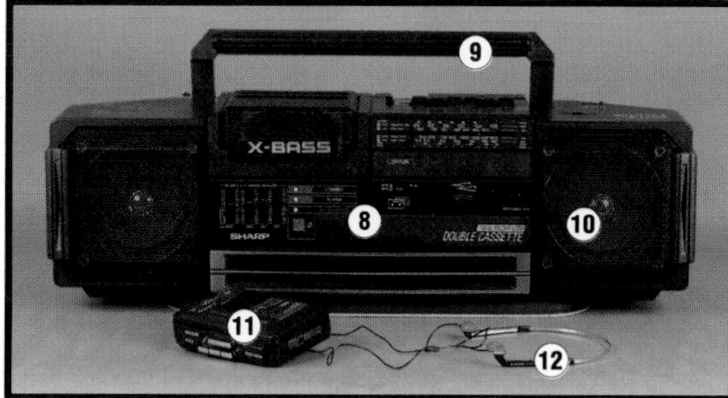

videokamera **1** camcorder

mikrofon **2** microphone

hledáček **3** viewfinder

videokazeta **4** (video)tape

gramofonová deska **5** record

kazeta **6** cassette

kompaktní disk **7** compact disc/CD

radiomagnetofon **8** radio cassette recorder (*US also* AM/FM cassette recorder)

držadlo **9** handle

reproduktor **10** speaker

walkman **11** Walkman (*Brit also* personal stereo)

sluchátka **12** headphones

hi-fi věž **13** stereo/stereo system (*US also* sound system) (*Brit also* hi-fi)

gramofon **14** turntable

rádio **15** radio

zesilovač **16** amplifier

grafický equalizér **17** graphic equalizer

kazetový přehrávač **18** cassette deck/tape deck

CD přehrávač **19** compact disc player/ CD player

Postal Services 1 page 31

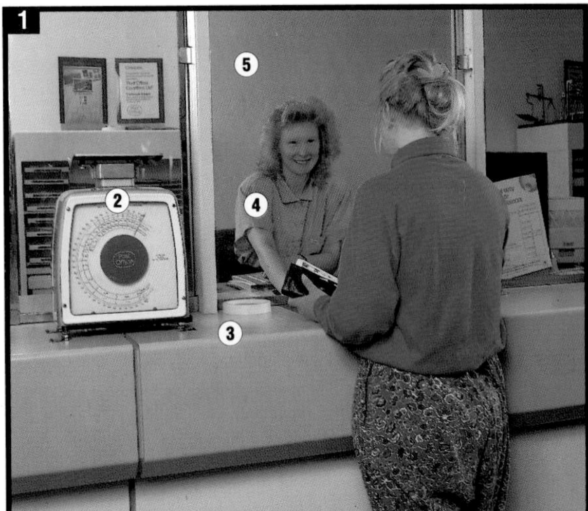

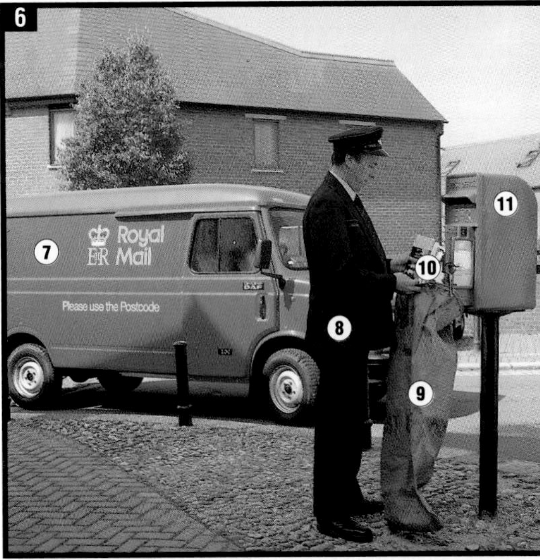

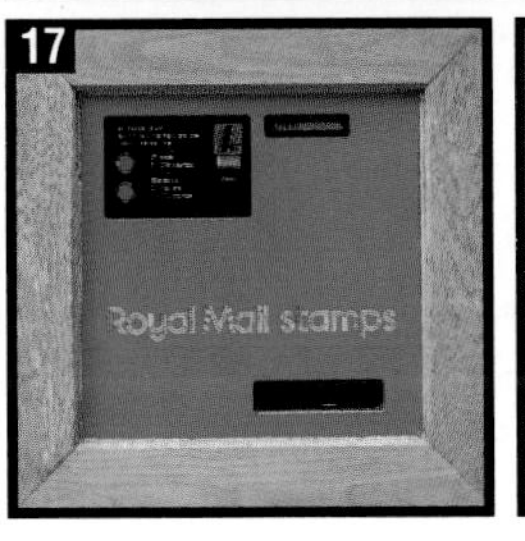

poštovní úřad	**1**	post office
váha	**2**	scales (*US* scale)
přepážka	**3**	counter
poštovní úřednice	**4**	counter assistant (*US* postal clerk)
okýnko	**5**	window
vybírání schránky	**6**	collection
poštovní dodávka	**7**	post office van (*US* mail truck)
listonoš	**8**	postman (*US* mailman)
poštovní vak	**9**	mailbag
pošta	**10**	post (*US* mail)
poštovní schránka	**11**	letter-box/postbox (*US* mailbox)
doručování pošty	**12**	delivery
poštovní brašna	**13**	postbag (*esp US* mailbag)
schránka na dopisy	**14**	letter-box (*US* mailbox)
doručování kurýrem	**15**	delivery by courier (*US* delivery by messenger)
kurýr	**16**	despatch-rider (*US* messenger)
automat na poštovní známky	**17**	stamp machine
arch poštovních známek	**18**	sheet of stamps
poštovní známka	**19**	stamp
blok poštovních známek	**20**	book of stamps

page 32

Postal Services 2

Britské **British** Americké **American**

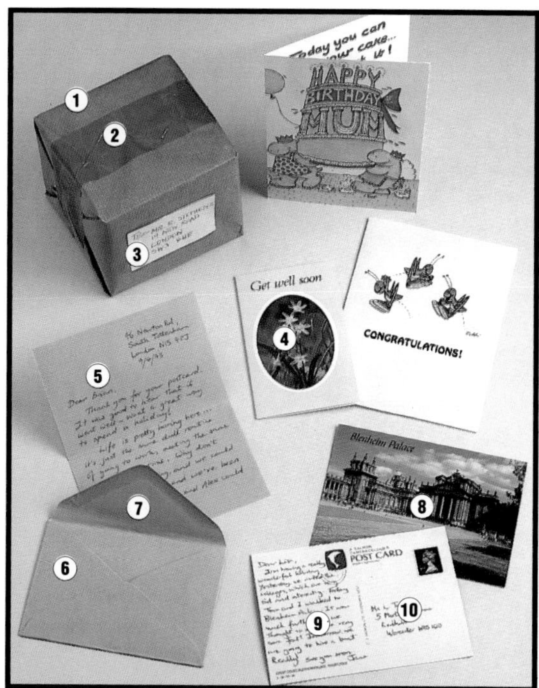

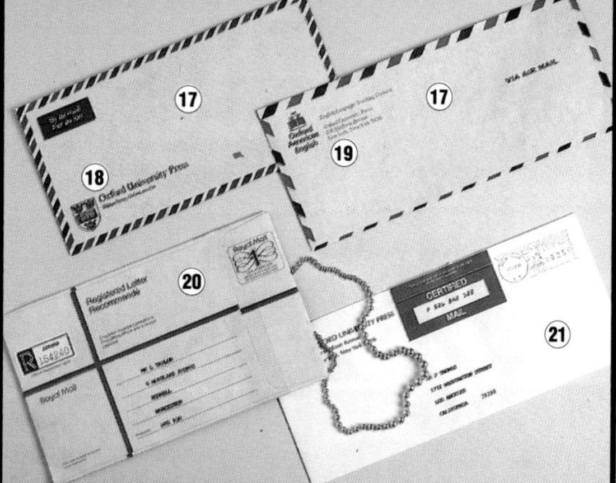

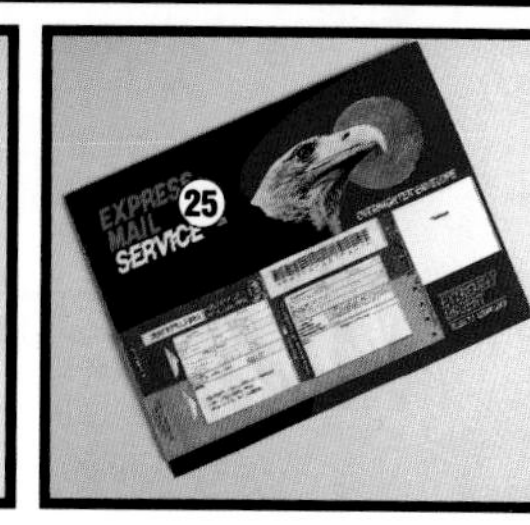

balíček	**1** parcel (*esp US* package)
lepicí páska	**2** tape
štítek	**3** label
blahopřání	**4** greetings card (*US* greeting card)
dopis	**5** letter
obálka	**6** envelope
chlopeň	**7** flap
pohlednice	**8** postcard
sdělení	**9** message
adresa	**10** address
pošta 1. třídy	**11** first-class post (*Brit*)
poštovní razítko	**12** postmark
poštovní směrovací číslo	**13** postcode (*also* postal code) (*Brit*)
pošta 1. třídy	**14** first class mail (*US*)
pošta 2. třídy	**15** second-class post (*Brit*)
poštovní směrovací číslo	**16** zip code (*US*)
letecká pošta	**17** airmail
zpáteční adresa	**18** address of sender (*Brit*)
zpáteční adresa	**19** return address (*US*)
doporučený dopis	**20** registered post (*Brit*)
doporučený dopis	**21** certified mail (*US*)
peněžní poukázka	**22** postal order (*Brit*)
peněžní poukázka	**23** money order (*US*)
spěšná zásilka/expres	**24** Special Delivery (*Brit*)
spěšná zásilka/expres	**25** Express Mail (*US*)

Numbers/The Date page 33

JULY 1998					
Sunday		5	12	19	26
Monday		6	13	20	27
Tuesday		7	14	21	28
Wednesday	1	8	15	22	29
Thursday	2	9	16	23	30
Friday	3	10	17	24	31
Saturday	4	11	18	25	

jeden	**1**	one
dva	**2**	two
tři	**3**	three
čtyři	**4**	four
pět	**5**	five
šest	**6**	six
sedm	**7**	seven
osm	**8**	eight
devět	**9**	nine
deset	**10**	ten
jedenáct	**11**	eleven
dvanáct	**12**	twelve
třináct	**13**	thirteen
čtrnáct	**14**	fourteen
patnáct	**15**	fifteen
šestnáct	**16**	sixteen
sedmnáct	**17**	seventeen
osmnáct	**18**	eighteen
devatenáct	**19**	nineteen
dvacet	**20**	twenty
dvacet jedna	**21**	twenty-one
třicet	**30**	thirty
čtyřicet	**40**	forty
padesát	**50**	fifty
šedesát	**60**	sixty
sedmdesát	**70**	seventy
osmdesát	**80**	eighty
devadesát	**90**	ninety
sto	**100**	one hundred
sto jedna	**101**	one hundred and one
tisíc	**1000**	one thousand
dva tisíce dvě stě deset	**2210**	two thousand, two hundred and ten
milion	**1000000**	one million

1. první	**1st**	first
2. druhý	**2nd**	second
3. třetí	**3rd**	third
4. čtvrtý	**4th**	fourth
5. pátý	**5th**	fifth
6. šestý	**6th**	sixth
7. sedmý	**7th**	seventh
8. osmý	**8th**	eighth
9. devátý	**9th**	ninth
10. desátý	**10th**	tenth
11. jedenáctý	**11th**	eleventh
12. dvanáctý	**12th**	twelfth
13. třináctý	**13th**	thirteenth
20. dvacátý	**20th**	twentieth
21. dvacátý první	**21st**	twenty-first
22. dvacátý druhý	**22nd**	twenty-second
23. dvacátý třetí	**23rd**	twenty-third
30. třicátý	**30th**	thirtieth
31. třicátý první	**31st**	thirty-first

britská angličtina ***British***

3.5.98 3rd May 1998
3/5/98 3 May 1998

třetího května devatenáct set devadesát osm — The third of May nineteen ninety-eight/ May the third, nineteen ninety-eight.

americká angličtina ***American***

5/3/98 May 3, 1998

třetího května devatenáct set devadesát osm — May third, nineteen ninety-eight.

page 34 At the Bank

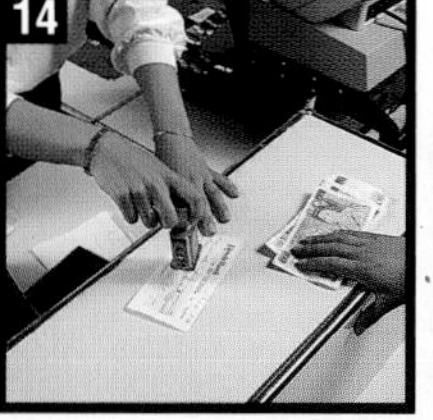

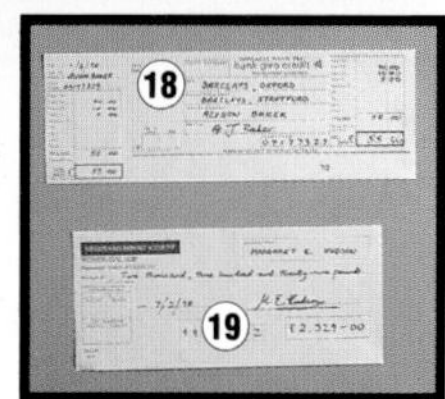

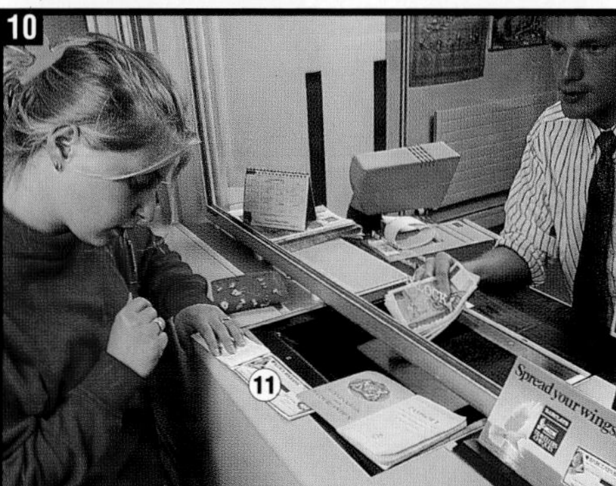

šeková knížka	**1**	cheque book (*US* checkbook)
kontrolní ústřižek	**2**	counterfoil/cheque stub (*US* check stub)
šeková karta	**3**	cheque (guarantee) card (*Brit only*)
kreditní karta	**4**	credit card
bankovní výpis	**5**	bank statement (*esp US* monthly statement)
stav (bankovního) konta	**6**	(bank) balance
číslo (bankovního) konta	**7**	(bank) account number
devizový kurz	**8**	exchange rates
pokladník	**9**	cashier (*US* teller)
proplácení cestovního šeku	**10**	changing a traveller's cheque (*US* cashing a traveler's check)
cestovní šek	**11**	traveller's cheque (*US* traveler's check)
výměna peněz	**12**	changing money
cizí měna	**13**	foreign currency
proplácení šeku	**14**	cashing a cheque (*US* cashing a check)
vybírání hotovosti	**15**	withdrawing cash
peněžní automat	**16**	cash dispenser/cashpoint (*US* cash machine/ automatic teller)
ukládání peněz	**17**	paying in (*US* making a deposit)
vkladní lístek	**18**	paying-in slip (*US* deposit slip)
výběrní lístek	**19**	withdrawal slip

American Money

mince	**1 coins**
cent	**2** a penny
péticent/niklák	**3** a nickel
desetník	**4** a dime
čtvrtdolar	**5** a quarter
bankovky	**6 bills**
dolarová bankovka	**7** a dollar bill
pětidolarová bankovka	**8** a five dollar bill
desetidolarová bankovka	**9** a ten dollar bill
dvacetidolarová bankovka	**10** a twenty dollar bill
padesátidolarová bankovka	**11** a fifty dollar bill

Placení v hotovosti	**Paying (in) cash**
dvacet dolarů	**12** twenty dollars
sedm dolarů devadesát pět centů	**13** seven dollars and ninety-five cents/ seven ninety-five
paragon	**14** receipt
celková částka	**15** total
peníze nazpět	**16** change

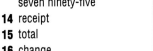

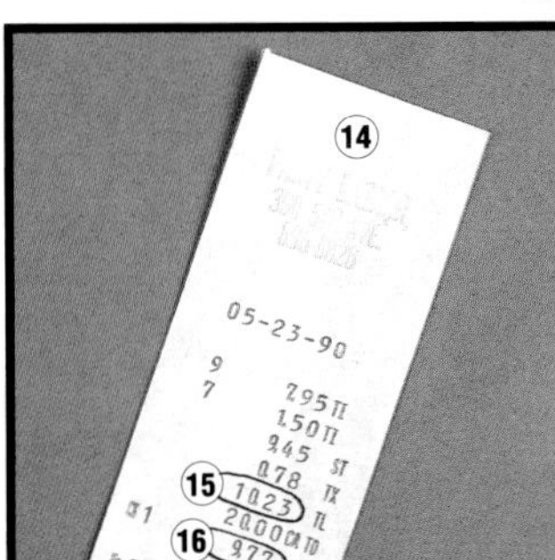

British Money

mince	**1 coins**
pence	**2** a one pence piece/a penny
dvoupence	**3** a two pence piece
pětipence	**4** a five pence piece
desetipence	**5** a ten pence piece
dvacetipence	**6** a twenty pence piece
padesátipence	**7** a fifty pence piece
libra	**8** a pound coin
dvoulibrová mince	**9** a two pound coin

bankovky	**10 notes**
pětilibrová bankovka	**11** a five pound note
desetilibrová bankovka	**12** a ten pound note
dvacetilibrová bankovka	**13** a twenty pound note
padesátilibrová bankovka	**14** a fifty pound note

Kolik to stojí?	**How much is it?**
dvacet pencí	**15** twenty pence (also 20p)
deset pencí	**16** ten pence (also 10p)
padesát pencí	**17** fifty pence (also 50p)
tři libry osmdesát dva pencí	**18** three pounds eighty-two pence/ three pounds eighty-two
dvě libry	**19** two pounds

Time page 37

24 hours = 1 day
7 days = 1 week (wk)
365 days = 1 year (yr)
100 years = 1 century (c)

tři hodiny	**1** three o'clock
ciferník	**2** clock-face
minutová ručička	**3** minute-hand
hodinová ručička	**4** hour-hand
vteřinová ručička	**5** second-hand
devět hodin pět minut	**6** five past nine (*US also* five after nine)/
devět pět	nine o five
devět hodin deset minut	**7** ten past nine (*US also* ten after nine)/
devět deset	nine ten
čtvrt na deset	**8** a quarter past nine (*US also* a quarter after nine)/
devět patnáct	nine fifteen
půl desáté/devět třicet	**9** half past nine/nine thirty
devět hodin čtyřicet minut/za dvacet minut deset	**10** twenty to ten/nine forty
tři čtvrtě na deset/ devět čtyřicet pět	**11** a quarter to ten/ nine forty-five
za deset minut deset/devět padesát	**12** ten to ten/nine fifty
dvanáct hodin/poledne *také* půlnoc	**13** twelve o'clock/midday (*esp US* noon) *also* midnight
dvanáct hodin sedm minut	**14** seven minutes past twelve (*US also* seven minutes after twelve)/twelve o seven
sedm hodin ráno	**15** seven am (*US* A.M.)/ seven o'clock in the morning
pět hodin odpoledne	**16** five pm (*US* P.M.)/ five o'clock in the afternoon
osm hodin večer	**17** eight pm (*US* P.M.)/ eight o'clock in the evening
půl dvanácté v noci	**18** eleven thirty pm (*US* P.M.) half past eleven at night

Emergency Services

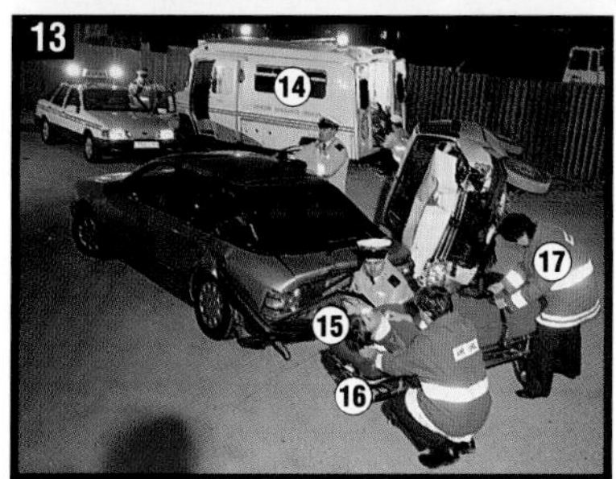

Policie	**Police**
policejní stanice	**1** police station
policejní auto	**2** police car
policistka	**3** police officer
Hasičská stanice	**Fire Brigade (*US* Fire Department)**
hasičský vůz	**4** fire-engine
žebřík	**5** ladder
voda	**6** water
kouř	**7** smoke
požár	**8** fire
hasicí přístroj	**9** fire extinguisher
hasič	**10** fireman (*esp US* fire fighter)
hydrant	**11** hydrant
hadice	**12** hose
Záchranná služba	**Ambulance Service**
autonehoda	**13** car accident
sanitka	**14** ambulance
zraněný	**15** injured man
nosítka	**16** stretcher
pracovník záchranné služby	**17** paramedic
rozlišovací číslo	**18** international code
směrové číslo země	**19** country code
národní směrové číslo	**20** area code
telefonní číslo	**21** (tele)phone number
telefonní budka	**22** (tele)phone box (*esp US* telephone booth)
sluchátko	**23** receiver
telefonní karta	**24** phonecard (*Brit only*)
otvor na mince	**25** slot
číselník	**26** dial

(18) 00 (19) 44 1865 556767

01865 (20) 556767 (21)

In Britain the telephone number for the police, fire and ambulance services is 999. In the US the emergency number is 911.

Telefonní číslo policie, požární a záchranné služby v Británii je 999. Ve Spojených státech je číslo pohovosti 911.

Jobs 1 page 39

umělec **1** artist
zahradník **2** gardener
diskžokej **3** disc jockey (*US* disk jockey)
hlasatelka **4** newsreader (*esp US* newscaster)

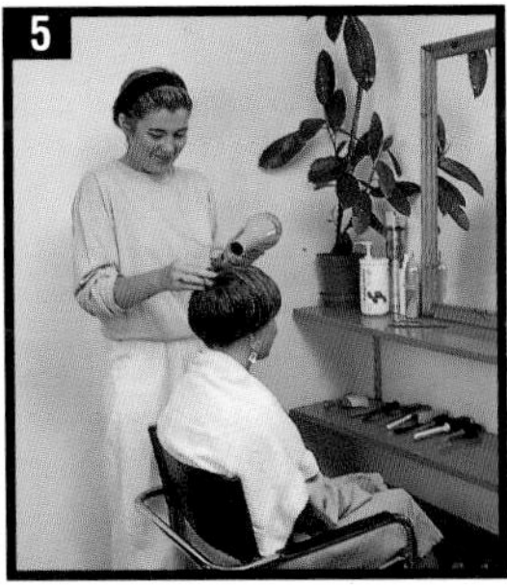

kadeřnice **5** hairdresser
lékárnice **6** pharmacist
pekař **7** baker
řezník **8** butcher

zemědělec/farmář **9** farmer
rybář **10** fisherman
námořník **11** sailor
voják **12** soldier

page 40

Jobs 2

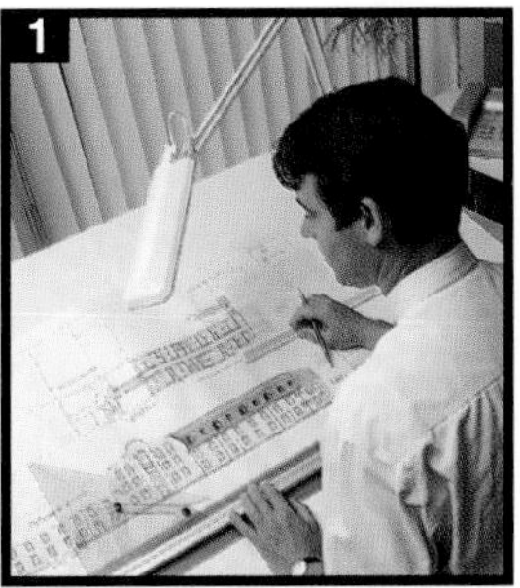

architekt **1** architect
řidič nákladního auta **2** lorry driver (*US* truck driver)
pracovnice cestovní kanceláře **3** travel agent
fotograf **4** photographer

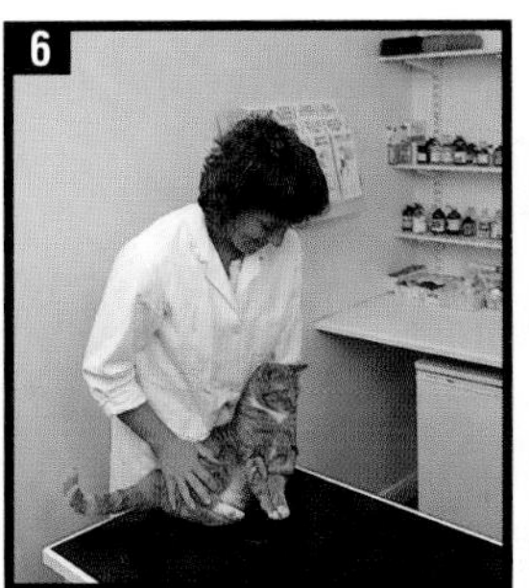

programátor **5** computer programmer
veterinářka **6** vet
elektrikář **7** electrician
truhlář **8** carpenter

svářeč **9** welder
instalatér **10** plumber

mechanik **11** mechanic
zedník **12** bricklayer

Daily Routine page 41

Probouzí se. **1** He wakes up.
Vstává/Vstává z postele. **2** He gets up/He gets out of bed.
Jde (dolů) ze schodů. **3** He goes downstairs.
Jde běhat. **4** He goes jogging.

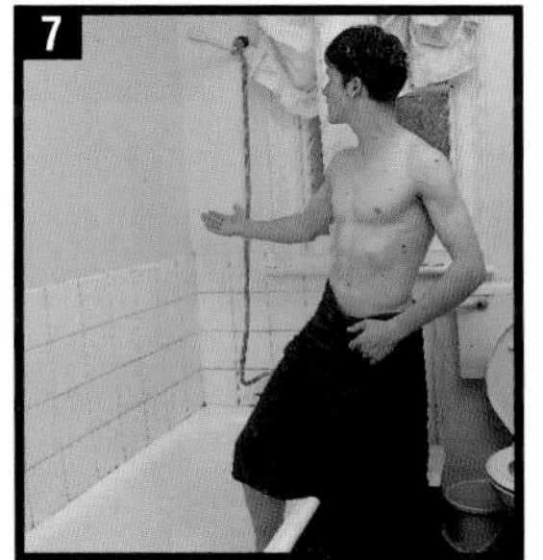

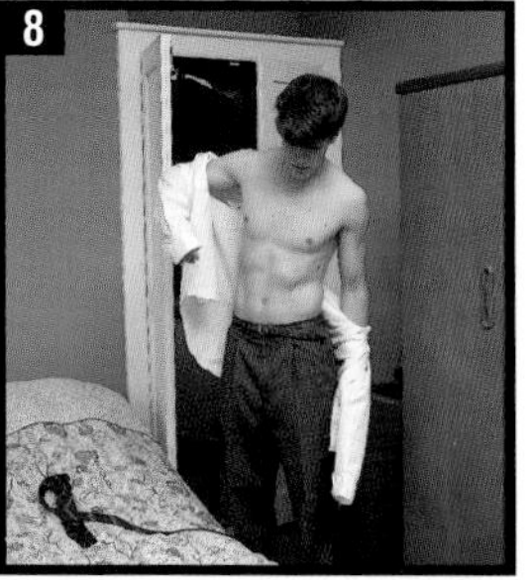

Vrací se. **5** He comes back.
Sbírá poštu. **6** He picks up the post (*US* mail).
Sprchuje se. **7** He has a shower.
(*esp US* He takes a shower.)
Obléká se. **8** He gets dressed.

Snídá. **9** He has breakfast/He eats breakfast.
Odchází z domova. **10** He leaves home.
Kupuje noviny. **11** He buys a newspaper.
Poslouchá hudbu. **12** He listens to music.

page 42

Daily Routine 2

Nastupuje do vlaku. **13** He catches the train.

Čte noviny. **14** He reads the newspaper.

Začíná pracovat. **15** He starts work.

Pije kávu. **16** He has a cup of coffee.
He drinks some coffee.

Obědvá. **17** He has lunch/He eats lunch.

Končí práci. **18** He finishes work.

Jede do sportovního střediska. **19** He drives to the sports centre (*US* health club).

Setkává se s přáteli. **20** He meets his friends.

Hraje squash. **21** He plays squash.

Večeří. **22** He has dinner/He eats dinner.

Dívá se na televizi. **23** He watches television/TV.

Jde spát. **24** He goes to bed.

Office Verbs page 43

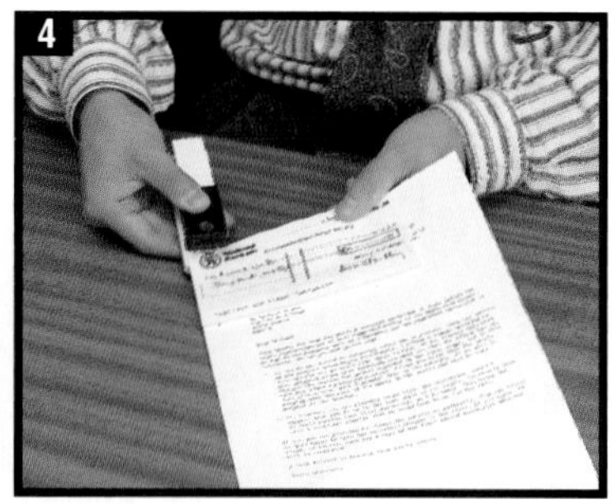

Diktuje dopis. **1** She is dictating a letter.
diktafon **2** Dictaphone/dictating machine
Píše na stroji dopis. **3** He is typing a letter.
He is typing.
Sešívačkou připevňuje šek k dopisu. **4** He is stapling a cheque to a letter. (*US* check)

Vyplňuje formulář. **5** She is filling in a form.
(*US* She is filling out a form.)
Podepisuje dopis. **6** She is signing a letter.
podpis **7** signature
Poznamenává si schůzku. **8** She is making a note of an appointment.

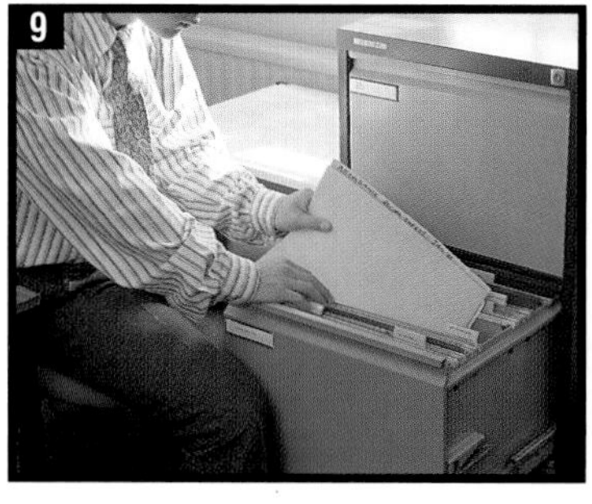

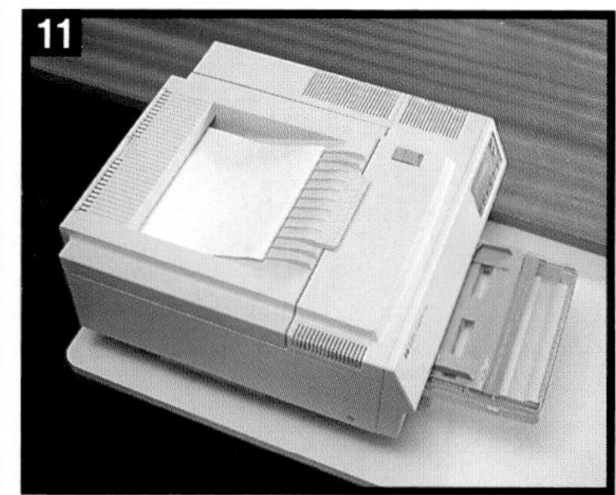

Zařazuje. **9** He is filing.
Posílá fax. **10** He is sending a fax.
Faxuje dopis. He is faxing a letter.
Tiskne. **11** It is printing.
Tiskne kopii. It is printing a copy.

The Office

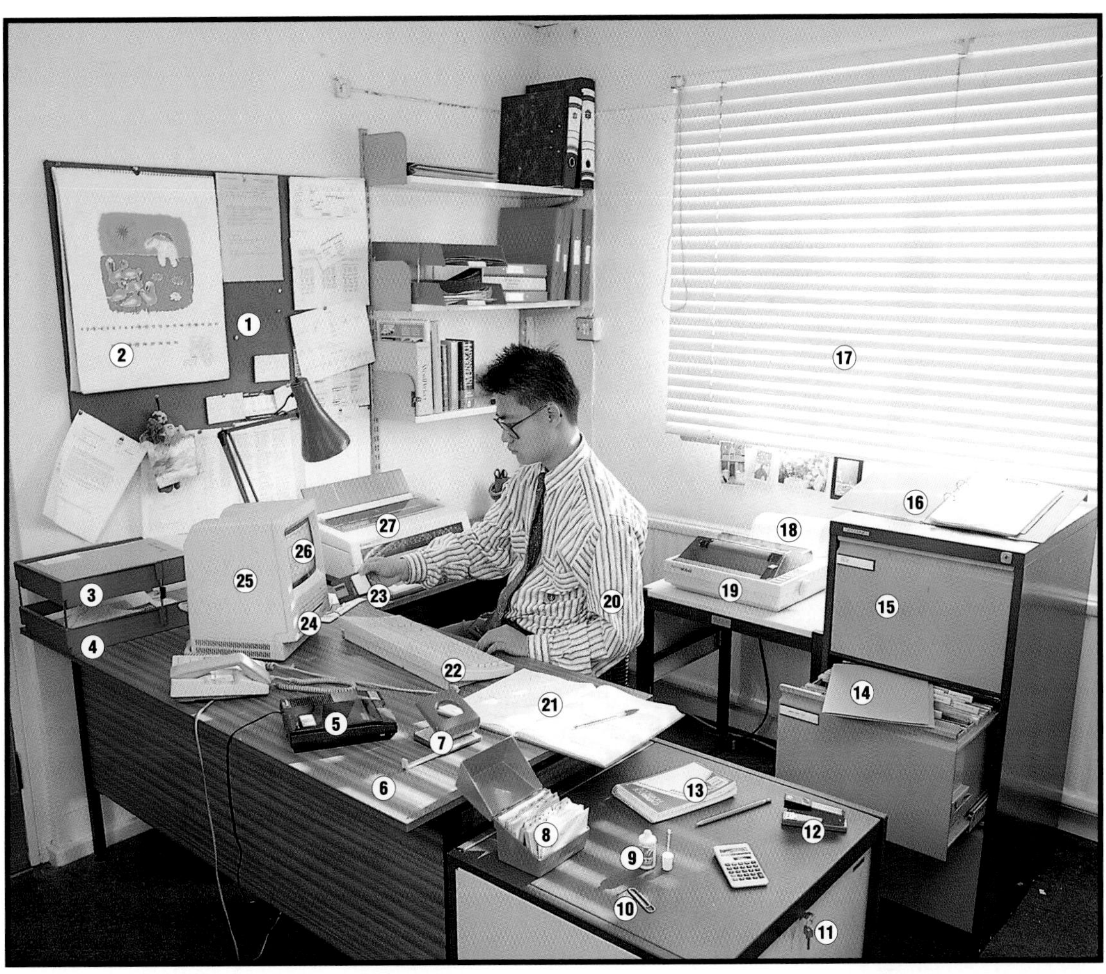

nástěnka	**1**	notice-board (*US* bulletin board)
kalendář	**2**	calendar
přihrádka na došlou poštu	**3**	in-tray (*US* in box)
přihrádka na vyřízenou poštu	**4**	out-tray (*US* out box)
telefonní záznamník	**5**	answering machine (*Brit also* answerphone)
psací stůl	**6**	desk
děrovačka	**7**	hole-punch
kartotéka	**8**	card index (*US* card file)
opravný lak	**9**	Tipp-Ex (*esp US* correction fluid)
kancelářská sponka	**10**	paper-clip
klíč	**11**	key
sešívačka	**12**	stapler
poznámkový blok	**13**	notebook
desky	**14**	file
registratura	**15**	filing cabinet (*US* file cabinet)
pořadač	**16**	ring binder
okenní žaluzie	**17**	venetian blind
výtisk	**18**	printout
tiskárna	**19**	printer
sekretář	**20**	secretary
diář	**21**	diary (*US* appointment book)
klávesnice	**22**	keyboard
disketa	**23**	floppy disk
disketová jednotka	**24**	disk drive
osobní počítač	**25**	personal computer/PC
obrazovka	**26**	screen
psací stroj	**27**	typewriter

A Science Laboratory 1 page 45

ochranné brýle	**1**	goggles
zkumavka	**2**	test-tube
plamen	**3**	flame
gumová hadice	**4**	rubber tubing
Bunsenův hořák	**5**	Bunsen burner
stojan	**6**	rack
těrka	**7**	pestle
třecí miska	**8**	mortar
baňka s plochým dnem	**9**	flat bottom flask
trychtýř/nálevka	**10**	funnel
filtrační papír	**11**	filter paper
hranol	**12**	prism
laboratorní kleště	**13**	tongs
lupa	**14**	magnifying glass
píst	**15**	plunger
stříkačka	**16**	syringe
kónická baňka	**17**	conical flask
U-trubice	**18**	U-tube
stolička	**19**	stool
stojan s úchytkou	**20**	clamp stand (*US* ring stand)
teploměr	**21**	thermometer
baňka s kulatým dnem	**22**	round bottom flask
chladič	**23**	condenser
odměrná kádinka	**24**	measuring beaker (*US* graduated beaker)
drátěná mřížka	**25**	gauze (*US* wire mesh screen)
trojnožka	**26**	tripod

page 46

A Science Laboratory 2

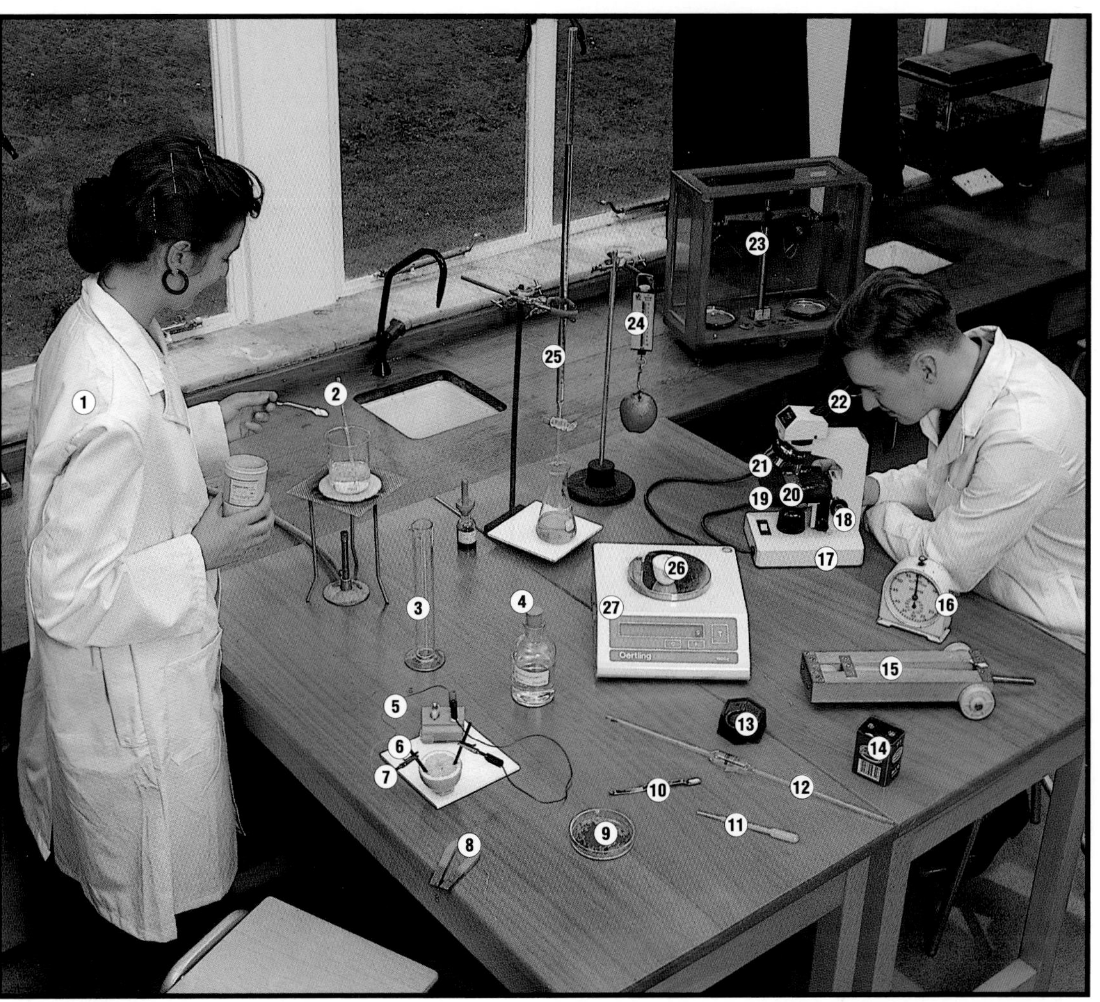

laboratorní plášť	**1** lab coat
skleněná tyčinka	**2** glass rod
odměrný válec	**3** measuring cylinder (*US* graduated cylinder)
zátka	**4** stopper
drát	**5** wire
elektroda	**6** electrode
svorka/krokodýl	**7** crocodile clip (*US* alligator clip)
magnet	**8** magnet
Petriho miska	**9** Petri dish (*US* petri dish)
špachtle	**10** spatula
kapátko	**11** dropper
pipeta	**12** pipette
závaží	**13** weight
baterie	**14** battery
vozík	**15** trolley (*US* cart)
stopky	**16** stop clock (*US* timer)
mikroskop	**17** microscope
zaostřovací šroub	**18** focusing control (*US also* focusing knob)
stolek (mikroskopu)	**19** stage
sklíčko	**20** slide
objektiv	**21** objective lens
okulár	**22** eyepiece
laboratorní váhy	**23** balance/scales (*US* scale)
mincíř	**24** spring balance
byreta	**25** burette
kelímek	**26** crucible
mikrováhy	**27** microbalance

Shapes and Lines page 47

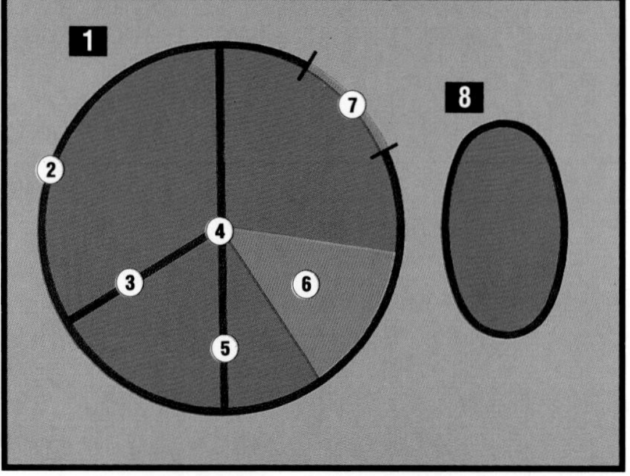

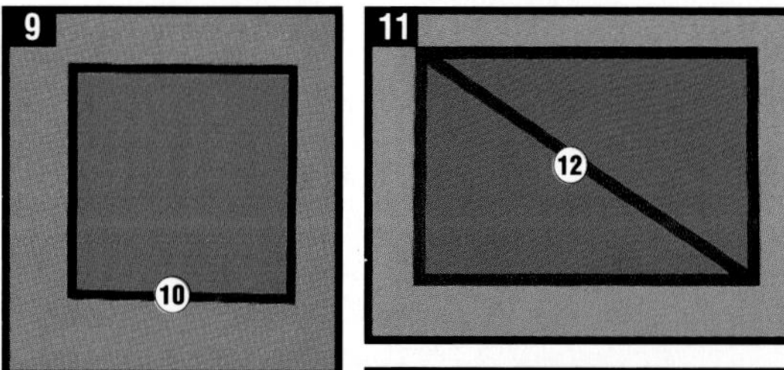

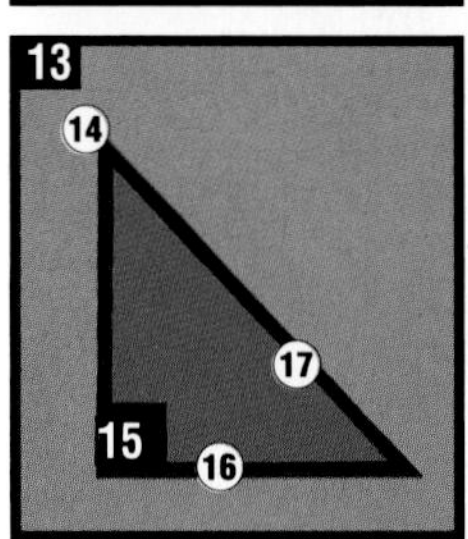

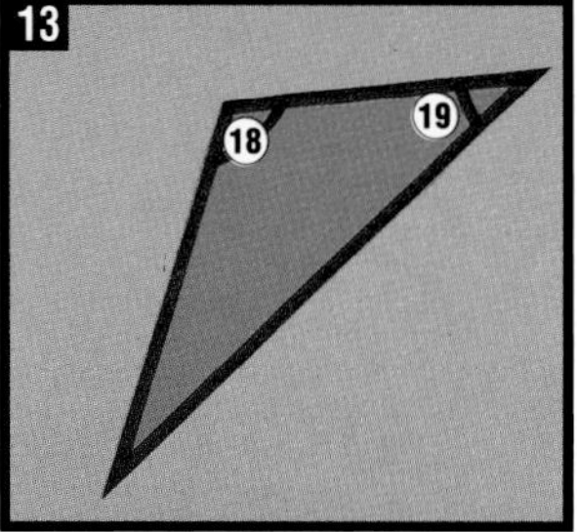

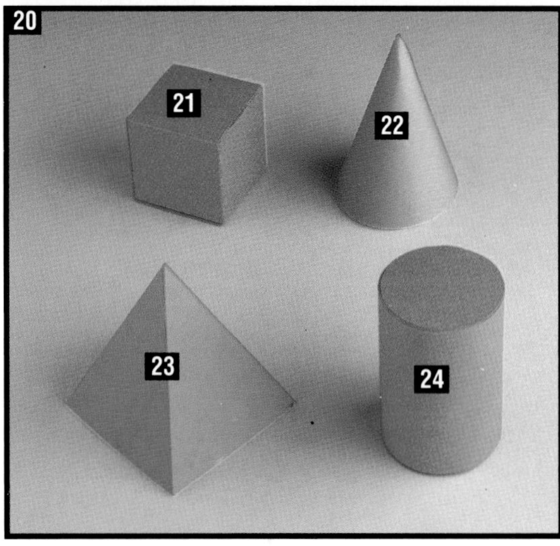

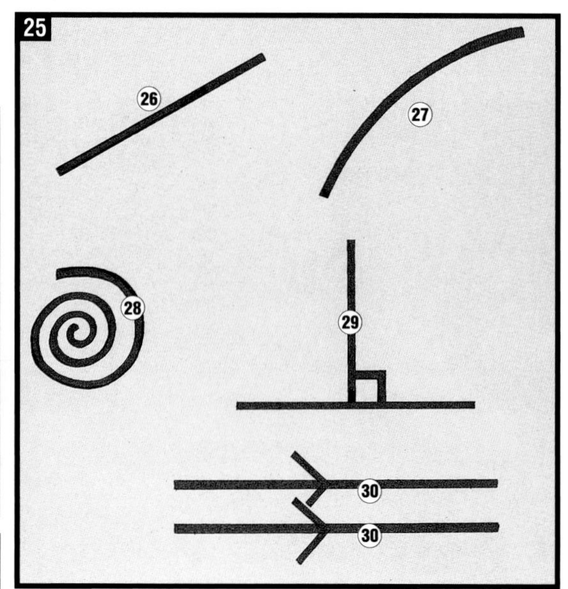

kruh	**1** circle
obvod kruhu	**2** circumference
poloměr	**3** radius
střed	**4** centre (*US* center)
průměr	**5** diameter
výseč	**6** sector
oblouk	**7** arc
ovál	**8** oval
čtverec	**9** square
strana	**10** side
obdélník	**11** rectangle
úhlopříčka	**12** diagonal
trojúhelník	**13** triangle
vrchol	**14** apex
pravý úhel	**15** right angle
základna	**16** base
přepona	**17** hypotenuse
tupý úhel	**18** obtuse angle
ostrý úhel	**19** acute angle
tělesa	**20** solid figures
krychle	**21** cube
kužel	**22** cone
jehlan	**23** pyramid
válec	**24** cylinder
čáry	**25** lines
přímka	**26** straight line
křivka	**27** curve
spirála	**28** spiral
kolmice	**29** perpendicular line
rovnoběžky	**30** parallel lines

Measurement

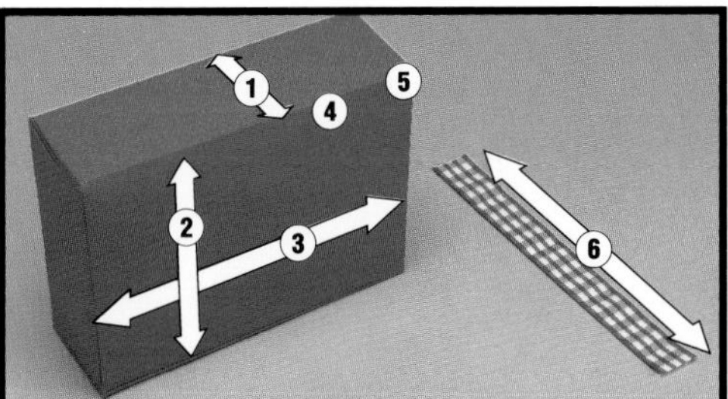

$$7 \overset{11}{+} 11 = 18$$

$$80 \overset{12}{-} 13 = 67$$

$$40 \overset{13}{\times} 4 = 160$$

$$32 \overset{14}{\div} 8 \overset{15}{=} 4$$

(16) 2.5 (17) 50%

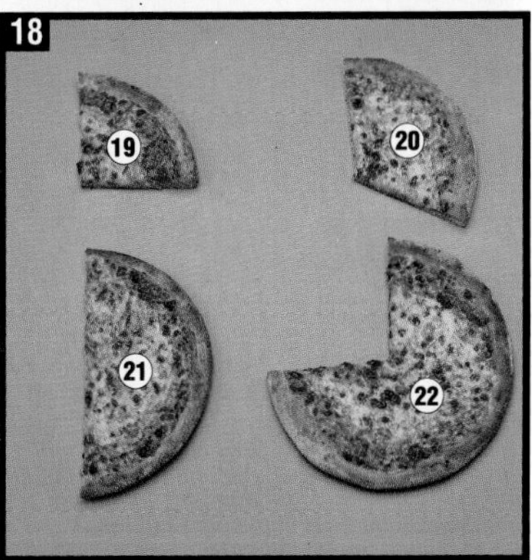

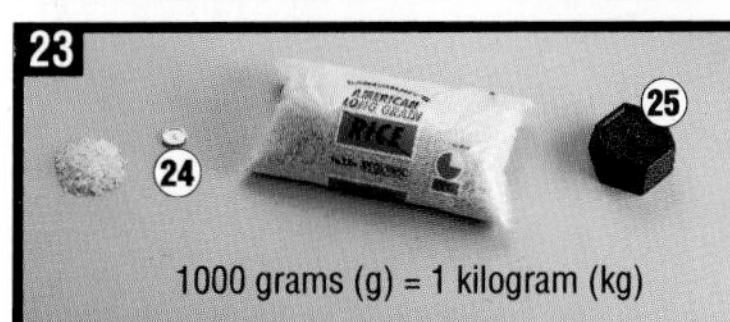

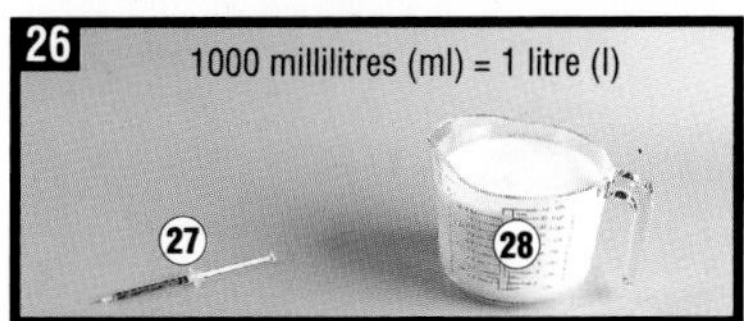

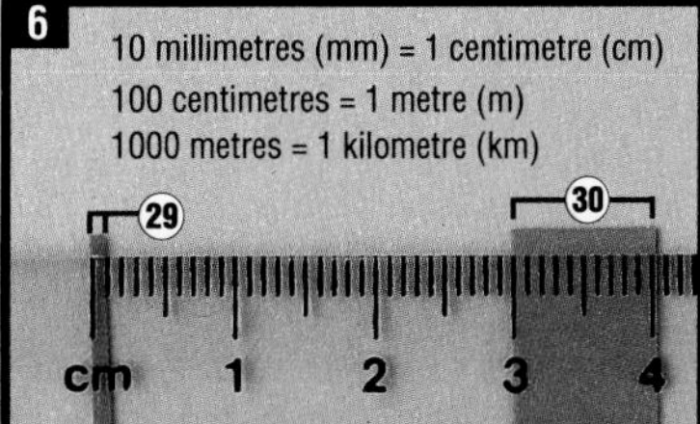

hloubka	**1**	depth
výška	**2**	height
šířka	**3**	width
hrana	**4**	edge
roh	**5**	corner
délka	**6**	length
přední stěna	**7**	front
dno	**8**	bottom
boční stěna	**9**	side
zadní stěna	**10**	back
plus	**11**	plus
minus	**12**	minus
násobeno/krát	**13**	multiplied by/times
děleno	**14**	divided by
rovná se	**15**	equals
dvě celé pět	**16**	two point five
padesát procent	**17**	fifty per cent
zlomky	**18**	fractions
čtvrtina	**19**	a quarter/ $\frac{1}{4}$
třetina	**20**	a third/ $\frac{1}{3}$
polovina	**21**	a half/ $\frac{1}{2}$
tři čtvrtiny	**22**	three quarters/ $\frac{3}{4}$
váha	**23**	weight
10 gramů	**24**	10 grams*
kilogram	**25**	kilogram*
objem	**26**	capacity
mililitr	**27**	millilitre (*US* milliliter)*
litr	**28**	litre (*US* liter)*
milimetr	**29**	millimetre (*US* millimeter)*
centimetr	**30**	centimetre (*US* centimeter)*

Tyto míry se obvykle neužívají v americké angličtině.

**These measurements are not usually used in US English.*

The Classroom page 49

tabule **1** blackboard (*US also* chalkboard)
žák **2** pupil (*esp US* student)
učebnice **3** textbook
sešit **4** exercise book (*US* notebook)
kalkulačka **5** calculator
trojúhelník **6** set square (*US* triangle)
úhloměr **7** protractor
školní taška **8** school bag
(dlaždicová) podlaha **9** (tiled) floor
židle **10** chair
globus **11** globe
nůžky **12** scissors
(malířský) stojan **13** easel
štětec **14** paintbrush
barvy **15** paintbox
učitelka **16** teacher
obraz **17** picture
mapa **18** map

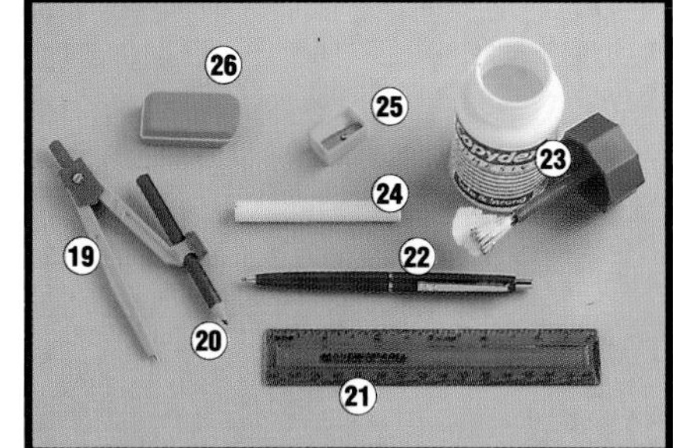

kružítko **19** (pair of) compasses (*also* compass)
tužka **20** pencil
pravítko **21** ruler
kuličkové pero **22** pen
lepidlo **23** glue
křída **24** (piece of) chalk
ořezávátko **25** pencil-sharpener
guma **26** rubber (*US* eraser)

page 50

Space

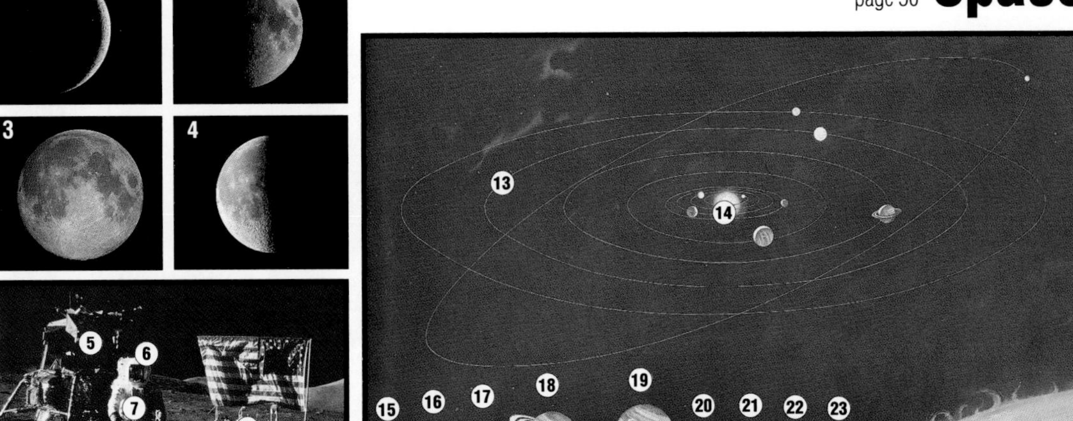

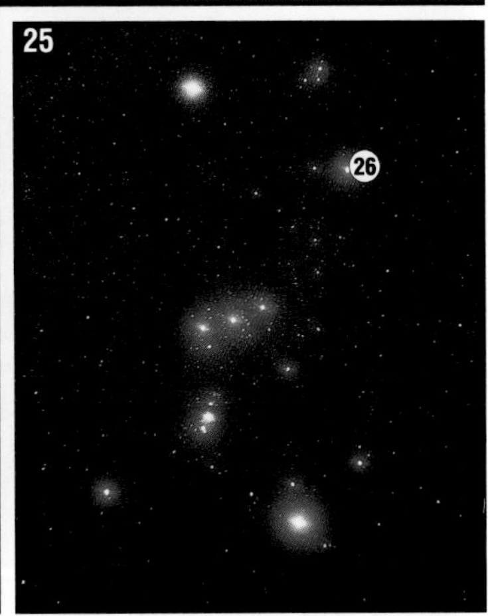

nový měsíc	**1** new moon (*esp US* crescent moon)
první čtvrt	**2** half moon (*US also* first quarter)
úplněk	**3** full moon
poslední čtvrt	**4** old moon (*US* half moon/last quarter)
lunární modul	**5** lunar module
kosmonaut	**6** astronaut
skafandr	**7** spacesuit
lunární vozidlo	**8** lunar vehicle
družice/satelit	**9** satellite
raketa	**10** rocket
raketoplán	**11** space shuttle
startovací plošina	**12** launch pad

Sluneční soustava	**The Solar System**
oběžná dráha	**13** orbit
Slunce	**14** Sun
Planety	**The Planets**
Pluto	**15** Pluto
Neptun	**16** Neptune
Uran	**17** Uranus
Saturn	**18** Saturn
Jupiter	**19** Jupiter
Mars	**20** Mars
Země	**21** Earth
Venuše	**22** Venus
Merkur	**23** Mercury
Vesmír	**Outer Space**
galaxie	**24** galaxy
souhvězdí	**25** constellation
hvězda	**26** star

The Weather page 51

Svítí slunce. **1** It's sunny.
Prší. **2** It's raining. (*US also* It's rainy.)
Sněží. **3** It's snowing. (*US also* It's snowy.)
sníh **4** snow
Je vítr. **5** It's windy.

Je opar. **6** It's misty.
Je mlha. **7** It's foggy.
Je oblačno. **8** It's cloudy.
Bude bouřka. **9** It's stormy.

bouřka **10** thunderstorm
blesk **11** lightning
duha **12** rainbow
Je jasno. **13** It's bright.
Je pošmourno. **14** It's dull. (*US* It's dark.)

page 52

The Temperature
The Seasons

9

10

11

12

Teplota	The Temperature
stupně Fahrenheita	**1** degrees Fahrenheit
stupně Celsia	**2** degrees Celsius (*or* centigrade)
Je horko.	**3** It's hot.
Je teplo.	**4** It's warm.
Je chladno.	**5** It's cool.
Je zima.	**6** It's cold.
Mrzne.	**7** It's freezing.
Je minus šest (stupňů).	**8** It's minus six (degrees). (*US* It's six (degrees) below zero.)

Roční období	The Seasons
na jaře	**9** in (the) spring
v létě	**10** in (the) summer
na podzim	**11** in (the) autumn (*US* in the fall)
v zimě	**12** in (the) winter

Měsíce	The Months
leden	January
únor	February
březen	March
duben	April
květen	May
červen	June
červenec	July
srpen	August
září	September
říjen	October
listopad	November
prosinec	December

The World page 53

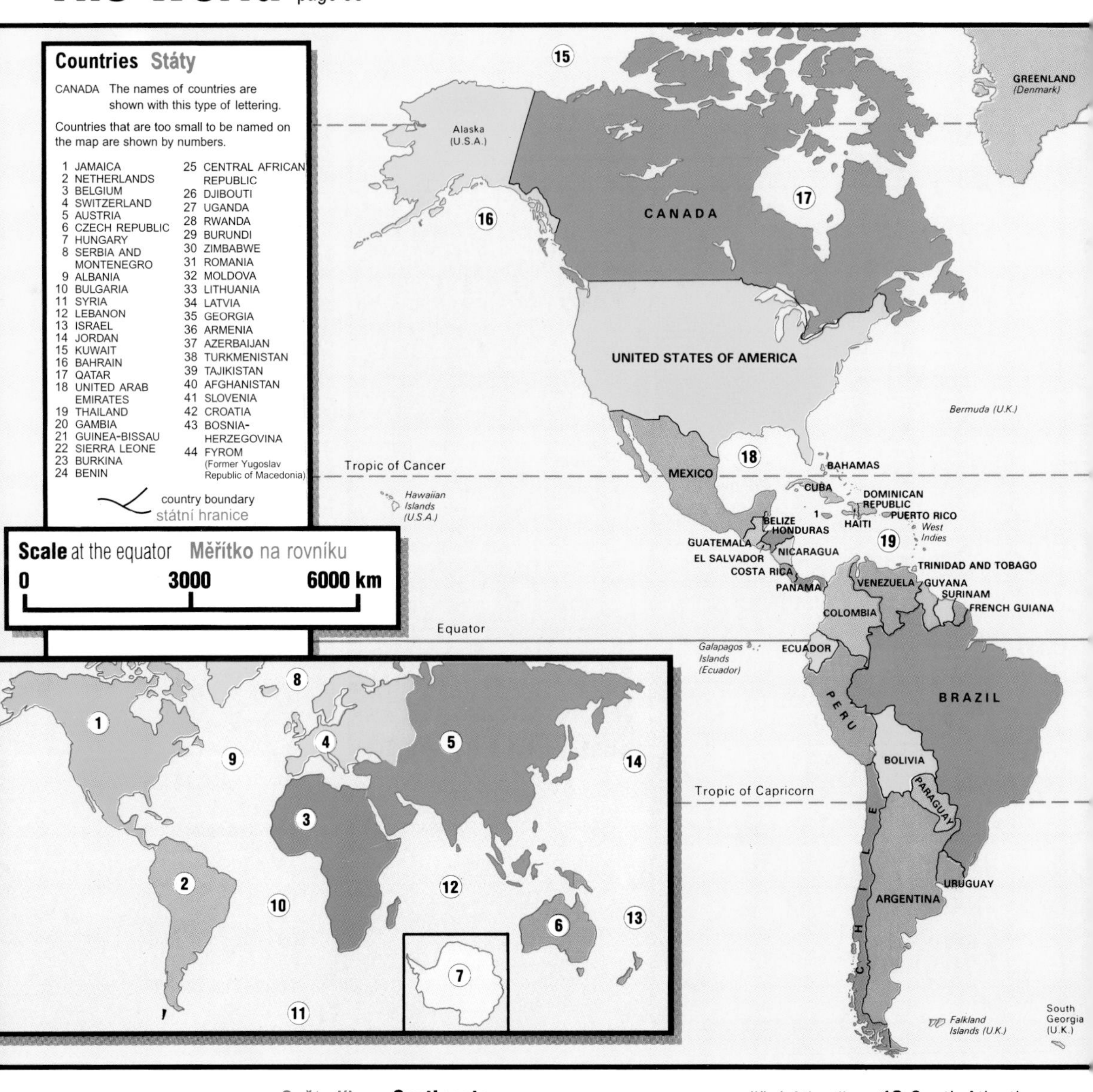

Světadíly	**Continents**
Severní Amerika	**1** North America
Jižní Amerika	**2** South America
Afrika	**3** Africa
Evropa	**4** Europe
Asie	**5** Asia
Austrálie	**6** Australia
Antarktida	**7** Antarctica
Oceány	**Oceans**
Severní ledový oceán	**8** Arctic
severní Atlantik	**9** North Atlantic
jižní Atlantik	**10** South Atlantic
Jižní ledové moře	**11** Antarctic
Indický oceán	**12** Indian
jižní Pacifik	**13** South Pacific
severní Pacifik	**14** North Pacific
Moře a zálivy	**Seas, Gulfs, and Bays**
Beaufortovo moře	**15** Beaufort Sea
Aljašský záliv	**16** Gulf of Alaska
Hudsonův záliv	**17** Hudson Bay
Mexický záliv	**18** Gulf of Mexico
Karibské moře	**19** Caribbean Sea

page 54 **The World**

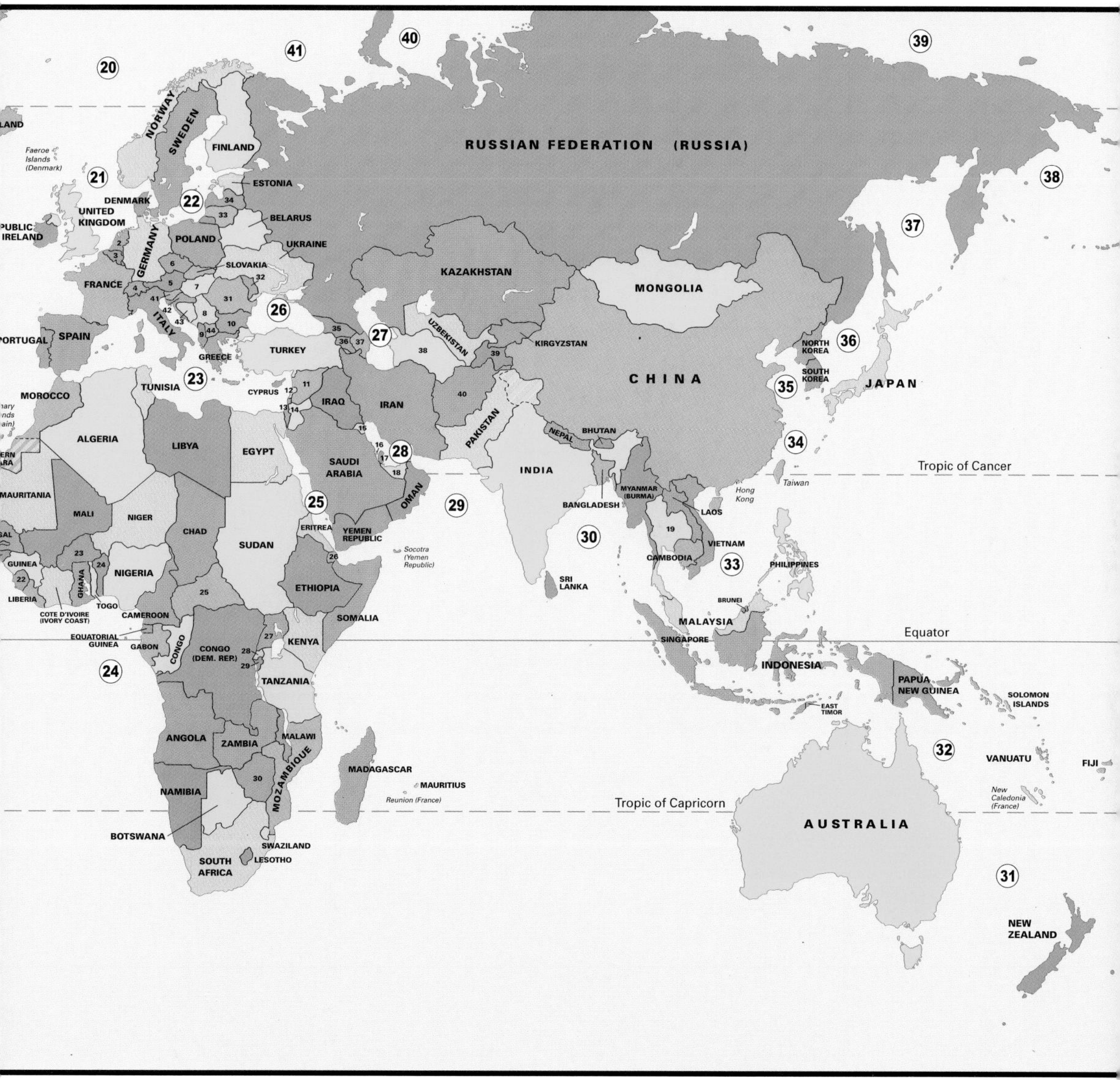

Norské moře	**20**	Norwegian Sea	Tasmanovo moře	**31**	Tasman Sea
Severní moře	**21**	North Sea	Korálové moře	**32**	Coral Sea
Baltské moře	**22**	Baltic Sea	Jihočínské moře	**33**	South China Sea
Středozemní moře	**23**	Mediterranean Sea	Východočínské moře	**34**	East China Sea
Guinejský záliv	**24**	Gulf of Guinea	Žluté moře	**35**	Yellow Sea
Rudé moře	**25**	Red Sea	Japonské moře	**36**	Sea of Japan *or* East Sea
Černé moře	**26**	Black Sea	Ochotské moře	**37**	Sea of Okhotsk
Kaspické moře	**27**	Caspian Sea	Beringovo moře	**38**	Bering Sea
Perský záliv	**28**	Persian Gulf	Moře Laptěvů	**39**	Laptev Sea
Arabské moře	**29**	Arabian Sea	Karelské moře	**40**	Kara Sea
Bengálský záliv	**30**	Bay of Bengal	Barentsovo moře	**41**	Barents Sea

The USA

page 55

Spojené státy americké (*zkr.* USA) = 50 států a federální oblast District of Columbia

the United States (of America) (*abbrs* (the) US, USA) = 50 States and the District of Columbia

state line hranice státu	lake jezero	mountain pohoří	main river hlavní řeka	island ostrov	• city *or* town velkoměsto *nebo* město

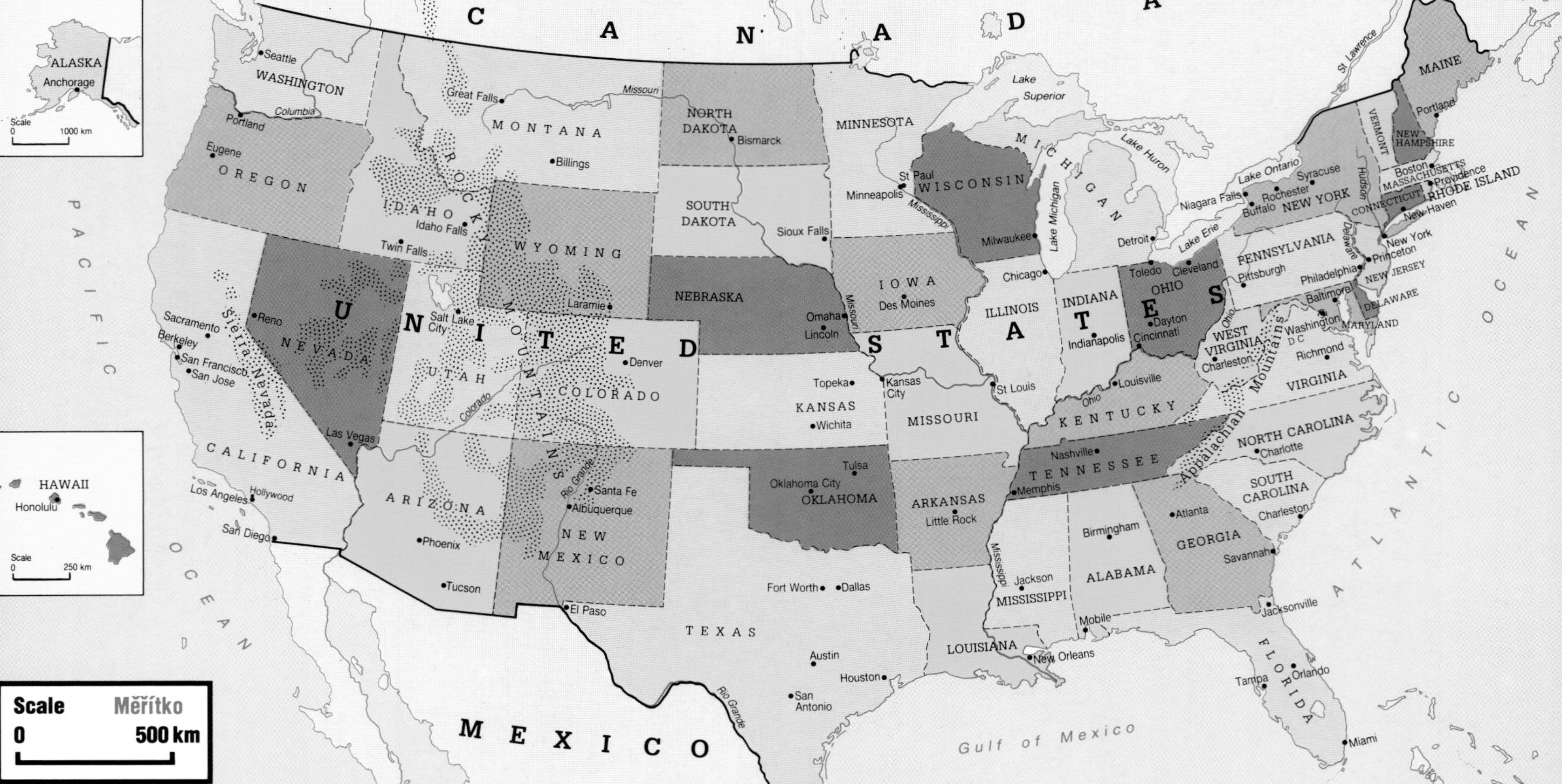

The British Isles

international boundary
national boundary
capital city
city or town
0 50 100 km
Great Britain (abbr GB) (also Britain) = England Scotland Wales
the United Kingdom (abbr (the) UK) = Great Britain Northern Ireland
the British Isles = Great Britain Ireland
Shetland Islands
Orkney Islands
Outer Hebrides
Inner Hebrides
SCOTLAND
Inverness
Aberdeen
Dundee
St Andrews
Stirling
Glasgow
Edinburgh
Berwick-upon-Tweed
Atlantic Ocean
NORTHERN IRELAND
Londonderry
Belfast
ISLE OF MAN
Douglas
Carlisle
Newcastle upon Tyne
Durham
Keswick
Middlesbrough
North Sea
Irish Sea
York
Blackpool
Leeds
Bradford
Kingston upon Hull
Galway
Dublin
Anglesey
Holyhead
Caernarfon
Liverpool
Manchester
Sheffield
ENGLAND
Chester
Lincoln
Limerick
Stoke-on-Trent
Derby
Nottingham
Shrewsbury
Leicester
Birmingham
Norwich
WALES
Coventry
Warwick
Ely
Worcester
Cambridge
Cork
Hereford
Stratford-upon-Avon
Ipswich
REPUBLIC OF IRELAND
Gloucester
Luton
Colchester
Oxford
Swansea
Cardiff
London
Bristol
Bath
Reading
Ramsgate
Canterbury
Dover
Taunton
Salisbury
Southampton
Hastings
Brighton
Strait of Dover
Exeter
Bournemouth
Poole
Portsmouth
Eastbourne
Isle of Wight
Plymouth
Isles of Scilly
English Channel

Prepositions 1 page 57

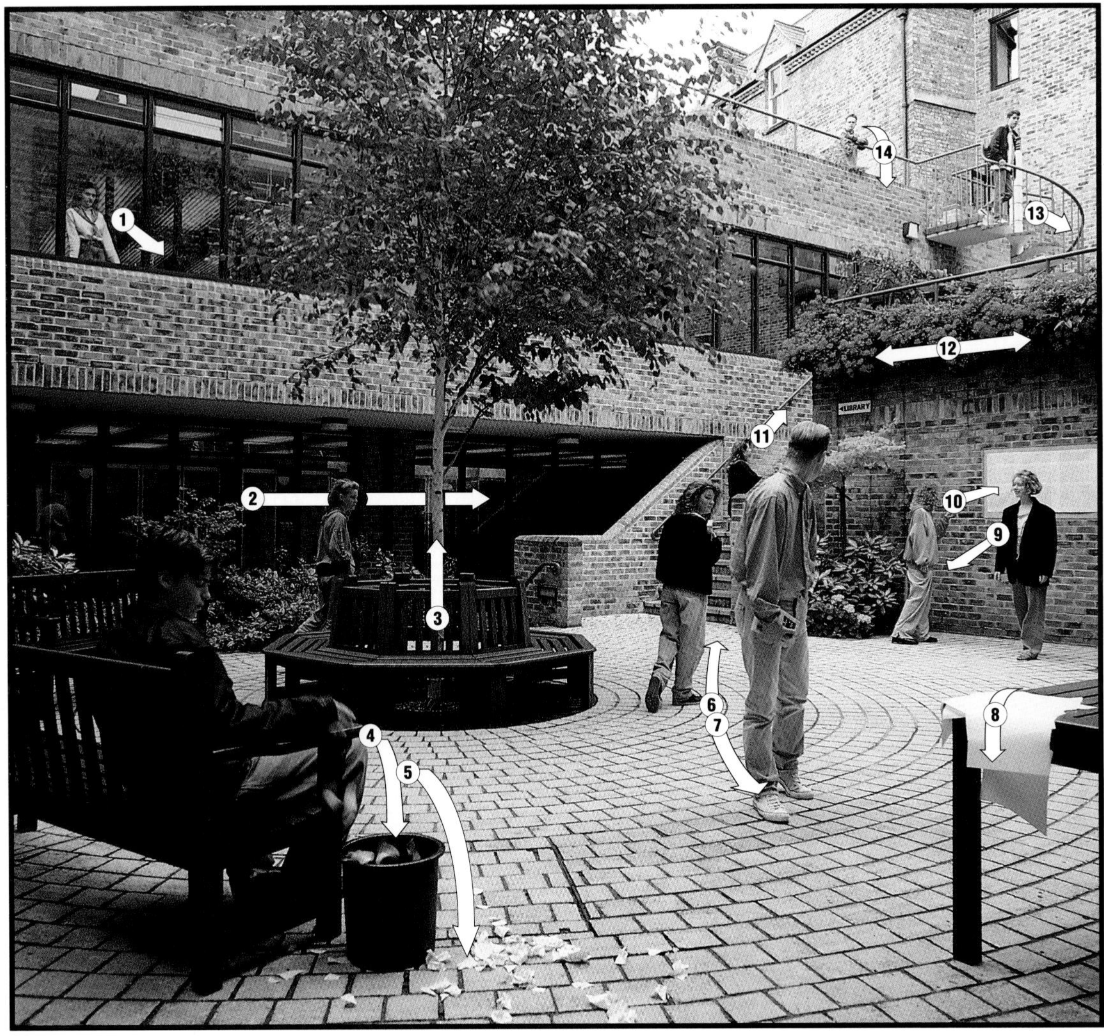

Dívá se **z** okna.	**1** She is looking **out of** the window.
Jde **přes** dvůr.	**2** She is walking **across** the courtyard.
Strom roste **skrz** lavičku.	**3** The tree is growing **through** the seat.
Vyhazuje papír **do** odpadkového koše.	**4** He is throwing some paper **into** the bin (*US* trash can).
Hází papír **na** zem.	**5** He is throwing some paper **onto** the ground.
Jde **do** knihovny.	**6** She is going **to** the library.
Přichází **z** knihovny.	**7** He is coming **from** the library.
Papír padá **ze** stolu.	**8** The paper is falling **off** the table.
Jde (**směrem**) **od** vývěsní tabule.	**9** She is walking **away from** the notice (*US* sign).
Jde (**směrem**) **k** vývěsní tabuli.	**10** She is walking **towards** (*esp US* **toward**) the notice (*US* sign).
Jde **do** schodů.	**11** She is walking **up** the steps.
Květiny rostou **podél** zdi.	**12** The flowers are growing **along** the wall.
Jde **ze** schodů.	**13** He is walking **down** the steps.
Dívá se **přes** zábradlí balkonu.	**14** He is looking **over** the balcony.

page 58

Prepositions 2

Keř je **za** oknem.	**1** The bush is **outside** the window.
Stuha je **okolo** koše.	**2** The ribbon is **round** the basket (*esp US* **around** the basket).
Kazety jsou **uvnitř v** zásuvce.	**3** The cassettes are **in/inside** the drawer.
Kniha je opřená **o** stůl.	**4** The book is **against** the table.
Hrnek je **pod** stolkem.	**5** The mug is **under/underneath** the table.
Stolek je **u/poblíž** krbu.	**6** The table is **by/near** the fireplace.
Sušené květiny jsou **v** krbu.	**7** The dried flowers are **in** the fireplace.
Hodiny jsou **mezi** svíčkami.	**8** The clock is **between** the candles.
Svíčka je **na** krbové římse.	**9** The candle is **on** the mantelpiece (*US* mantel).
Obraz je **nad** krbovou římsou.	**10** The picture is **over** the mantelpiece (*US* mantel).
Rostlina je (**nahoře**) **na** knihovně.	**11** The plant is **on top of** the bookcase.
Ozdobný předmět je **nahoře v** knihovně.	**12** The ornament is **at the top of** the bookcase.
Talíř je **uprostřed** knihovny.	**13** The plate is **in the middle of** the bookcase.
Knihy jsou **dole v** knihovně.	**14** The books are **at the bottom of** the bookcase.
Talíře jsou **nad** knihami.	**15** The plates are **above** the books.
Šálky jsou **pod** konvicí.	**16** The cups are **below** the teapot.
Konvice je **vedle** talíře.	**17** The teapot is **beside/next to** the plate.
Televizor je **před** časopisy.	**18** The television is **in front of** the magazines.
Časopisy jsou **za** televizorem.	**19** The magazines are **behind** the television.

The City 1 page 59

dopravní značka	**1**	road sign
parkovací značka	**2**	parking notice (*US* parking sign)
poštovní schránka	**3**	letter-box/pillar-box (*US* mailbox)
kavárna	**4**	café (*also* cafe)
policista	**5**	police officer
chodník	**6**	pavement (*US* sidewalk)
poklop kanálové šachty	**7**	manhole cover
stružka	**8**	gutter
obrubník	**9**	kerb (*US* curb)
ulice	**10**	street
roh ulice	**11**	street corner
obchod	**12**	shop (*esp US* store)
provoz	**13**	traffic
odpadkový koš	**14**	litter-bin (*US* trash can/garbage can)
novinový stánek	**15**	news-stand
noviny	**16**	newspaper
kamelot	**17**	news-vendor (*Brit only*)
obchodní dům	**18**	department store
prapor	**19**	flag

reklama	**20**	advertisement
přístřešek u autobusové zastávky	**21**	bus shelter
autobusová zastávka	**22**	bus stop
továrna	**23**	factory
přechod pro chodce	**24**	pedestrian crossing (*US* crosswalk)

page 60

The City 2

budova	**1** building
park	**2** park
kočárek	**3** pram (*US* baby carriage)
sportovní kočárek (skládací)	**4** pushchair (*US* stroller)
postranní ulice	**5** side street
taxi/taxík	**6** taxi/cab
stožár pouličního osvětleni	**7** lamppost
chodec	**8** pedestrian
železný plot	**9** railings
tabule s názvem ulice	**10** street sign
člun	**11** boat
výšková budova/mrakodrap	**12** tower block (*esp US* skyscraper)
obloha	**13** sky
silueta/obzor	**14** skyline
most	**15** bridge
přístavní molo	**16** pier
řeka	**17** river
břeh	**18** bank
Na předměstí	**In the suburbs**
semafor	**19** traffic-lights (*US* traffic light)
cyklista	**20** cyclist (*US* bicyclist)
křižovatka	**21** crossroads (*US* intersection)
dvojitá žlutá čára	**22** double yellow lines (*Brit only*)
ukazatel	**23** signpost
automobil	**24** car
poschoďový autobus	**25** double-decker bus
kruhový objezd	**26** roundabout (*US* traffic circle/rotary)

Roads and Road Signs 1 page 61

dej přednost v jízdě	**1**	give way (*US* yield)
stůj!	**2**	stop
vjezd zakázán	**3**	no entry (*US* do not enter)
provoz oběma směry	**4**	two-way traffic
zákaz otáčení	**5**	no U-turn
omezení rychlosti	**6**	speed limit
zákaz odbočení vlevo	**7**	no left turn
dvojitá zatáčka (první vpravo)	**8**	bend to right (*US* curve to right)
stezka pro pěší a cyklisty	**9**	cycle and pedestrian route (*US* bike and pedestrian path)
jednosměrná ulice	**10**	one-way street
motorest	**11**	service station (*US* service area)
přikázaný směr doprava	**12**	turn right
práce na silnici	**13**	roadworks (*US* road work)
výklopný vůz/dampr	**14**	dumper (truck) (*esp US* dump truck)
stavební dělník	**15**	construction worker
pneumatická sbíječka	**16**	pneumatic drill (*US also* jackhammer)
kužel (dopravní)	**17**	cone
buldozer s rýpadlem	**18**	JCB (*US* backhoe)
zemina	**19**	soil

page 62

Roads and Road Signs 2

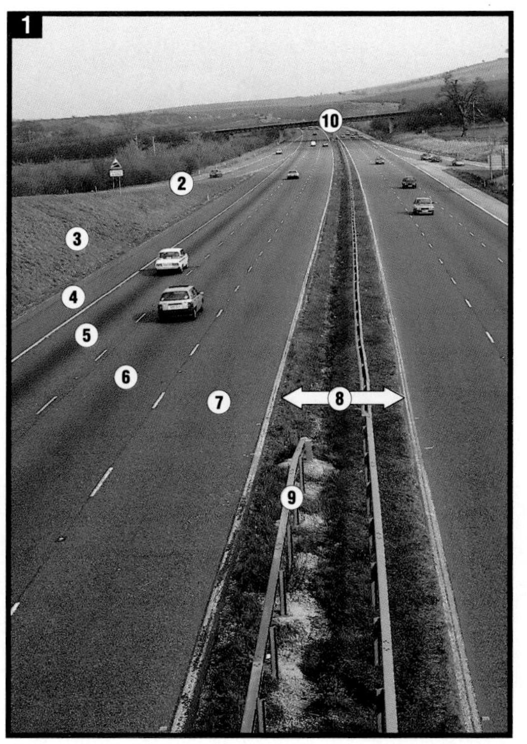

dálnice	**1**	motorway (*Brit*)
vjezd na dálnici	**2**	slip-road (*Brit*)
násep	**3**	embankment (*Brit*)
zpevněná krajnice	**4**	hard shoulder (*Brit*)
vnitřní pruh/pomalý pruh	**5**	inside lane/slow lane (*Brit*)
střední pruh	**6**	middle lane/centre lane (*Brit*)
vnější pruh/rychlý pruh	**7**	outside lane/fast lane (*Brit*)
dělicí pás	**8**	central reservation (*Brit*)
svodidlo	**9**	crash barrier (*Brit*)
nadjezd	**10**	flyover (*Brit*)
dálnice	**11**	freeway/ interstate highway (*US*)
výjezd z dálnice	**12**	exit ramp (*US*)
násep	**13**	bank (*US*)
zpevněná krajnice	**14**	shoulder (*US*)
pravý pruh/pomalý pruh	**15**	right lane/slow lane (*US*)
střední pruh	**16**	center lane/middle lane (*US*)
levý pruh/rychlý pruh	**17**	left lane/fast lane/ passing lane (*US*)
dělicí pás	**18**	median strip (*US*)
svodidlo	**19**	guardrail (*US*)
nadjezd	**20**	overpass (*US*)

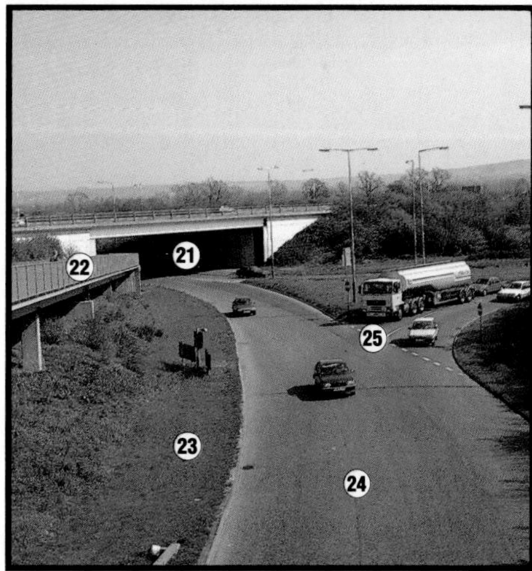

podjezd	**21**	underpass
můstek pro pěší	**22**	footbridge
travnatá krajnice	**23**	grass verge (*US* shoulder)
silnice	**24**	road (*US* highway)
křižovatka	**25**	junction (*esp US* intersection)

Vehicles page 63

transportér	**1** transporter
dálkový autobus	**2** coach (*US* bus)
cisternový vůz	**3** tanker (*US* fuel truck)
nákladní automobil	**4** lorry (*US* truck)
dodávka	**5** van
míchačka betonu	**6** cement-mixer (*US* cement truck)
dodávka pick-up	**7** pick-up truck
vysokozdvižný vozík	**8** fork-lift truck
obytný přívěs/karavan	**9** caravan (*US* trailer)
džíp	**10** jeep
sportovní auto	**11** sports car
sedan	**12** saloon (*US* sedan)
kabriolet	**13** convertible
kombi (větší, pětidveřové)	**14** estate (*US* station wagon)
kombi (menší, třídveřové)	**15** hatchback

page 64

The Car

čerpací stanice	**1** filling-station (*US also* gas station)
vnější zpětné zrcátko	**2** wing mirror (*US* side mirror)
blinkr	**3** indicator (*US* turn signal)
přední světlo	**4** headlight
státní poznávací značka	**5** number-plate (*US* license plate)
výfuk	**6** exhaust-pipe
nárazník	**7** bumper
zadní světlo	**8** rear-light (*US* taillight)
kufr	**9** boot (*US* trunk)
stěrač zadního skla	**10** rear windscreen wiper (*US* rear windshield wiper)
benzinové čerpadlo	**11** petrol pump (*US* gas pump)
hadice	**12** hose
hubice	**13** nozzle
kapota	**14** bonnet (*US* hood)
motor	**15** engine
vzduchový filtr	**16** air filter
hlava válce	**17** cylinder head
mřížka chladiče	**18** radiator grille
přední sklo	**19** windscreen (*US* windshield)
přístrojová deska	**20** dashboard
řadicí páka	**21** gear lever (*US* gearshift)
volant	**22** steering-wheel
palivoměr	**23** fuel gauge (*US also* gas gauge)
tachometr	**24** speedometer
zapalování	**25** ignition
spojka	**26** clutch
nožní brzda	**27** footbrake
pedál plynu/plyn	**28** accelerator (*US also* gas pedal)

Bikes page 65

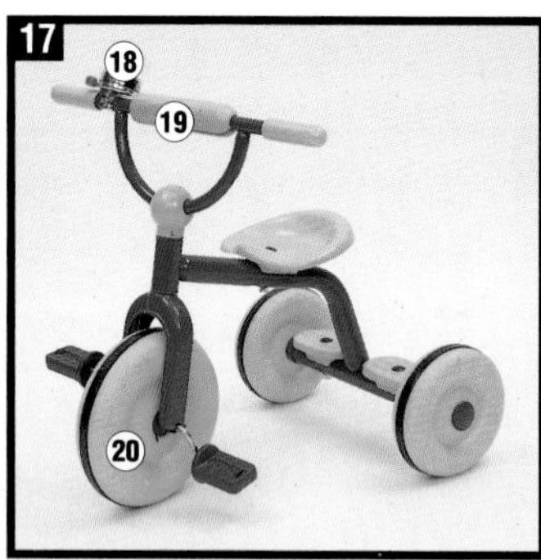

jízdní kolo/kolo	**1** bicycle/bike
sedlo	**2** saddle (*esp US* seat)
pumpička	**3** pump
rám	**4** frame
klika pedálu	**5** crank
zámek	**6** lock
paprsky/dráty	**7** spokes
řetěz	**8** chain
pedál	**9** pedal
řetězové kolo	**10** chain-wheel
ventilek	**11** valve
náboj kola	**12** hub
přehazovačka	**13** gear lever (*US* gear changer)
odrazové sklo	**14** reflector
lanko	**15** cable
brzdová páka	**16** brake lever

tříkolka	**17** tricycle
zvonek	**18** bell
řídítka	**19** handlebar
kolo	**20** wheel
skútr	**21** scooter
blatník	**22** mudguard (*US* fender)
sedlo	**23** seat
kufr	**24** top box (*US* top case)
motocykl	**25** motor cycle (*Brit also* motor bike)
plyn	**26** accelerator/throttle
pneumatika	**27** tyre (*US* tire)
motor	**28** engine
tlumiče (nárazů)	**29** shock absorbers

page 66

The Railway (*US* Railroad)

stavědlo	**1** signal-box (*US* signal tower)
(úrovňový) železniční přejezd	**2** level crossing (*US* grade crossing)
lokomotiva	**3** engine
vagon	**4** coach (*US* passenger car)
Metro	**The Underground (*US* The Subway)**
východ (označení)	**5** exit sign
nástupiště	**6** platform
trať/kolej	**7** line(s) (*esp US* track)
vlak	**8** train
tunel	**9** tunnel
Na nádraží	**At the Station**
výdejna jízdenek/pokladna	**10** ticket office (*US* ticket counter)
okýnko	**11** window
fronta	**12** queue (*US* line)
taška	**13** bag
kufr	**14** suitcase
jízdní řád	**15** timetable
batoh	**16** rucksack (*esp US* backpack)
tabule s odjezdy	**17** departures board (*US* departure board)
číslo nástupiště	**18** platform number (*US* track number)
kontrolor jízdenek	**19** ticket-collector (*US* ticket taker)
cestující	**20** passenger
vstup (na nástupiště 10)	**21** entrance (to platform 10)
bariéra	**22** barrier (*esp US* gate)

At the Airport 1 page 67

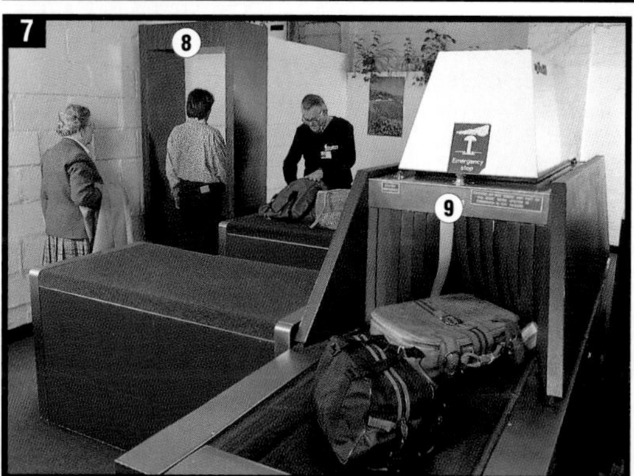

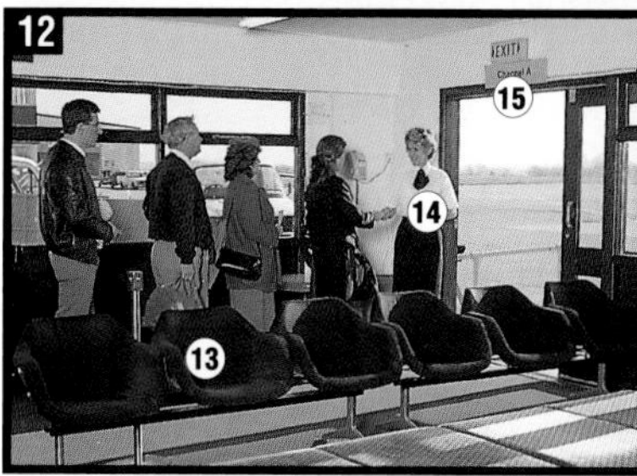

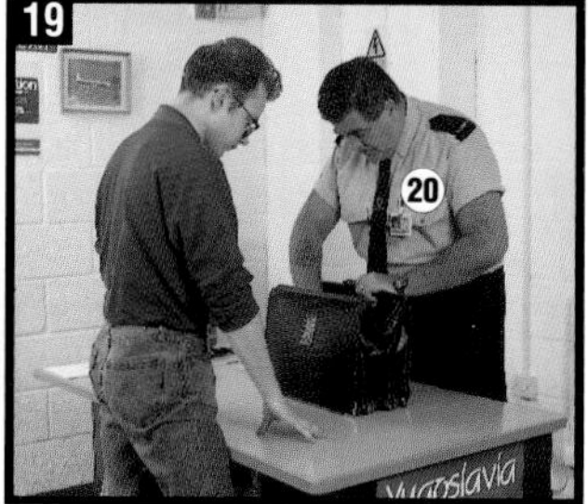

V letištní budově	**In the terminal**
odbavení	**1** check-in
letenka	**2** airline ticket
palubní karta	**3** boarding pass
odbavovací přepážka	**4** check-in desk (*US* check-in counter)
pasová kontrola	**5** passport control
pas	**6** passport
bezpečnostní odbavení	**7** security
detektor kovů	**8** metal detector
rentgenový snímač	**9** X-ray scanner
prodejna bezcelního zboží	**10** duty-free shop
parfém	**11** perfume
odletová hala	**12** departures lounge (*US* departure lounge/ waiting area)
sedadlo	**13** seat
letuška	**14** steward (*US* flight attendant)
východ (k letadlům)	**15** gate
výdej zavazadel	**16** luggage reclaim (*US* baggage reclaim)
zavazadla	**17** luggage
vozík	**18** trolley (*US* cart)
celní prohlídka	**19** customs
celník	**20** customs officer

page 68

At the Airport 2

nástup do letadla	**1** boarding
cestující	**2** passenger
vozík	**3** trailer (*US* cart)
řídicí věž	**4** control tower
letecký dispečer	**5** air traffic controller
start	**6** take-off
rozjezdová/přistávací dráha	**7** runway
přistání	**8** landing
vrtulník/helikoptéra	**9** helicopter
vrtule (nosná)/rotor	**10** rotor
pilot	**11** pilot
letadlo	**12** plane
nos	**13** nose
pilotní kabina	**14** cockpit
vrtule	**15** propeller
křídlo	**16** wing
trup	**17** fuselage
ocas	**18** tail
tryskový/proudový motor	**19** jet engine

In Port 1 page 69

plachetnice	**1** sailing-ship
stěžeň	**2** mast
plachta	**3** sail
paluba	**4** deck
kajuta	**5** cabin
lano	**6** cable (*US* line)
veslový člun	**7** rowing-boat (*US* rowboat)
veslo	**8** oar
říční člun/hausbót	**9** barge
přístaviště	**10** marina
motorový člun	**11** motor boat
jachta	**12** yacht (*US also* sailboat)
kajutová jachta	**13** cabin cruiser
rybářský člun	**14** fishing boat
uvázání lodi	**15** mooring
příď	**16** bow
záď	**17** stern
záchranný člun	**18** lifeboat
kajak	**19** canoe (*US* kayak)
pádlo	**20** paddle

page 70

In Port 2

dok	**1** dock
jeřáb	**2** crane
skladiště	**3** warehouse
náklad	**4** cargo
loď	**5** ship
tanker	**6** (oil-)tanker
člun na podvodních křídlech	**7** hydrofoil
vznášedlo	**8** hovercraft
trajekt	**9** ferry
komín	**10** funnel (*US* smokestack)
osobní linková loď	**11** liner (*esp US* ocean liner)
maják	**12** lighthouse
skály	**13** rocks
nafukovací člun	**14** inflatable dinghy (*US* rubber raft)
přívěsný lodní motor	**15** outboard motor
kotva	**16** anchor

Holidays 1 (*US* Vacations) page 71

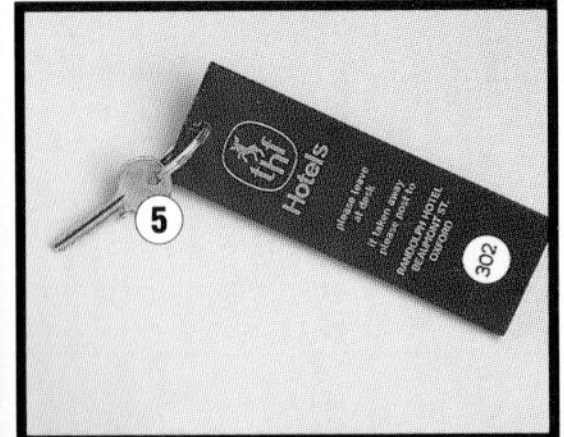

hotelová recepce	**1** hotel reception (*US* front desk)
hotelový sluha/nosič	**2** porter (*US also* bellhop)
host	**3** guest
recepční	**4** receptionist
klíč od pokoje	**5** room key
jednolůžkový pokoj	**6** single room
pokoj s dvojlůžkem	**7** double room
dvoulůžkový pokoj	**8** twin room (*US* room with twin beds)
prohlídka památek	**9** sightseeing
průvodkyně	**10** tour guide
skupina turistů	**11** party of tourists
turistka	**12** tourist
hrad	**13** castle
zámek	**14** country house
vesnice	**15** village
venkov/krajina	**16** the countryside
piknik	**17** picnic
stanování/táboření	**18** camping
stan	**19** tent
podlážka	**20** groundsheet
spací pytel	**21** sleeping-bag
vařič	**22** camping stove (*US* camp stove)
pěší turistika	**23** hiking
pěší turista	**24** hiker
batoh	**25** rucksack (*esp US* backpack)
autokempink pro přívěsy	**26** caravan site (*US* trailer camp)
obytný přívěs/karavan	**27** caravan (*US* trailer)

page 72

Holidays 2 (*US* Vacations)

pobřeží	**1** the seaside (*esp US* the beach)
letovisko	**2** holiday resort
pláž	**3** beach
pobřežní zeď	**4** sea wall
promenáda	**5** promenade (*esp US* seafront)
výletní plavba	**6** cruise
lehátko	**7** sunbed
slunící se člověk	**8** sunbather
slunečník	**9** sunshade
plachtění	**10** sailing
dovolená na lodi	**11** boating holiday (*US* boating vacation)
kanál	**12** canal
rybaření	**13** fishing
sportovní rybář	**14** angler
rybářský prut	**15** fishing-rod
jízda na ponících	**16** pony-trekking (*US* horseback riding)
safari	**17** safari
parašutismus	**18** parachuting
padák	**19** parachute
létání balonem	**20** ballooning
balon na horký vzduch	**21** hot-air balloon
létání na rogalu	**22** hang-gliding
rogalo	**23** hang-glider
horolezectví	**24** climbing
horolezec	**25** climber
úvaz	**26** harness

The Environment page 73

hora	**1**	mountain
vrchol	**2**	peak
údolí	**3**	valley
jezero	**4**	lake
les	**5**	forest
vodopád	**6**	waterfall
potok	**7**	stream
moře	**8**	sea
skály	**9**	rocks
pláž	**10**	beach
útes	**11**	cliff
kopec	**12**	hill
nádrž	**13**	reservoir
přehrada	**14**	dam
poušť	**15**	desert
písek	**16**	sand
duna	**17**	sand-dune
náhorní plošina	**18**	plateau
lesík	**19**	wood (*esp US* woods)
farma	**20**	farm
obytné stavení	**21**	farmhouse
stodola	**22**	barn
rybník	**23**	pond
pole	**24**	field
kombajn	**25**	combine harvester (*US* combine)
obilné pole	**26**	cornfield
zrní	**27**	grain
traktor	**28**	tractor
pluh	**29**	plough (*esp US* plow)
brázda	**30**	furrow

page 74

Hobbies

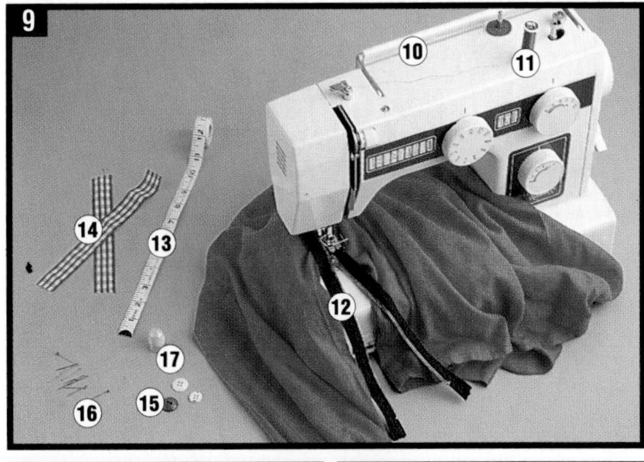

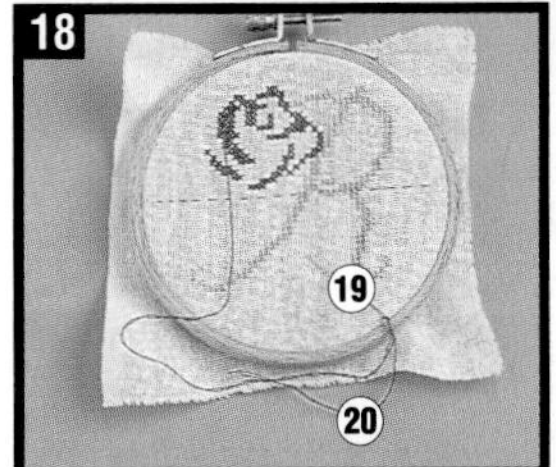

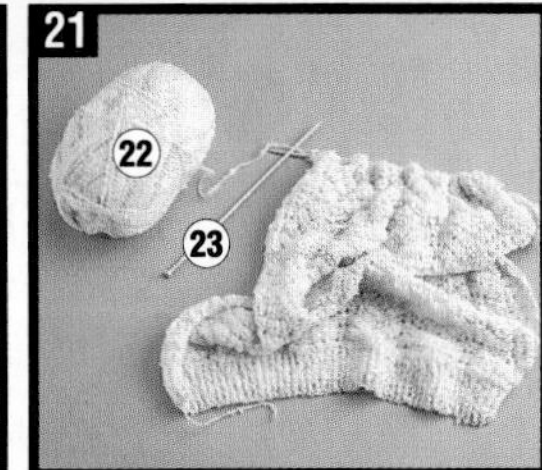

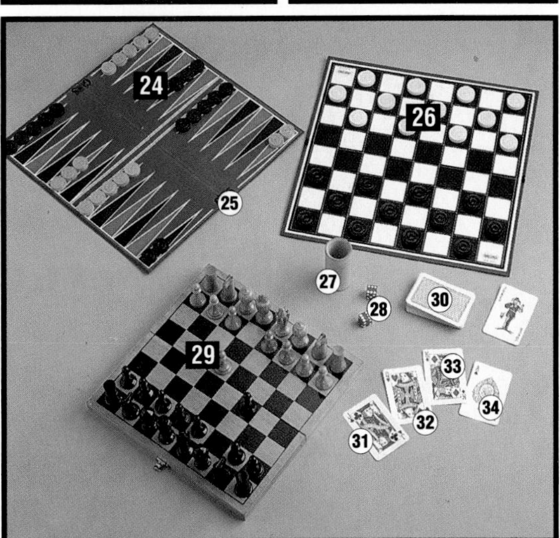

malování	**1** painting
kreslení	**2** drawing
hrnčířství	**3** pottery
sbírání známek/filatelie	**4** stamp collecting
album na známky	**5** stamp album
modelářství	**6** making models
modelářská stavebnice	**7** kit
model	**8** model
šití	**9** sewing
šicí stroj	**10** sewing-machine
cívka nitě	**11** reel of cotton (*US* spool of thread)
zip	**12** zip (*esp US* zipper)
krejčovský metr	**13** tape-measure
stuha	**14** ribbon
knoflík	**15** button
špendlík	**16** pin
náprstek	**17** thimble
vyšívání	**18** embroidery
jehla	**19** needle
nit	**20** thread
pletení	**21** knitting
vlna	**22** wool
pletací jehlice	**23** knitting-needle
lurč	**24** backgammon
hrací deska	**25** board
dáma	**26** draughts (*US* checkers)
pohárek (na vrhání kostek)	**27** shaker
kostky	**28** dice
šachy	**29** chess
sada karet	**30** pack of playing-cards
křížový kluk	**31** jack/knave of clubs
srdcová dáma	**32** queen of hearts
kárový král	**33** king of diamonds
pikové eso	**34** ace of spades

Musical Instruments

page 75

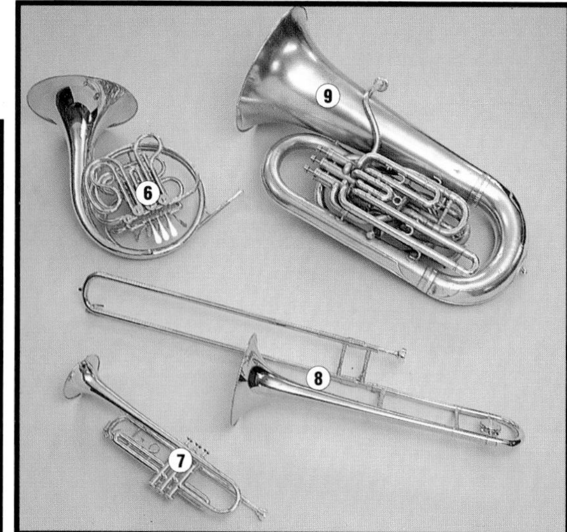

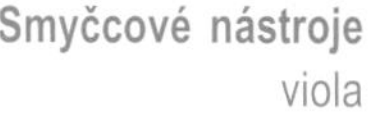

Smyčcové nástroje	**Strings**
viola	**1** viola
smyčec	**2** bow
cello/violoncello	**3** cello
housle	**4** violin
kontrabas/basa	**5** (double-)bass
Žesťové nástroje	**Brass**
lesní roh	**6** French horn
trubka	**7** trumpet
pozoun/trombon	**8** trombone
tuba	**9** tuba
Dechové nástroje	**Woodwind**
pikola	**10** piccolo
zobcová flétna	**11** recorder
flétna	**12** flute
hoboj	**13** oboe
klarinet	**14** clarinet
fagot	**15** bassoon
saxofon	**16** saxophone
Bicí nástroje	**Percussion**
tympán	**17** kettledrum
tamburína	**18** tambourine
paličky	**19** drumsticks
bonga	**20** bongos
činely	**21** cymbals
conga	**22** conga
Jiné nástroje	**Other instruments**
akordeon	**23** accordion
klávesy	**24** keys
harmonika (foukací)	**25** harmonica

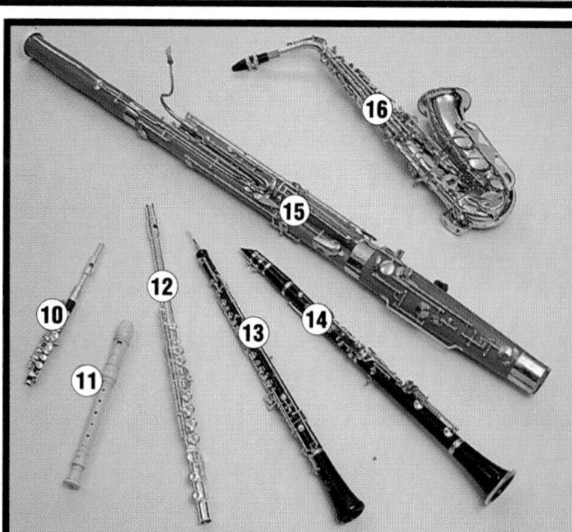

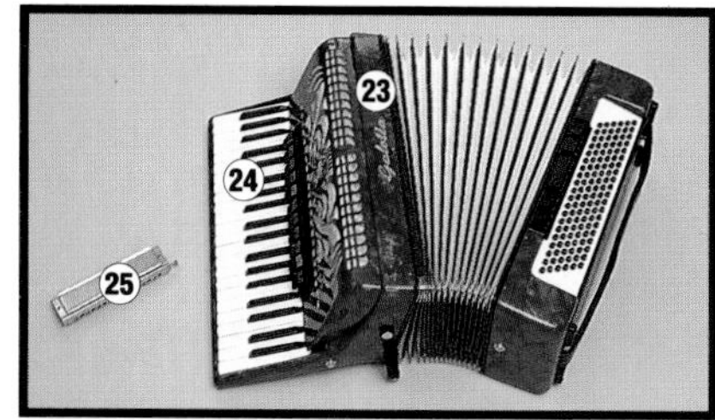

page 76

Music and Theatre (*US* Theater)

Hudba	**Music**
orchestr	**1** orchestra
hudebník	**2** musician
klavír	**3** piano
dirigent	**4** conductor
taktovka	**5** baton
noty	**6** sheet music
skupina pop music	**7** pop group
kytara (elektrická)	**8** (electric) guitar
zpěvák	**9** singer/vocalist
buben	**10** drum
bubeník	**11** drummer
hráč na klávesové nástroje	**12** keyboard player
syntezátor	**13** synthesizer
Divadlo	**The Theatre (*US* Theater)**
výprava/kulisy	**14** scenery
jeviště	**15** stage
herec	**16** actor
herečka	**17** actress
(postranní) zákulisí	**18** wings
orchestřiště	**19** orchestra pit
přízemí	**20** stalls (*US* orchestra seats)
balkon	**21** circle/balcony (*US* mezzanine)
galerie	**22** gallery (*US* balcony)
Kino	**The Cinema (*US* Movie Theater)**
promítací plátno	**23** screen
filmová hvězda	**24** film star (*US* movie star)
uvaděč	**25** usher
uvaděčka	**26** usher (*Brit also* usherette)
ulička	**27** aisle
obecenstvo	**28** audience

Sports 1 page 77

bruslení	**1** ice-skating
bruslit	**2** skate (*verb*)
bruslařka	**3** skater
brusle	**4** ice-skate
kluziště	**5** ice-rink (*esp US* rink)
lyžování	**6** skiing
lyžovat	**7** ski (*verb*)
hůlka	**8** pole
lyže	**9** ski
vodní lyžování	**10** water-skiing
jezdit na vodních lyžích	**11** water-ski (*verb*)
vodní lyžař	**12** water-skier
surfing	**13** surfing
vlna	**14** wave
surfovat	**15** surf (*verb*)
surfař	**16** surfer
prkno na surfing	**17** surfboard
windsurfing	**18** windsurfing
windsurfař	**19** windsurfer
prkno na windsurfing	**20** sailboard
potápění s akvalungem	**21** scuba-diving
kyslíková bomba	**22** (air)tank
potápění s dýchací trubicí	**23** snorkelling (*US* snorkeling)
dýchací trubice	**24** snorkel
plavání	**25** swimming
plavat	**26** swim (*verb*)
plavec	**27** swimmer
plavecký bazén	**28** swimming-pool
skočit po hlavě	**29** dive (*verb*)
skokan do vody	**30** diver

page 78

Sports 2

baseball	**1** baseball
pálkařská přilba	**2** batting helmet
pálkař	**3** batter
baseballová rukavice	**4** baseball glove/mitt
maska chytače	**5** face mask/catcher's mask
chytač	**6** catcher
diváci	**7** crowd
basketbal	**8** basketball
síťka	**9** net
střílet	**10** shoot (*verb*)
americký fotbal	**11** American football (*US* football)
fotbalový míč	**12** football
hodit	**13** throw (*verb*)
ragby	**14** rugby
složit	**15** tackle (*verb*)
pozemní hokej	**16** hockey (*US* field hockey)
hokejista	**17** hockey player
hokejka	**18** hockey stick
hokejový míček	**19** hockey ball
volejbal	**20** volleyball
vyskočit	**21** jump (*verb*)
squash	**22** squash
raketa	**23** racket (*also* racquet)
badminton	**24** badminton
badmintonový míček	**25** shuttlecock
stolní tenis	**26** table tennis (*esp US* ping-pong)
pálka na stolní tenis	**27** table tennis bat (*US* paddle)
odpálit	**28** hit (*verb*)

Sports 3 page 79

šipky	**1** darts
terč na šipky	**2** dartboard
mířit	**3** aim (*verb*)
kulečník	**4** snooker
tágo	**5** cue
stůl	**6** table
kapsa	**7** pocket
bowling/americké kuželky	**8** bowling
kuželková dráha	**9** bowling-alley
kuželky	**10** pins
golf	**11** golf
nosič holí	**12** caddy
golfová dráha	**13** fairway
jamkoviště/green	**14** green
golfová hůl	**15** club
jamka	**16** hole
box	**17** boxing
roh	**18** corner
ring	**19** ring
provazy	**20** ropes
boxerská rukavice	**21** boxing glove
udeřit	**22** punch (*verb*)
zápas	**23** wrestling
zápasit	**24** wrestle (*verb*)
rozhodčí	**25** referee
judo	**26** judo
karate	**27** karate
seknout	**28** chop (*verb*)

page 80

Sports 4

gymnastika	**1** gymnastics
gymnasta	**2** gymnast
cyklistika	**3** cycling
jezdit na kole	**4** cycle (*verb*)
automobilové závody	**5** motor-racing (*US* auto racing)
závodní dráha	**6** racetrack
závodní automobil	**7** racing car (*US* race car)
automobilový závodník	**8** racing driver (*US* race car driver)
jízda na koni	**9** riding (*US* horseback riding)
jezdit na koni	**10** ride (*verb*)
jezdec	**11** rider
sedlo	**12** saddle
třmeny	**13** stirrups
otěže	**14** reins
atletika	**15** athletics (*US* track and field)
doplňkové sektory	**16** field
závodní dráha	**17** track
diváci	**18** spectators
běžecká dráha	**19** lane
atlet	**20** athlete
běžet	**21** run (*verb*)
startovací blok	**22** starting-block
dostihy	**23** horse-racing
jet dostih	**24** race (*verb*)
dostihový kůň	**25** racehorse
žokej	**26** jockey
startovací box	**27** starting-gate
dostihová dráha	**28** racecourse (*esp US* racetrack)

Sports 5 page 81

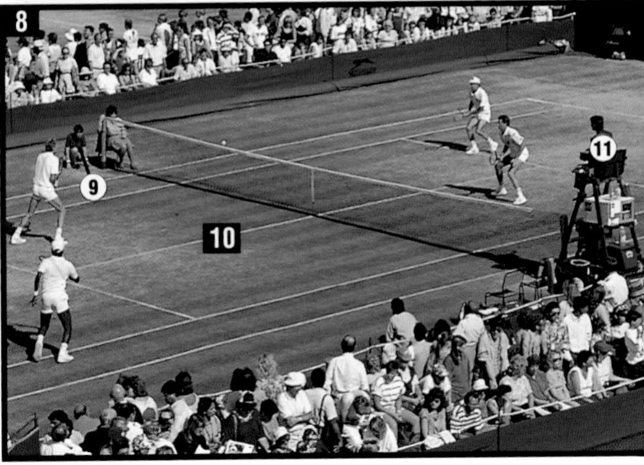

Tenis	**Tennis**
dvouhra	**1** singles match
podávat	**2** serve (*verb*)
podávající hráč	**3** server
základní čára	**4** baseline
servisová čára	**5** service line
postranní čáry	**6** tramlines (*US* sidelines)
síť	**7** net
čtyřhra	**8** doubles match
sběrač míčků	**9** ballboy
tenisový kurt	**10** tennis-court
rozhodčí	**11** umpire

Kriket	**Cricket**
kriketový zápas	**12** cricket match
polař u branky	**13** wicket-keeper
pálkař	**14** batsman
chrániče	**15** pads
prostor mezi brankami	**16** pitch
nadhazovač	**17** bowler
nadhazovat	**18** bowl (*verb*)
branka	**19** wicket/stumps
rozhodčí	**20** umpire
polař	**21** fielder
pole	**22** field
Fotbal	**Football (*esp US* Soccer)**
skórování	**23** scoring a goal
tribuna	**24** stand
pomezní rozhodčí	**25** linesman
vstřelit gól	**26** score (*verb*)
tyč	**27** goalpost
branka	**28** goal
minout	**29** miss (*verb*)
brankář	**30** goalkeeper

page 82

Keeping Fit (*US* Keeping in Shape)

chodit **1** walk (*verb*)
běhat **2** jog (*verb*)
joggistka **3** jogger
skákání na trampolíně **4** trampolining
padat **5** fall (*verb*)
trampolína **6** trampoline
trenér **7** instructor
odrazit se **8** bounce (*verb*)

házet **9** throw (*verb*)
chytat **10** catch (*verb*)
houpat se **11** swing (*verb*)
lano **12** rope
lézt **13** climb (*verb*)
ribstol **14** wall bars
tělocvična **15** gym/gymnasium
přeskakovat **16** vault (*verb*)
žíněnka **17** mat
švédská bedna **18** vaulting-horse
vytáhnout se **19** stretch (*verb*)
zaklonit se **20** bend over backwards (*verb*) (*US* bend over backward)
klečet **21** kneel (*verb*)
předklonit se **22** bend over (*verb*)
pískat **23** blow a whistle (*verb*)
píšťalka **24** whistle
dělat stojku **25** do a handstand (*verb*)
švihadlo **26** skipping-rope (*US* jump rope)
skákat **27** skip (*verb*)

Verbs 1 page 83

Žehlí košili. **1** He is **ironing**/He's **ironing** a shirt.
Vaří jídlo. **2** He is **cooking**/He's **cooking** a meal.
Myje okno. **3** He is **cleaning**/He's **cleaning** a window.
Šije. **4** He is **sewing**.

Zametá cestičku. **5** He is **sweeping**/He's **sweeping** the path (*US also* walk).
Zavazuje pytel. **6** He is **tying up** a bag/He's **tying** a bag **up**.
Ryje půdu. **7** He is **digging**/He's **digging** the soil.
Navíjí hadici. **8** He is **winding up** a hose/He's **winding** a hose **up**.

Naplňuje konvici. **9** She is **filling** a kettle (*US* an electric teakettle).
Voda **se vaří**. **10** The water is **boiling**.
Nalévá vodu do čajové konvice. **11** She is **pouring** the water into a teapot.
Míchá si čaj. **12** She is **stirring** her tea.

page 84

Verbs 2

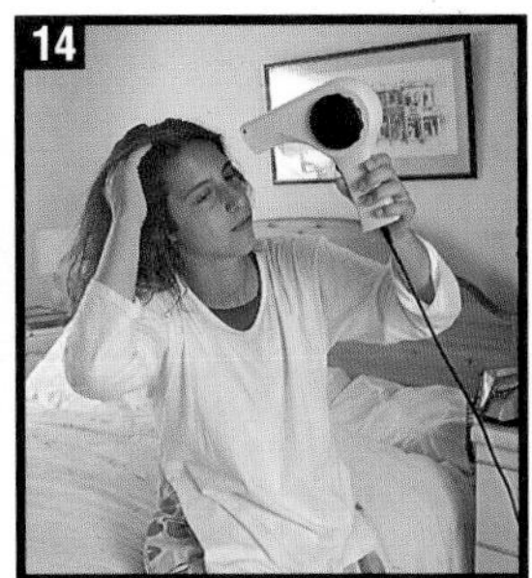

Myje si vlasy. **13** She is **washing** her hair.
Suší si vlasy. **14** She is **drying** her hair.
Češe si vlasy. **15** She is **combing** her hair.
Kartáčuje si vlasy. **16** She is **brushing** her hair.

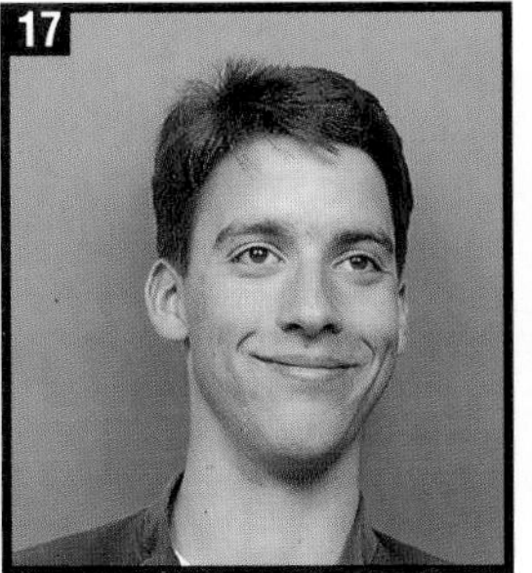

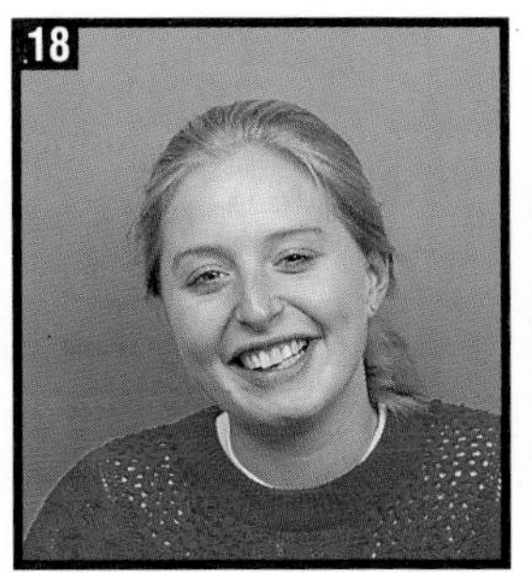

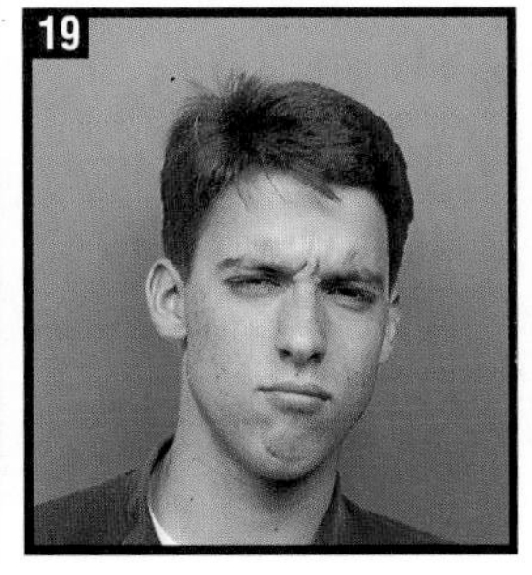

Usmívá se. **17** He is **smiling**.
Směje se. **18** She is **laughing**.
Mračí se. **19** He is **frowning**.
Pláče. **20** She is **crying**.

Sedí. **21** He is **sitting**.
Stojí. **22** He is **standing**.
Leží. **23** He is **lying down**.
Spí. **24** He is **sleeping**.

Verbs 3 page 85

Podávají si ruce.	**1** They are **shaking** hands.
Líbá dítě.	**2** She is **kissing** the child.
Objímá dítě.	**3** She is **hugging** the child.
Mává dítěti.	**4** She is **waving** to the child.

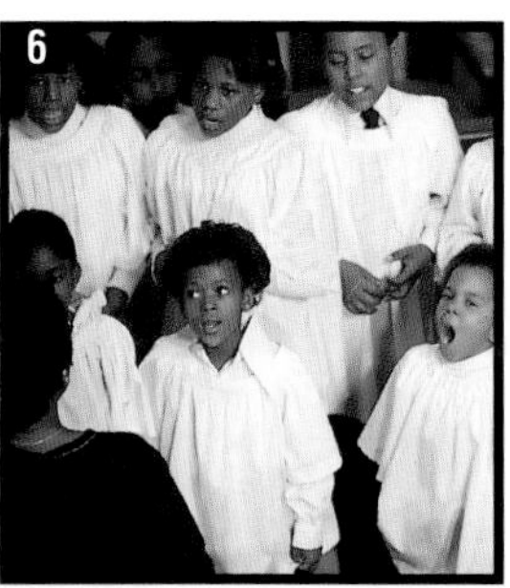

Mluví s ním.	**5** She is **speaking** to him/She is **talking** to him.
Zpívají.	**6** They are **singing**.
Tancují.	**7** They are **dancing**.
Tleskají.	**8** They are **clapping**.

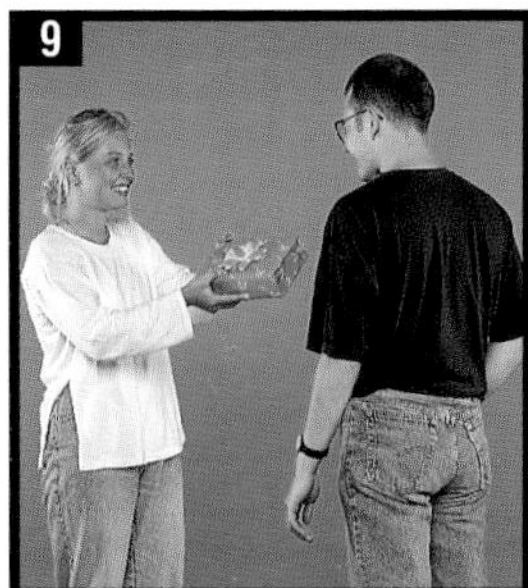
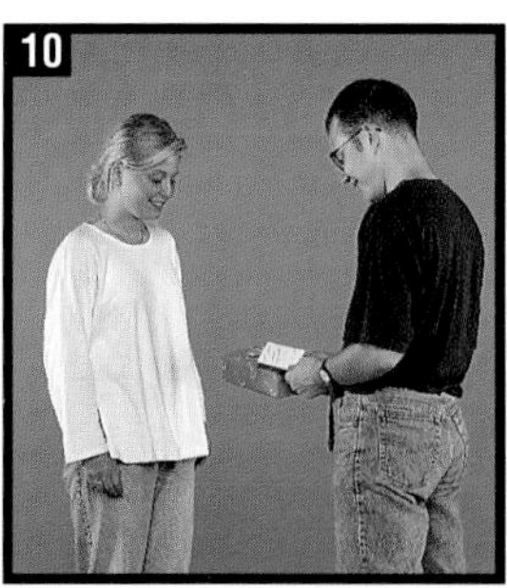
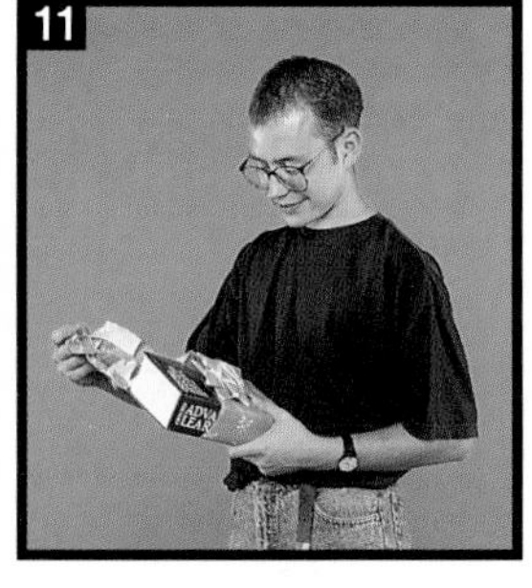

Dává mu dárek.	**9** She is **giving** him a present.
Bere si od ní dárek.	**10** He is **taking** the present from her.
Rozbaluje dárek.	**11** He is **opening** the present.
Čte knihu.	**12** He is **reading** the book.

13

14

15

16

Zvedá kufr. **13** She is **lifting** the suitcase.
Nese kufr. **14** She is **carrying** the suitcase.
Drží kufr. **15** She is **holding** the suitcase.
Pokládá kufr. **16** She is **putting** the suitcase **down**.

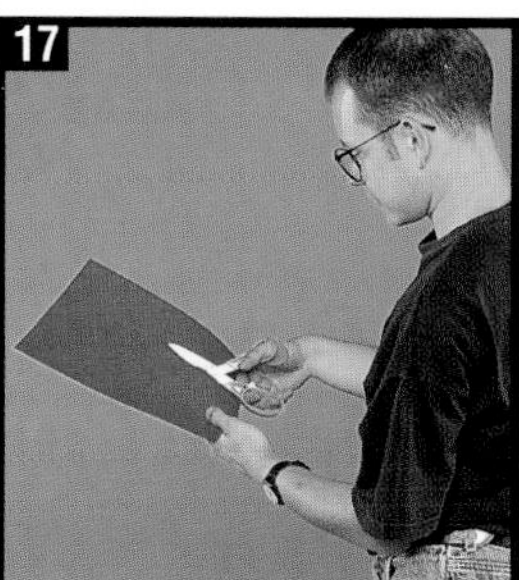
17

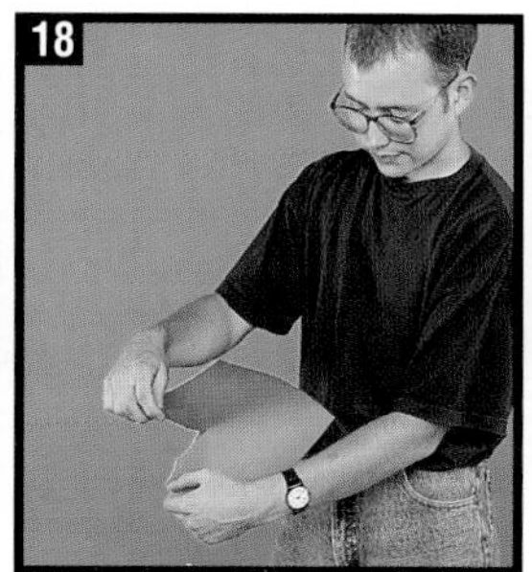
18

19

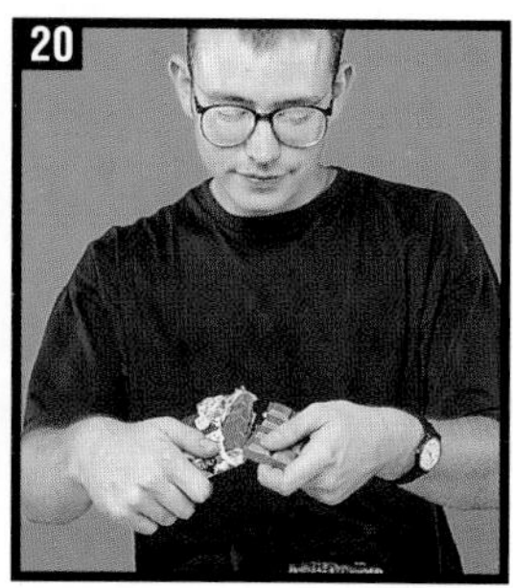
20

Stříhá kus papíru. **17** He is **cutting** a piece of paper.
Trhá kus papíru. **18** He is **tearing** a piece of paper.
Překládá kus papíru. **19** He is **folding** a piece of paper.
Láme tabulku čokolády. **20** He is **breaking** a bar of chocolate.

21

22

23

24

Tlačí vozík. **21** She is **pushing** a trolley (*US* cart).
Táhne vozík. **22** She is **pulling** a trolley (*US* cart).
Zapaluje svíčku. **23** He is **lighting** a candle.
Svíčka hoří. **24** The candle is **burning**.

Contrastive Adjectives 1 page 87

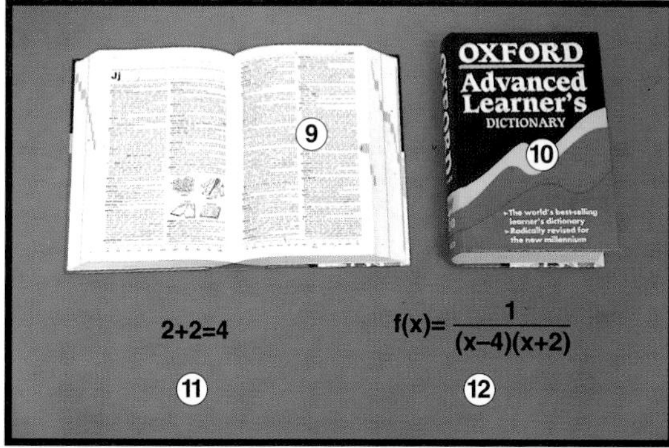

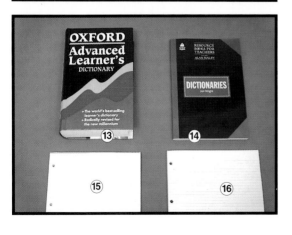

rovný	**1** straight
křivý	**2** crooked
velký	**3** big/large
malý	**4** little/small
starý	**5** old
nový	**6** new
levný	**7** cheap
drahý	**8** expensive
otevřený	**9** open
zavřený	**10** closed
snadný	**11** easy
obtížný	**12** difficult
tlustý	**13** thick
tenký	**14** thin
široký	**15** wide
úzký	**16** narrow
vysoký	**17** high
nízký	**18** low
hluboký	**19** deep
mělký	**20** shallow
slabý	**21** weak
silný	**22** strong
rychlý	**23** fast
pomalý	**24** slow

Contrastive Adjectives 2

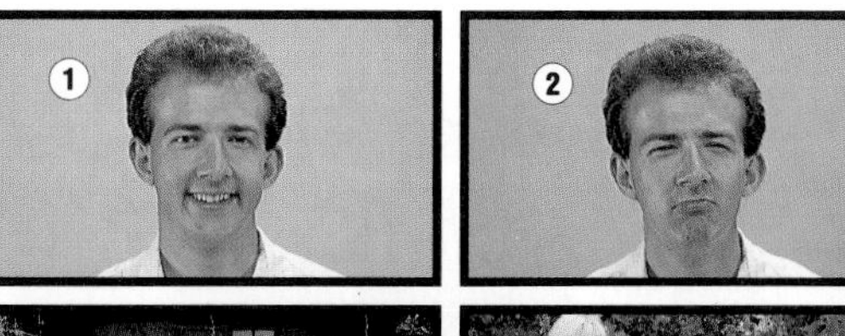

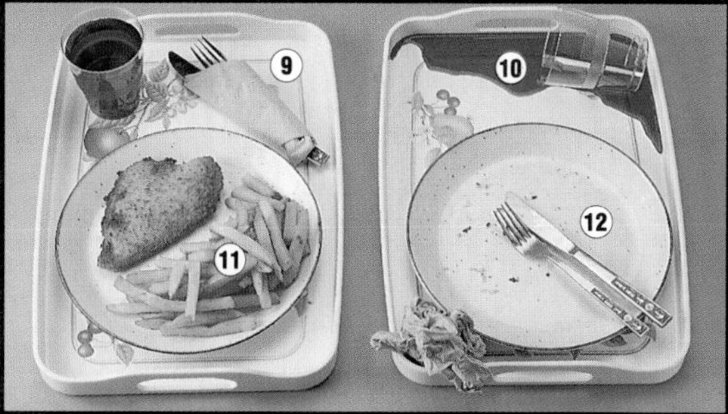

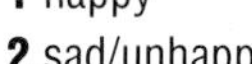
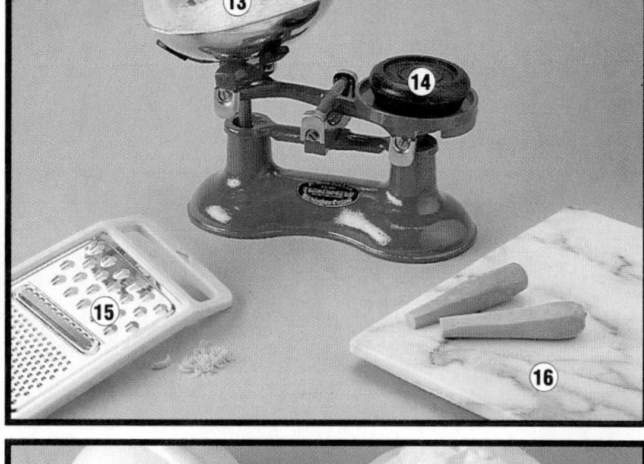
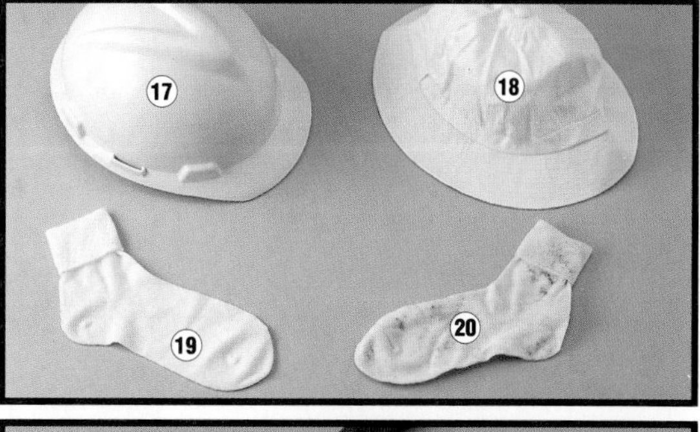
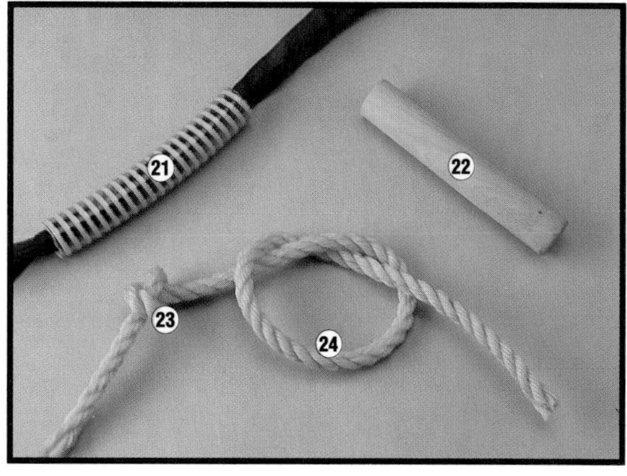

šťastný	**1** happy
smutný/nešťastný	**2** sad/unhappy
hlasitý	**3** loud
tichý	**4** quiet
dobrý	**5** good
špatný	**6** bad
uklizený	**7** tidy (*esp US* neat)
neuklizený	**8** untidy (*esp US* messy)
suchý	**9** dry
mokrý	**10** wet
plný	**11** full
prázdný	**12** empty
lehký	**13** light
těžký	**14** heavy
drsný	**15** rough
hladký	**16** smooth
tvrdý	**17** hard
měkký	**18** soft
čistý	**19** clean
špinavý	**20** dirty
dutý	**21** hollow
plný	**22** solid
pevný	**23** tight
volný	**24** loose

Animals 1 page 89

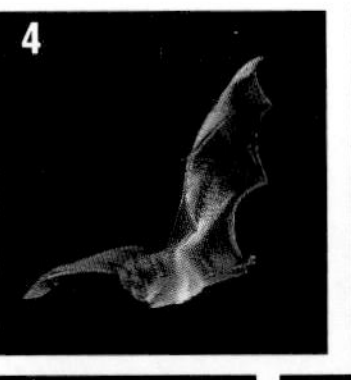

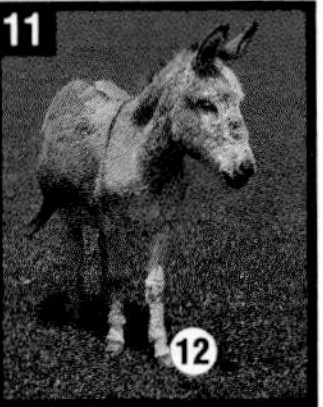

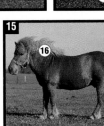

kráva	**1** cow
tele	**2** calf
býk	**3** bull
netopýr	**4** bat
ježek	**5** hedgehog
veverka	**6** squirrel
liška	**7** fox
koza	**8** goat
ovce	**9** sheep
jehně	**10** lamb
osel	**11** donkey
kopyto	**12** hoof
kůň	**13** horse
hříbě	**14** foal
poník	**15** pony
hříva	**16** mane
ohon	**17** tail

Pets Domácí zvířata

kočka	**18** cat
vousy	**19** whiskers
srst	**20** fur
kotě	**21** kitten

pes	**22** dog
štěně	**23** puppy
tlapa	**24** paw
křeček	**25** hamster
králík	**26** rabbit

Animals 2

page 90

jelen	**1**	deer
paroh	**2**	antler
vlk	**3**	wolf
medvěd	**4**	bear
dráp	**5**	claw
polární medvěd	**6**	polar bear
panda	**7**	panda
klokan	**8**	kangaroo
vak	**9**	pouch
velbloud	**10**	camel
hrb	**11**	hump
lama	**12**	llama
opice	**13**	monkey
gorila	**14**	gorilla
zebra	**15**	zebra
lev	**16**	lion
tygr	**17**	tiger
leopard	**18**	leopard
buvol	**19**	buffalo
roh	**20**	horn
nosorožec	**21**	rhinoceros
hroch	**22**	hippopotamus
žirafa	**23**	giraffe
slon	**24**	elephant
kel	**25**	tusk
chobot	**26**	trunk
tuleň	**27**	seal
ploutev	**28**	flipper
delfín	**29**	dolphin
velryba	**30**	whale

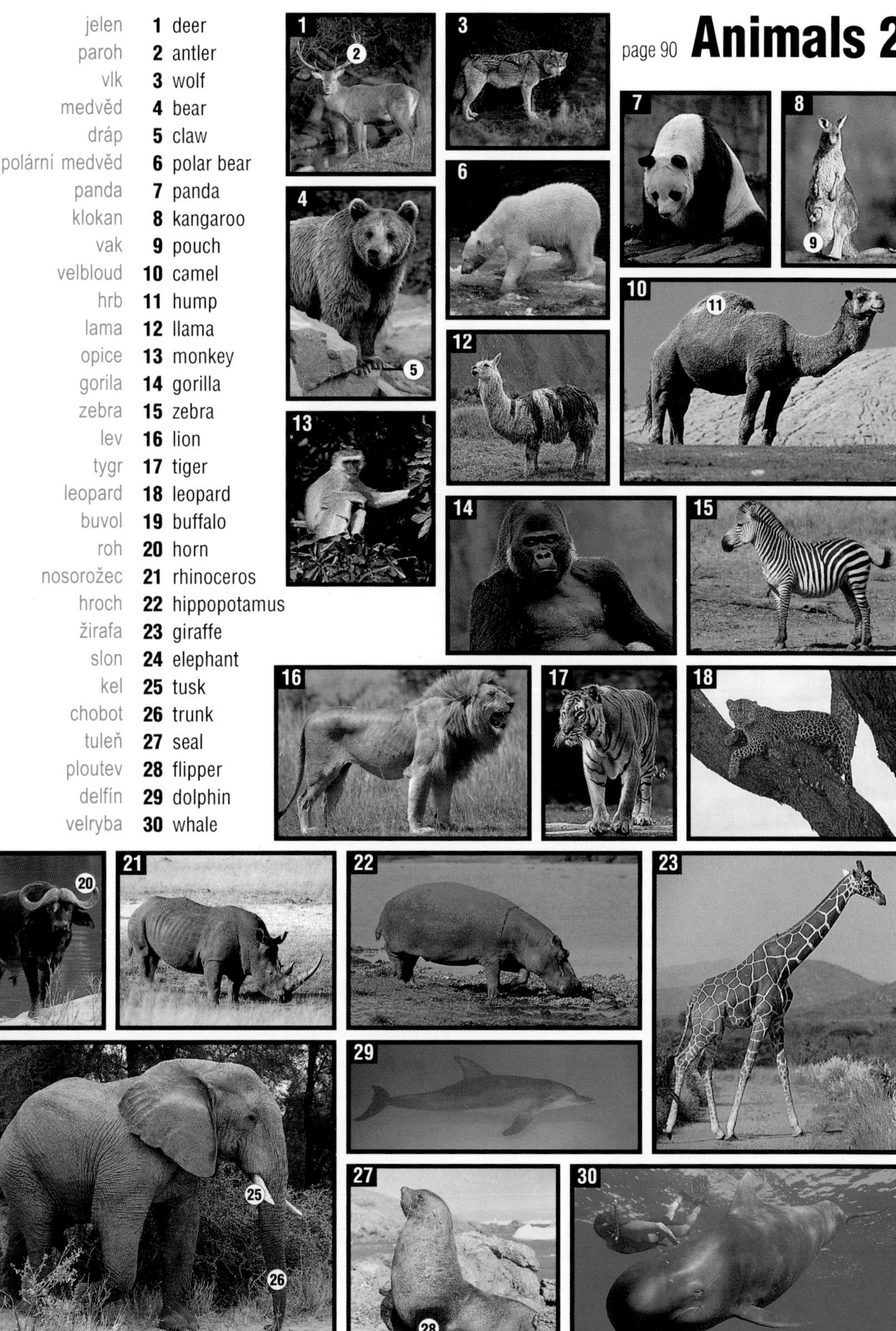

Fish and Reptiles page 91

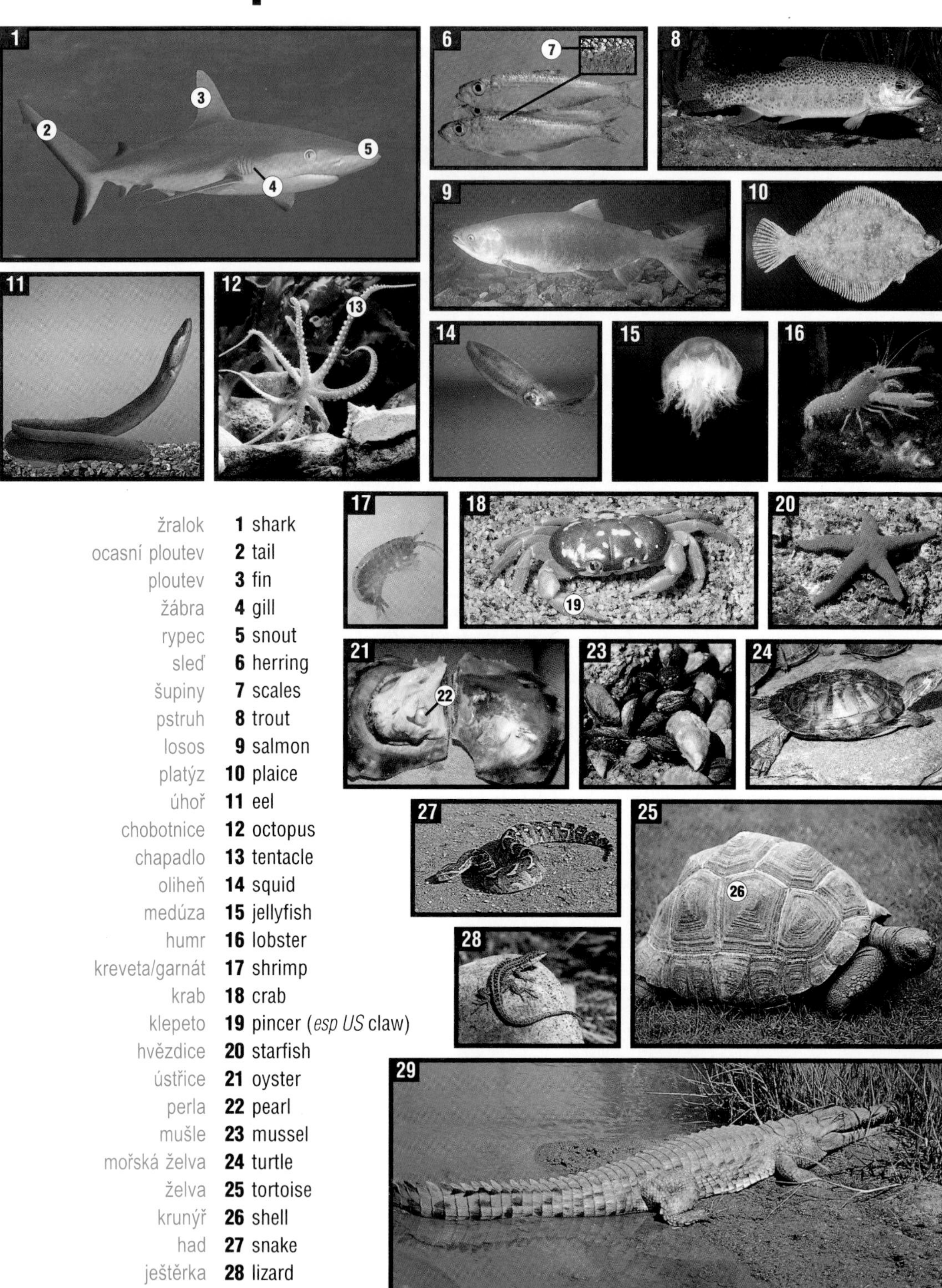

žralok	**1** shark
ocasní ploutev	**2** tail
ploutev	**3** fin
žábra	**4** gill
rypec	**5** snout
sleď	**6** herring
šupiny	**7** scales
pstruh	**8** trout
losos	**9** salmon
platýz	**10** plaice
úhoř	**11** eel
chobotnice	**12** octopus
chapadlo	**13** tentacle
oliheň	**14** squid
medúza	**15** jellyfish
humr	**16** lobster
kreveta/garnát	**17** shrimp
krab	**18** crab
klepeto	**19** pincer (*esp US* claw)
hvězdice	**20** starfish
ústřice	**21** oyster
perla	**22** pearl
mušle	**23** mussel
mořská želva	**24** turtle
želva	**25** tortoise
krunýř	**26** shell
had	**27** snake
ještěrka	**28** lizard
krokodýl	**29** crocodile

page 92

Insects and Other Animals

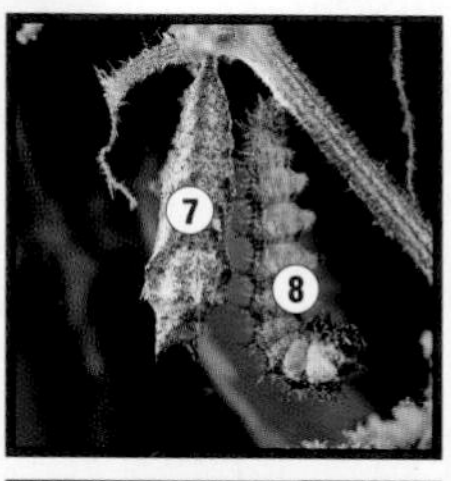

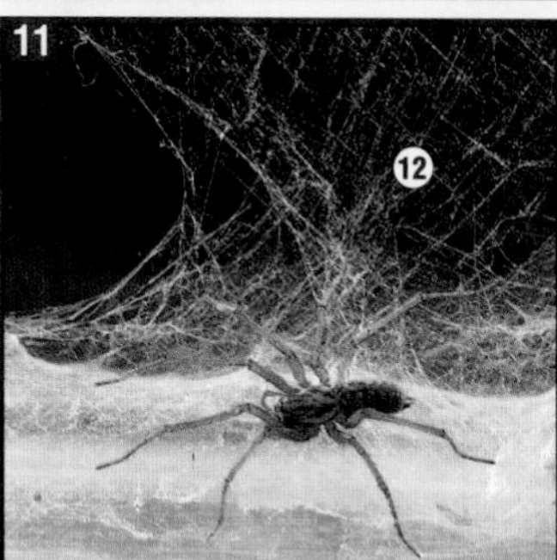

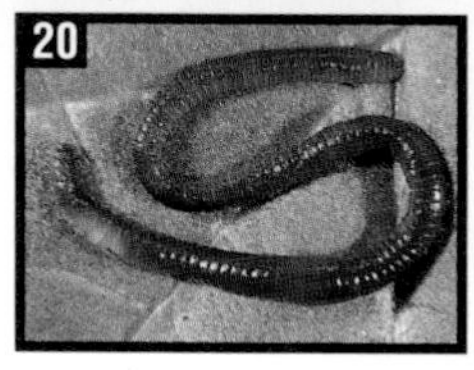
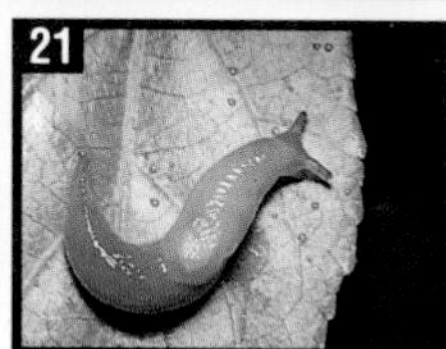

moucha **1** fly
včela **2** bee
vosa **3** wasp
komár **4** mosquito
vážka **5** dragonfly
motýl **6** butterfly
kukla **7** cocoon
housenka **8** caterpillar
můra **9** moth
tykadlo **10** antenna
pavouk **11** spider
pavučina **12** (cob)web
brouk **13** beetle
sluníčko sedmitečné **14** ladybird (*US* ladybug)
mravenec **15** ant
šváb **16** cockroach (*also* roach)
kobylka luční **17** grasshopper
cvrček **18** cricket
kudlanka nábožná **19** praying mantis
žížala **20** worm
slimák **21** slug
hlemýžď **22** snail
škorpión **23** scorpion
žihadlo **24** sting
žába **25** frog

Birds page 93

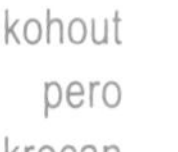

kur domácí	**1** chicken
slepice	**2** hen
kuře	**3** chick
kohout	**4** cock (*US* rooster)
pero	**5** feather
krocan	**6** turkey
bažant	**7** pheasant
orel	**8** eagle
zobák	**9** beak
jestřáb	**10** hawk
vrána	**11** crow
sova	**12** owl
hnízdo	**13** nest
holub	**14** pigeon
vrabec	**15** sparrow
kolibřík	**16** hummingbird
křídlo	**17** wing
kanár	**18** canary
papoušek	**19** parrot
andulka	**20** budgerigar (*US* parakeet)
vlaštovka	**21** swallow
pštros	**22** ostrich
tučňák	**23** penguin
páv	**24** peacock
plameňák	**25** flamingo
zobák	**26** bill
husa	**27** goose
kachna	**28** duck
noha s plovací blánou	**29** webbed foot
racek	**30** (sea)gull
labuť	**31** swan

Klíč k fonetickým symbolům

Samohlásky a dvojhlásky

1	iː	jako v	**see** / siː /	11	ɜː	jako v	**fur** / fɜː(r) /
2	ɪ	jako v	**sit** / sɪt /	12	ə	jako v	**ago** / ə'gəʊ /
3	e	jako v	**ten** / ten /	13	eɪ	jako v	**page** / peɪdʒ /
4	æ	jako v	**hat** / hæt /	14	əʊ	jako v	**home** / həʊm /
5	ɑː	jako v	**arm** / ɑːm /	15	aɪ	jako v	**five** / faɪv /
6	ɒ	jako v	**got** / gɒt /	16	aʊ	jako v	**now** / naʊ /
7	ɔː	jako v	**saw** / sɔː /	17	ɔɪ	jako v	**join** / dʒɔɪn /
8	ʊ	jako v	**put** / pʊt /	18	ɪə	jako v	**near** / nɪə(r) /
9	uː	jako v	**too** / tuː /	19	eə	jako v	**hair** / heə(r) /
10	ʌ	jako v	**cup** / kʌp /	20	ʊə	jako v	**pure** / pjʊə(r) /

Souhlásky

1	p	jako v	**pen** / pen /	13	s	jako v	**so** / səʊ /
2	b	jako v	**bad** / bæd /	14	z	jako v	**zoo** / zuː /
3	t	jako v	**tea** / tiː /	15	ʃ	jako v	**she** / ʃiː /
4	d	jako v	**did** / dɪd /	16	ʒ	jako v	**vision** / 'vɪʒn /
5	k	jako v	**cat** / kæt /	17	h	jako v	**how** / haʊ /
6	g	jako v	**got** / gɒt /	18	m	jako v	**man** / mæn /
7	tʃ	jako v	**chin** / tʃɪn /	19	n	jako v	**no** / nəʊ /
8	dʒ	jako v	**June** / dʒuːn /	20	ŋ	jako v	**sing** / sɪŋ /
9	f	jako v	**fall** / fɔːl /	21	l	jako v	**leg** / leg /
10	v	jako v	**voice** / vɔɪs /	22	r	jako v	**red** / red /
11	θ	jako v	**thin** / θɪn /	23	j	jako v	**yes** / jes /
12	ð	jako v	**then** / ðen /	24	w	jako v	**wet** / wet /

/ ' / označuje *hlavní přízvuk* jako v **about** / ə'baʊt /
/ ˌ / označuje *vedlejší přízvuk* jako v **academic** / ˌækə'demɪk /

(r) 'r' v kulatých závorkách se v britské angličtině vyslovuje, jestliže hned po něm následuje samohláska. Jinak se vynechává. V americké výslovnosti se žádné 'r' z fonetického přepisu ani z běžného pravopisu nevynechává.

Značení britských a amerických termínů

Brit motorway (*Brit*)
značí, že výraz se používá pouze v britské angličtině

US zip code (*US*)
značí, že výraz se používá pouze v americké angličtině

jug (*US* pitcher)
značí, že výraz (jug), který se užívá pouze v britské angličtině, znamená totéž jako výraz (pitcher) užívaný pouze v americké angličtině

Brit also red (*Brit also* ginger)
značí, že výraz (red) užívaný jak v britské, tak v americké angličtině znamená totéž jako výraz (ginger), který se užívá pouze v britské angličtině

US also blackboard (*US also* chalkboard)
značí, že výraz (blackboard) užívaný jak v britské, tak v americké angličtině znamená totéž jako výraz (chalkboard), který se užívá pouze v americké angličtině

esp US sofa (*esp US* couch)
značí, že výraz, který se užívá hlavně v britské angličtině, ale kterého lze použít také v americké angličtině (sofa), znamená totéž jako výraz (couch), který je obvyklejší v americké angličtině

Index

Aberconwy and Colwyn /ˌæbəˈkɒnwi ənd ˈkɒlwɪn/ **56**
Aberdeen /ˌæbəˈdiːn/ **56**
Aberdeenshire /ˌæbəˈdiːnʃə(r)/ **56**
above /əˈbʌv/ **58**/15
accelerator /əkˈseləreɪtə(r)/ **64**/28, **65**/26
accident /ˈæksɪdənt/ **6**, **38**/13
accordion /əˈkɔːdɪən/ **75**/23
ace /eɪs/ **74**/34
across /əˈkrɒs/ **57**/2
actor /ˈæktə(r)/ **76**/16
actress /ˈæktrɪs/ **76**/17
acute angle /əˌkjuːt ˈæŋgl/ **47**/19
address /əˈdres; *US* ˈædres/ **32**/10, 18, 19
adhesive tape /ədhiːsɪv ˈteɪp/ **7**/10
adjective /ˈædʒɪktɪv/ **87**/**88**
adult /ˈædʌlt, *also* əˈdʌlt/ **5**/4, 5
administrative area /ədˌmɪnɪstrətɪv ˈeərɪɪ/ **56**
advertisement /ədˈvɜːtɪsmənt; *US* ˌædvərˈtaɪzmənt/ **59**/20
Afghanistan /æfˈgænɪstɑːn; *US* æfˈgænɪstæn/ **54**
Africa /ˈæfrɪkə/ **53**/3
after /ˈɑːftə(r); *US* ˈæftər/ **37**/6, 7, 8, 14
after-shave lotion /ˈæftərʃeɪv ˌləʊʃn/ **17**/21
afternoon /ɑːftəˈnuːn; *US* æf-/ **37**/16
aftershave /ˈɑːftəʃeɪv/ **17**/21
against /əˈgenst, əˈgeɪnst/ **58**/4
age /eɪdʒ/ **5**
aim (verb) /eɪm/ **79**/3
air filter /ˈeə fɪltə(r)/ **64**/16
air traffic controller /ˌeə træfɪk kənˈtrəʊlə(r)/ **68**/5
airline ticket /ˈeəlaɪn tɪkɪt/ **67**/2
airmail /ˈeəmeɪl/ **32**/17
airport /ˈeəpɔːt/ **67**/**68**
(air)tank /ˈeətæŋk/ **77**/22
aisle /aɪl/ **76**/27
Alabama /ˌæləˈbæmə/ **55**
alarm clock /əˈlɑːm klɒk/ **18**/14
Alaska /əˈlæskə/ **55**
Albania /ælˈbeɪnɪə/ **54**
Albuquerque /ˈælbəˌkɜːrkɪ/ **55**
Algeria /ælˈdʒɪərɪə/ **54**
alligator clip /ˈælɪgeɪtər klɪp/ **46**/7
almond /ˈɑːmənd/ **28**/17
along /əˈlɒŋ/ **57**/12
am (*US* A.M.) /eɪˈem/ **37**/15
AM/FM /ˈeɪ em, ˌef em/ **30**/8
ambulance /ˈæmbjʊləns/ **38**/14
ambulance service /ˈæmbjʊləns sɜːvɪs/ **38**
America /əˈmerɪkə/ **53**, **55**
American /əˈmerɪkən/ **32**, **33**, **35**
American football /əmerɪkən ˈfʊtbɔːl/ **78**/11
amplifier /ˈæmplɪfaɪə(r)/ **30**/16
anchor /ˈæŋkə(r)/ **70**/16
Anchorage /ˈæŋkərɪdʒ/ **55**
angler /ˈæŋglə(r)/ **72**/14
Anglesey /ˈæŋglsɪ/ **56**
Angola /æŋˈgəʊlə/ **54**
Angus /ˈæŋgəs/ **56**
animal /ˈænɪml/ **89**/**90**
ankle /ˈæŋkl/ **3**/16, **6**/14
answering machine /ˈɑːnsərɪŋ (*US* ˈænsərɪŋ) məˌʃiːn/ **44**/5
answerphone /ˈɑːnsəfəʊn; *US* ˈænsər/ **44**/5
ant /ænt/ **92**/15
Antarctic /æntˈɑːktɪk/ **53**/11
Antarctica /æntˈɑːktɪkə/ **53**/7
antenna /ænˈtenə/ **14**/20, **92**/10
antler /ˈæntlə(r)/ **90**/2
Antrim /ˈæntrɪm/ **56**
apartment house /əˈpɑːrtməntˌhaʊs/ **13**/10
apex /ˈeɪpeks/ **47**/14
Appalachian Mountains /æpəˌleɪʃn ˈmaʊntnz/ **55**
appetizer /ˈæpɪtaɪzə(r)/ **28**
apple /ˈæpl/ **24**/4
apple pie /æpl ˈpaɪ/ **28**/8
appointment /əˈpɔɪntmənt/ **43**/8
appointment book /əˈpɔɪntmənt bʊk/ **44**/21
April /ˈeɪprəl/ **52**
Arabian Sea /əˌreɪbɪən ˈsiː/ **54**/29
arc /ɑːk/ **47**/7
arch /ɑːtʃ/ **14**/10
architect /ˈɑːkɪtekt/ **40**/1
Arctic /ˈɑːktɪk/ **53**/8
Ards /ɑːdz/ **56**
area code /ˈeərɪə kəʊd/ **38**/20
Argentina /ˌɑːdʒənˈtiːnə/ **53**
Argyll and Bute /ɑːˈgaɪl ənd ˈbjuːt/ **56**
Arizona /ˌærɪˈzəʊnə/ **55**
Arkansas /ˈɑːrkənsɔː/ **55**
arm /ɑːm/ **3**/7
Armagh /ɑːˈmɑː/ **56**
armchair /ˈɑːmtʃeə(r)/ **16**/22
Armenia /ɑːˈmiːnɪə/ **54**
around /əˈraʊnd/ **58**/2
arrangement /əˈreɪndʒmənt/ **25**/10
artist /ˈɑːtɪst/ **39**/1
Asia /ˈeɪʃə/ **53**/5
asparagus /əˈspærəgəs/ **23**/5
astronaut /ˈæstrənɔːt/ **50**/6
at the bottom of /æt ðə ˈbɒtəm əv/ **58**/14
at the top of /æt ðə ˈtɒp əv/ **58**/12
athlete /ˈæθliːt/ **80**/20
athletics /æθˈletɪks/ **80**/15
Atlanta /ətˈlæntə/ **55**
Atlantic /ətˈlæntɪk/ **53**
aubergine /ˈəʊbəʒiːn/ **23**/20
audience /ˈɔːdɪəns/ **76**/28
August /ˈɔːgəst/ **52**
aunt /ɑːnt; *US* ænt/ **1**/3
Austin /ˈɒstɪn/ **55**
Australia /ɒˈstreɪlɪə; *US* ɔːˈstreɪljə/ **53**/6
Austria /ˈɒstrɪə/ **54**
auto racing /ˈɔːtəʊ ˌreɪsɪŋ/ **80**/5
automatic teller /ˌɔːtəmætɪk ˈtelər/ **34**/16
autumn /ˈɔːtəm/ **52**/11
avocado /ˌævəˈkɑːdəʊ/ **24**/13
away from /əˈweɪ frɒm/ **57**/9
Ayrshire /ˈeəʃə(r)/ **56**
Azerbaijan /ˌæzəbaɪˈdʒɑːn/ **54**

baby /ˈbeɪbɪ/ **5**/1
baby carriage /ˈbeɪbɪ kærɪdʒ/ **60**/3
back /bæk/ **3**/9, **48**/10
back garden /ˌbæk ˈgɑːdn/ **22**/1
back teeth /ˌbæk ˈtiːθ/ **8**/12
backbone /ˈbækbəʊn/ **4**/14
backgammon /ˈbækgæmən/ **74**/24
backhoe /ˈbækhəʊ/ **61**/18
backpack /ˈbækpæk/ **66**/16, **71**/25
backward /ˈbækwərd/ **82**/20
backwards /ˈbækwədz/ **82**/20
backyard /ˌbækˈjɑːrd/ **22**/1
bad /bæd/ **88**/6
badminton /ˈbædmɪntən/ **78**/24
bag /bæg/ **24**/12, **26**/10, 16, **66**/13, **83**/6
baggage reclaim /ˌbægɪdʒ rɪˈkleɪm/ **67**/16
Bahamas /bəˈhɑːməz/ **53**
Bahrain /bɑːˈreɪn/ **54**
baked potato /ˌbeɪkt pəˈteɪtəʊ/ **28**/25
baker /ˈbeɪkə(r)/ **39**/7
balance /ˈbæləns/ **46**/23
balcony /ˈbælkənɪ/ **13**/12, **57**/14, **76**/21, 22
bald /bɔːld/ **5**/7
ball /bɔːl/ **26**/2, **78**/19
ballboy /ˈbɔːlbɔɪ/ **81**/9
ballooning /bəˈluːnɪŋ/ **72**/20
Ballymena /ˌbælɪˈmiːnə/ **56**
Ballymoney /ˌbælɪˈmʌnɪ/ **56**
Baltic Sea /ˌbɔːltɪk ˈsiː/ **54**/22
Baltimore /ˈbɒltɪmɔːr/ **55**
banana /bəˈnɑːnə; *US* bəˈnænə/ **24**/3
Banbridge /ˈbænbrɪdʒ/ **56**
Band-Aid /ˈbændeɪd/ **7**/3
bandage /ˈbændɪdʒ/ **7**/2
Bangladesh /ˌbæŋgləˈdeʃ/ **54**
bangs /bæŋz/ **5**/14
bank /bæŋk/ **34**, **60**/18, **62**/13
(bank) account number /bæŋk əˈkaʊnt ˌnʌmbə(r)/ **34**/7
(bank) balance /bæŋk ˈbæləns/ **34**/6
bank statement /ˈbæŋk steɪtmənt/ **34**/5
bar /bɑː(r)/ **17**/8, **26**/11, **86**/20
barbecue /ˈbɑːbɪkjuː/ **22**/16
Barents Sea /ˌbɑːrənts ˈsiː/ **54**/41
barge /bɑːdʒ/ **69**/9
bark /bɑːk/ **25**/8
barn /bɑːn/ **73**/22
barrier /ˈbærɪə(r)/ **66**/22
base /beɪs/ **47**/16
baseball /ˈbeɪsbɔːl/ **78**/1
baseball glove /ˈbeɪsbɔːl glʌv/ **78**/4
baseball mitt /ˈbeɪsbɔːl mɪt/ **78**/4
baseline /ˈbeɪslaɪn/ **81**/4
basement window /ˈbeɪsmənt wɪndəʊ/ **13**/9
basin /ˈbeɪsn/ **8**/5
basket /ˈbɑːskɪt; *US* ˈbæskɪt/ **24**/2, 22, **25**/6, **58**/2
basketball /ˈbɑːskɪtbɔːl/ **78**/8
bassoon /bəˈsuːn/ **75**/15
bat /bæt/ **78**/27, **89**/4
bath /bɑːθ; *US* bæθ/ **17**/15
bath-towel /ˈbɑːθtaʊəl/ **17**/11
bathing suit /ˈbeɪðɪŋ suːt/ **11**/1, 2
bathroom /ˈbɑːθruːm, rʊm; *US* ˈbæθruːm, rʊm/ **17**
bathroom cabinet /ˌbɑːθruːm, rʊm ˈkæbɪnɪt/ **17**/1
bathtub /ˈbæθtʌb/ **17**/15
baton /ˈbætn, ˈbætɒn; *US* bəˈtɒn/ **76**/5
batsman /ˈbætsmən/ **81**/14
batter /ˈbætə(r)/ **78**/3
battery /ˈbætərɪ/ **46**/14
batting helmet /ˈbætɪŋ helmɪt/ **78**/2
bay /beɪ/ **53**
Bay of Bengal /ˌbeɪ əv beŋˈgɔːl/ **54**/30
bay window /ˌbeɪ ˈwɪndəʊ/ **14**/11
be (verb) /biː/ **6**/1–3
beach /biːtʃ/ **72**/1, 3, **73**/10
beak /biːk/ **93**/9
bear /beə(r)/ **90**/4
beard /bɪəd/ **4**/24
Beaufort Sea /ˌbəʊfət ˈsiː/ **53**/15
bed /bed/ **18**/3, **41**/2, **42**/24
bed-linen /ˈbedlɪnɪn/ **18**/2

Bedfordshire /ˈbedfədʃə(r)/ **56**
bedroom /ˈbedruːm, rʊm/ **18**
bedside cabinet /ˌbedsaɪd ˈkæbɪnɪt/ **18**/10
bedspread /ˈbedspred/ **18**/4
bee /biː/ **92**/2
beet /biːt/ **23**/8
beetle /ˈbiːtl/ **92**/13
beetroot /ˈbiːtruːt/ **23**/8
behind /bɪˈhaɪnd/ **58**/19
Belarus /ˈbelərʊs/ **54**
Belfast /ˈbelfɑːst/ **56**
Belgium /ˈbeldʒəm/ **54**
Belize /beˈliːz/ **53**
bell /bel/ **65**/18
bellhop /ˈbelhɒp/ **71**/2
below /bɪˈləʊ/ **52**/8, **58**/16
belt /belt/ **12**/11
bench /bentʃ/ **22**/14
bend over (verb)/ bend ˈəʊvə(r)/ **82**/22
bend to right /ˌbend tʊ ˈraɪt/ **61**/8
Benin /ˈbenɪn/ **54**
Bering Sea /ˌberɪŋ ˈsiː/ **54**/38
Berkeley /ˈbɜːrklɪ/ **55**
Berkshire /ˈbɑːkʃə(r)/ **56**
Bermuda /bəˈmjuːdə/ **53**
beside /bɪˈsaɪd/ **58**/17
between /bɪˈtwiːn/ **58**/8
Bhutan /buːˈtɑːn/ **54**
bicycle /ˈbaɪsɪkl/ **65**/1
bicyclist /ˈbaɪsɪklɪst/ **60**/20
big /bɪg/ **87**/3
bike /baɪk/ **65**, **65**/1
bike and pedestrian path /baɪk ənd pəˈdestrɪən pæθ/ **61**/9
bill /bɪl/ **35**/6, **93**/26
Billings /ˈbɪlɪŋz/ **55**
bin /bɪn/ **57**/4
binoculars /bɪˈnɒkjʊləz/ **29**/7
bird /bɜːd/ **93**
Birmingham /ˈbɜːrmɪŋhæm/ **55**
Birmingham /ˈbɜːmɪŋəm/ **56**
biscuit /ˈbɪskɪt/ **27**/15, 16
biscuit tin /ˈbɪskɪt tɪn/ **16**/10
Bismarck /ˈbɪzmɑːk/ **55**
black /blæk/ **9**/13
black and white print /ˌblæk ənd waɪt ˈprɪnt/ **29**/14
black eye /blæk ˈaɪ/ **6**/20
Black Sea /ˌblæk ˈsiː/ **54**/26
blackboard /ˈblækbɔːd/ **49**/1
Blaenau Gwent /ˌblaɪnaɪ ˈgwent/ **56**
blanket /ˈblæŋkɪt/ **18**/5
blazer /ˈbleɪzə(r)/ **10**/3
blind /blaɪnd/ **17**/19
block of flats /blɒk əv ˈflæts/ **13**/10
blonde /blɒnd/ **5**/15
blood /blʌd/ **6**/19
blood pressure gauge /ˈblʌd preʃə ˌgeɪdʒ/ **7**/23
blouse /blaʊz; *US* blaʊs/ **10**/9
blow (verb) /bləʊ/ **82**/23
blue /bluː/ **9**/7
board /bɔːd/ **74**/25
boarding /ˈbɔːdɪŋ/ **68**/1
boarding pass /ˈbɔːdɪŋ pɑːs; *US* pæs/ **67**/3
boat /bəʊt/ **60**/11
boating /ˈbəʊtɪŋ/ **72**/11
boil (verb) /bɔɪl/ **83**/10
boiled potatoes /ˌbɔɪld pəˈteɪtəʊz/ **28**/26
Bolivia /bəˈlɪvɪə/ **53**
bolt /bəʊlt/ **21**/24
bongos /ˈbɒŋgəʊz/ **75**/20
bonnet /ˈbɒnɪt/ **64**/14
bonsai /ˈbɒnsaɪ; *US also* bəʊnˈsaɪ/ **25**/12
book /bʊk/ **31**/20, **58**/4, 14, 15, **85**/12
bookcase /ˈbʊkkeɪs/ **58**/11–14
boot /buːt/ **10**/13, **64**/9
Bosnia-Herzegovina /ˌbɒznɪə ˌhɜːtsəgəˈviːnə/ **54**
Boston /ˈbɒstən/ **55**
Botswana /bɒtˈswɑːnə/ **54**
bottle /ˈbɒtl/ **27**/25
bottom /ˈbɒtəm/ **3**/11, **48**/8
bounce (verb) /baʊns/ **82**/8
boundary /baʊndrɪ/ **53**, **56**
bow /baʊ/ **69**/16
bow /bəʊ/ **75**/2
bowl (verb) /bəʊl/ **81**/18
bowl /bəʊl/ **15**/13
bowler /ˈbəʊlə(r)/ **81**/17
bowling /ˈbəʊlɪŋ/ **79**/8
bowling-alley /ˈbəʊlɪŋ ælɪ/ **79**/9
box /bɒks/ **18**/9, **26**/9, **27**/1
boxer /ˈbɒksə(r)/ **12**/9
boxing /ˈbɒksɪŋ/ **79**/17
boxing glove /ˈbɒksɪŋ glʌv/ **79**/21
boy /bɔɪ/ **5**/2
bra /brɑː/ **11**/9
brace /breɪs/ **21**/15
bracelet /ˈbreɪslɪt/ **12**/23
Bradford /ˈbrædfəd/ **56**
braid /breɪd/ **5**/17
brake lever /ˈbreɪk liːvə(r)/ **65**/16
branch /brɑːntʃ; *US* bræntʃ/ **25**/7
brass /brɑːs; *US* bræs/ **75**
Brazil /brəˈzɪl/ **53**
bread /bred/ **27**/2
breadboard /ˈbredbɔːd/ **20**/18
break (verb) /breɪk/ **6**/13, **86**/20
breakfast /ˈbrekfəst/ **41**/9
breastbone /ˈbrestbəʊn/ **4**/12
brick /brɪk/ **13**/7, 16
bricklayer /ˈbrɪkleɪə(r)/ **40**/12
bridge /brɪdʒ/ **8**/17, **60**/15
Bridgend /ˌbrɪdʒˈend/ **56**
briefcase /ˈbriːfkeɪs/ **10**/12
bright /braɪt/ **51**/13
Brighton /ˈbraɪtn/ **56**
Bristol /ˈbrɪstl/ **56**
Britain /ˈbrɪtn/ **56**
British /ˈbrɪtɪʃ/ **32, 33, 36**
British Isles /ˌbrɪtɪʃ ˈaɪls/ **56**
broccoli /ˈbrɒkəlɪ/ **23**/17
brooch /brəʊtʃ/ **12**/22
broom /bruːm/ **22**/13
brother-in-law /ˈbrʌðər ɪn lɔː/ **1**/10
brown /braʊn/ **9**/4
bruise /bruːz/ **6**/15
Brunei /ˈbruːnaɪ/ **54**
brush (verb) /brʌʃ/ **84**/16
brush /brʌʃ/ **19**/5
Brussels sprout (*US* **brussels sprout**) /ˌbrʌslz ˈspraʊt/ **23**/15
bucket /ˈbʌkɪt/ **19**/6
Buckinghamshire /ˈbʌkɪŋəmʃə(r)/ **56**
buckle /ˈbʌkl/ **11**/19
bud /bʌd/ **25**/27
budgerigar /ˈbʌdʒərɪgɑː(r)/ **93**/20
Buffalo /ˈbʌfələʊ/ **55**
buffalo /ˈbʌfələʊ/ **90**/19
buffet /bəˈfeɪ/ **15**/18
building /ˈbɪldɪŋ/ **13**/**14**, **60**/1
building material /ˈbɪldɪŋ məˌtɪərɪəl/ **13**
built-in flash /ˌbɪltɪn ˈflæʃ/ **29**/20
bulb /bʌlb/ **25**/13
Bulgaria /bʌlˈgeərɪə/ **54**
bull /bʊl/ **89**/3
bulletin board /ˈbʊlətɪn bɔːrd/ **44**/1
bumper /ˈbʌmpə(r)/ **64**/7
bunch /bʌntʃ/ **24**/3, **24**/10, **25**/9
bungalow /ˈbʌŋgələʊ/ **14**/19
Bunsen burner /ˌbʌnsn ˈbɜːnə(r)/ **45**/5
bureau /bjʊˈrəʊ/ **18**/19
burette /bjʊəˈret/ **46**/25
Burkina /bɜːˈkiːnə/ **54**
Burma /ˈbɜːmə/ **54**
burn (verb) /bɜːn/ **86**/24
burner /ˈbɜːnə(r)/ **20**/27
Burundi /bʊˈrʊndɪ/ **54**
bus /bʌs/ **63**/2
bus shelter /ˈbʌs ʃeltə(r)/ **59**/21
bus stop /ˈbʌs stɒp/ **59**/22
bush /bʊʃ/ **22**/9, **58**/1
butcher /ˈbʊtʃə(r)/ **39**/8
butter /ˈbʌtə(r)/ **27**/29
butterfly /ˈbʌtəflaɪ/ **92**/6
buttocks /ˈbʌtəks/ **3**/11
button /ˈbʌtən/ **74**/15
buy (verb) /baɪ/ **41**/11
by /baɪ/ **58**/6

cab /kæb/ **60**/6
cabbage /ˈkæbɪdʒ/ **23**/21
cabin /ˈkæbɪn/ **69**/5
cabin cruiser /ˈkæbɪn ˌkruːzə(r)/ **69**/13
cabinet /ˈkæbɪnɪt/ **17**/1, **18**/10, **20**/20
cable /ˈkeɪbl/ **65**/15, **69**/6
cactus /ˈkæktəs/ **25**/21
caddy /ˈkædɪ/ **79**/12
Caenarfonshire and Merionethshire /kəˈnɑːvənʃər ənd ˌmerɪˈɒnəθʃə(r)/ **56**
Caerphilly /kəˈfɪlɪ/ **56**
café /ˈkæfeɪ; *US* kæˈfeɪ/ **59**/4
cake /keɪk/ **28**/13
calculator /ˈkælkjʊleɪtə(r)/ **49**/5
calendar /ˈkælɪndə(r)/ **44**/2
calf /kɑːf; *US* kæf/ **89**/2
California /ˌkælɪˈfɔːnɪə/ **55**
Cambodia /kæmˈbəʊdɪə/ **54**
Cambridge /ˈkeɪmbrɪdʒ/ / **56**
Cambridgeshire /ˈkeɪmbrɪdʒʃə(r)/ **56**
camcorder /ˈkæmkɔːdə(r)/ **30**/1
camel /ˈkæml/ **90**/10
camera /ˈkæmərə/ **29**/16, 19, 23
camera case /ˈkæmərə keɪs/ **29**/21
camera shop /ˈkæmərə ʃɒp/ **29**
camera store /ˈkæmərə stɔːr/ **29**
Cameroon /ˌkæməˈruːn/ **54**
camp stove /ˈkæmp stəʊv/ **71**/22
camping /ˈkæmpɪŋ/ **71**/18
camping stove /ˈkæmpɪŋ stəʊv/ **71**/22
can /kæn/ **27**/6, 26
can opener /ˈkæn əʊpənər/ **20**/10
Canada /ˈkænədə/ **53**
canal /kəˈnæl/ **72**/12
canary /kəˈneərɪ/ **93**/18
Canary Islands /kəˈneərɪ ˌaɪləndz/ **54**
candle /ˈkændl/ **15**/3, **58**/8, 9, **86**/23, 24

candy /ˈkændɪ/ **26**/10, 14, 15, 18
canoe /kəˈnu:/ **69**/19
cap /kæp/ **10**/2
capacity /kəˈpæsətɪ/ **48**/26
capital city /ˌkæpɪtl ˈsɪtɪ/ **56**
capsule /ˈkæpsju:l; *US* ˈkæpsl/ **7**/6
car /kɑ:(r)/ **60**/24, **64**
car accident /ˈkɑ:r ˌæksɪdənt/ **38**/13
car-park /ˈkɑ:pɑ:k/ **13**/15
caravan /ˈkærəvæn/ **63**/9, **71**/27
caravan site /ˈkærəvæn saɪt/ **71**/26
card file /ˈkɑ:d faɪl/ **44**/8
card index /ˈkɑ:d ɪndeks/ **44**/8
Cardiff /ˈka:dɪf/ **56**
cardigan /ˈkɑ:dɪgən/ **12**/7
Cardiganshire /ˈkɑ:dɪgənʃə(r)/ **56**
cargo /ˈkɑ:gəʊ/ **70**/4
Caribbean Sea /kærɪˌbi:ən ˈsi:/ **53**/19
Carlow /ˈkɑ:ləʊ/ **56**
Carmarthenshire /kəˈmɑ:ðənʃə(r)/ **56**
carnation /kɑ:ˈneɪʃn/ **25**/24
Carolina /kærəˈlaɪnə/ **55**
carpenter /ˈkɑ:pəntə(r)/ **40**/8
carpet /ˈkɑ:pɪt/ **16**/7
Carrickfergus /ˌkærɪkˈfɜ:gəs/ **56**
carrot /ˈkærət/ **23**/14
carry (verb) /ˈkærɪ/ **86**/14
cart /kɑ:rt/ **28**/6, **46**/15, **67**/18, **68**/3, **86**/21
carton /ˈkɑ:tən/ **27**/21
cash (verb) /kæʃ/ **34**/10, 14
cash /kæʃ/ **34**/15, **35**
cash dispenser /ˈkæʃ dɪspensə(r)/ **34**/16
cash machine /ˈkæʃ məʃi:n/ **34**/16
cash register /ˈkæʃ ˌredʒɪstə(r)/ **29**/3
cashier /kæˈʃɪə(r)/ **34**/9
cashpoint /ˈkæʃpɔɪnt/ **34**/16
Caspian Sea /ˌkæspɪən ˈsi:/ **54**/27
casserole /ˈkæsərəʊl/ **20**/1
cassette /kəˈset/ **30**/6, **58**/3
cassette deck /kəˈset dek/ **30**/18
cast /kæst/ **7**/13
castle /ˈkɑ:sl; *US* ˈkæsl/ **71**/13
Castlereagh /ˈkɑ:slreɪ/ **56**
cat /kæt/ **89**/18
catch (verb) /kætʃ/ **42**/13, **82**/10
catcher /ˈkætʃə(r)/ **78**/6
catcher's mask /ˈkætʃərz mæsk/ **78**/5
caterpillar /ˈkætəpɪlə(r)/ **92**/8
cauliflower /ˈkɒlɪflaʊər; *US* ˈkɔ:lɪ-/ **23**/4
Cavan /ˈkævən/ **56**
CD /ˌsi: ˈdi:/ **30**/7
CD player /ˌsi: ˈdi: ˌpleɪə(r)/ **30**/19
ceiling /ˈsi:lɪŋ/ **16**/1
celery /ˈselərɪ/ **23**/16
cello /ˈtʃeləʊ/ **75**/3
Celsius /ˈselsɪəs/ **52**/2
cement truck /sɪˈment trʌk/ **63**/6
cement-mixer /sɪˈmentmɪksə(r)/ **63**/6
cent /sent/ **35**/13
center /ˈsentər/ **47**/4
center lane /ˈsentər leɪn/ **62**/16
centigrade /ˈsentigreɪd/ **52**/2
centimetre /ˈsentɪmi:tə(r)/ **48**/30
Central African Republic /ˌsentrəl ˌæfrɪkən rɪˈpʌblɪk/ **54**
central reservation /ˌsentrəl rezəˈveɪʃn/ **62**/8
centre /ˈsentə(r)/ **47**/4
centre lane /ˈsentə leɪn/ **62**/6
century /ˈsentʃərɪ/ **37**
cereal /ˈsɪərɪəl/ **27**/1
certified mail /ˌsɜ:rtɪfaɪd ˈmeɪl/ **32**/21
Chad /tʃæd/ **54**
chain /tʃeɪn/ **12**/25, **65**/8
chain-wheel /ˈtʃeɪnwi:l; *US also* hwi:l/ **65**/10
chair /tʃeə(r)/ **49**/10
chalk /tʃɔ:k/ **49**/24
chalkboard /ˈtʃɔ:kbɔ:rd/ **49**/1
change (verb) /tʃeɪndʒ/ **34**/10, 12, **35**/16
Charleston /tʃɑ:rlstən/ **55**
Charlotte /ʃɑ:rlət/ **55**
cheap /tʃi:p/ **87**/7
check /tʃek/ **9**/19
check-in /ˈtʃekɪn/ **67**/1
check-in counter /ˈtʃekɪn ˌkaʊntər/ **67**/4
check-in desk /ˈtʃekɪn ˌdesk/ **67**/4
checked /tʃekt/ **9**/19
checkers /ˈtʃekərz/ **74**/26
cheek /tʃi:k/ **4**/19
cheese /tʃi:z/ **27**/22
cheesecake /ˈtʃi:zkeɪk/ **28**/9
cheque (*US* check) /tʃek/ **34**/14, **43**/4
cheque book (*US* checkbook) /ˈtʃek bʊk/ **34**/1
cheque card /ˈtʃek kɑ:d/ **34**/3
cheque stub (*US* check stub) /ˈtʃek stʌb/ **34**/2
cherry /ˈtʃerɪ/ **28**/1
Cheshire /ˈtʃeʃə(r)/ **56**
chess /tʃes/ **74**/29
chest /tʃest/ **3**/26
chest of drawers /ˈtʃest əv drɔ:z/ **18**/19
Chicago /ʃɪˈkɑ:gəʊ/ **55**
chick /tʃɪk/ **93**/3
chicken /ˈtʃɪkɪn/ **27**/10, **93**/1
child /tʃaɪld/ **5**/2, **85**/2–4
children /ˈtʃɪldrən/ **1**/19
Chile /ˈtʃɪlɪ/ **53**
chimney /ˈtʃɪmnɪ/ **14**/7
chin /tʃɪn/ **3**/28
China /ˈtʃaɪnə/ **54**
chips /tʃɪps/ **28**/27
chisel /ˈtʃɪzl/ **21**/14
chocolate /ˈtʃɒklət/ **26**/9, 11, 17, **28**/13
chop (verb) /tʃɒp/ **79**/28
Christmas tree /ˈkrɪsməs tri:/ **25**/1
chrysanthemum /krɪˈsænθəməm/ **25**/15
Cincinnati /ˌsɪnsɪˈnætɪ/ **55**
cinema /ˈsɪnəmɑ:, ˈsɪnəmə/ **76**
circle /ˈsɜ:kl/ **47**/1, **76**/21
circumference /səˈkʌmfərəns/ **47**/2
city /ˈsɪtɪ/ **55, 56, 59/60**
Clackmannanshire /klækˈmænənʃə(r)/ **56**
clamp stand /ˈklæmp stænd/ **45**/20
clap (verb) /klæp/ **85**/8
Clare /kleə(r)/ **56**
clarinet /klærɪˈnet/ **75**/14
classroom /ˈklɑ:sru:m, rʊm; *US* ˈklæs-/ **49**
claw /klɔ:/ **90**/5, **91**/19
clean (verb) /kli:n/ **83**/3
clean /kli:n/ **88**/19
Cleveland /ˈkli:vlənd/ **55**
cliff /klɪf/ **73**/11
climb (verb) /klaɪm/ **82**/13
climber /ˈklaɪmə(r)/ **72**/25
climbing /ˈklaɪmɪŋ/ **72**/24
clock /klɒk/ **15**/26, **58**/8
clock-face /ˈklɒkfeɪs/ **37**/2
closed /kləʊzd/ **87**/10
closet /ˈklɒzɪt/ **18**/17
clothes /kləʊðz; *US* kləʊz/ **9/11**
clothes-line /ˈkləʊðzlaɪn; *US* ˈkləʊz-/ **19**/22
clothes-peg /ˈkləʊðzpeg/ **19**/10
clothespin /ˈkləʊzpin/ **19**/10
cloudy /ˈklaʊdɪ/ **51**/8
club /klʌb/ **74**/31, **79**/15
clutch /klʌtʃ/ **64**/26
coach /kəʊtʃ/ **63**/2, **66**/4
coat /kəʊt/ **10**/17
coat-hanger /ˈkəʊthæŋə(r)/ **18**/18
(cob)web /ˈkɒbweb/ **92**/12
cock /kɒk/ **93**/4
cockpit /ˈkɒkpɪt/ **68**/14
cockroach /ˈkɒkrəʊtʃ/ **92**/16
cocktail /ˈkɒkteɪl/ **28**/11
coconut /ˈkəʊkənʌt/ **24**/7
cocoon /kəˈku:n/ **92**/7
coffee-pot /ˈkɒfɪˌpɒt; *US* ˈkɔ:fɪˌpɒt/ **15**/21
coffee-table /ˈkɒfɪˌteɪbl; *US* ˈkɔ:fɪ-/ **16**/8
coin /kɔɪn/ **35**/1, **36**/1
colander /ˈkʌləndə(r)/ **20**/9
cold /kəʊld/ **6**/7, **52**/6
cold water faucet /ˈkəʊld wɔ:tər ˌfɔ:sɪt/ **19**/19
cold(-water) tap /ˌkəʊldˈwɔ:tə ˌtæp/ **19**/19
Coleraine /ˈkəʊləˌreɪn/ **56**
collar /ˈkɒlə(r)/ **11**/15
collection /kəˈlekʃn/ **31**/6
Colombia /kəˈlʌmbɪə/ **53**
Colorado /ˌkɒləˈrɑ:dəʊ/ **55**
colour (*US* color) /ˈkʌlə(r)/ **9**
colour print (*US* color print) /ˈkʌlə prɪnt/ **29**/13
coloured pens (*US* colored pens) /ˈkʌləd penz/ **26**/5
Columbia /kəˈlʌmbɪə/ **55**
comb (verb) /kəʊm/ **84**/15
comb /kəʊm/ **17**/27
combine harvester (*US* combine) /ˌkɒmbaɪn ˈhɑ:vɪstə(r)/ **73**/25
come (verb) /kʌm/ **57**/7
come back (verb) /kʌm ˈbæk/ **41**/5
compact camera /ˌkɒmpækt ˈkæmərə/ **29**/19
compact disc /ˌkɒmpækt ˈdɪsk/ **30**/7
compact disc player /ˌkɒmpækt ˈdɪsk ˌpleɪə(r)/ **30**/19
compass /ˈkʌmpəs/ **49**/19
compasses /ˈkʌmpəsɪz/ **49**/19
computer programmer /kəmˈpju:tə ˌprəʊgræmə(r)/ **40**/5
concrete /ˈkɒŋkri:t/ **13**/18
concrete wall /ˌkɒŋkri:t ˈwɔ:l/ **14**/12
condenser /kənˈdensə(r)/ **45**/23
conductor /kənˈdʌktə(r)/ **76**/4
cone /kəʊn/ **47**/22, **61**/17
confectionery /kənˈfekʃənərɪ/ **26**
conga /ˈkɒŋgə/ **75**/22
Congo /ˈkɒŋgəʊ/ **54**
conical flask /ˈkɒnɪkl flɑ:sk; *US* flæsk/ **45**/17
Connecticut /kəˈnetɪkət/ **55**
constellation /ˌkɒnstəˈleɪʃn/ **50**/25
construction worker /kənˈstrʌkʃn ˌwɜ:kə(r)/ **61**/15
contact lens /ˌkɒntækt ˈlenz/ **8**/20
contact lens cleaner /ˌkɒntækt ˈlenz kli:nə(r)/ **8**/22
container /kənˈteɪnər/ **27**/19
continent /ˈkɒntɪnənt/ **53**
contrastive adjective /kənˈtrɑ:stɪv ˌædʒɪktɪv/ **87/88**

control tower /kən'trəʊl taʊə(r)/ **68**/4
convertible /kən'vɜ:təbl/ **63**/13
cook (verb) /kʊk/ **83**/2
cookbook /'kʊkbʊk/ **20**/4
cooked meat /ˌkʊkd 'mi:t/ **27**/7
cookery book /'kʊkərɪ bʊk/ **20**/4
cookie /'kʊkɪ/ **27**/15, 16
cookie tin /'kʊkɪ tɪn/ **16**/10
Cookstown /'kʊksˌtaʊn/ **56**
cool /ku:l/ **52**/5
coping saw /'kəʊpɪŋ ˌsɔ:/ **21**/20
copy /'kɒpɪ/ **43**/11
Coral Sea /ˌkɒrəl 'si:/ **54**/32
cord /kɔ:d/ **19**/11
Cork /kɔ:k/ **56**
corn /kɔ:n/ **28**/20
corner /'kɔ:nə(r)/ **48**/5, **79**/18
cornfield /'kɔ:nfi:ld/ **73**/26
Cornwall /'kɔ:nwəl/ **56**
correction fluid /kə'rekʃn flu:ɪd/ **44**/9
Costa Rica /ˌkɒstə 'ri:kə/ **53**
Côte d'Ivoire /ˌkəʊt di:'vwɑ:/ **54**
cottage /'kɒtɪdʒ/ **14**/13
cotton /'kɒtn/ **74**/11
cotton ball /'kɒtn bɔ:l/ **7**/4
cotton wool /ˌkɒtn 'wʊl/ **7**/4
couch /kaʊtʃ/ **16**/17
cough /kɒf; *US* kɔ:f/ **6**/9
counter /'kaʊntə(r)/ **20**/13, **31**/3
counter assistant /ˌkaʊntər ə'sɪstənt/ **31**/4
counterfoil /'kaʊntəfɔɪl/ **34**/2
country /'kʌntrɪ/ **53, 56**
country code /'kʌntrɪ kəʊd/ **38**/19
country house /ˌkʌntrɪ 'haʊs/ **71**/14
countryside /'kʌntrɪsaɪd/ **71**/16
county /'kaʊntɪ/ **56**
courgette /kɔ:'ʒet/ **23**/12
courier /'kʊrɪə(r)/ **31**/15
courtyard /'kɔ:tjɑ:d/ **57**/2
cousin /'kʌzn/ **1**/9
Coventry /'kɒvəntrɪ/ **56**
cow /kaʊ/ **89**/1
crab /kræb/ **91**/18
Craigavon /kreɪg'ævən/ **56**
crane /kreɪn/ **70**/2
crank /kræŋk/ **65**/5
crash barrier /'kræʃ bærɪə(r)/ **62**/9
cream /kri:m/ **9**/6, **28**/12
credit card /'kredɪt kɑ:d/ **34**/4
crescent /'kresnt/ **50**/1
cricket /'krɪkɪt/ **81, 92**/18
cricket match /'krɪkɪt mætʃ/ **81**/12
crisps /krɪsps/ **26**/16, 19
Croatia /krəʊ'eɪʃə/ **54**
crocodile /'krɒkədaɪl/ **91**/29
crocodile clip /'krɒkədaɪl ˌklɪp/ **46**/7
crooked /'krʊkɪd/ **87**/2
crossroads /'krɒsrəʊds/ **60**/21
crosswalk /'krɒswɔ:k/ **59**/24
crow /krəʊ/ **93**/11
crowd /kraʊd/ **78**/7
crucible /'kru:sɪbl/ **46**/26
cruise /kru:z/ **72**/6
crutch /krʌtʃ/ **7**/14
cry (verb) /craɪ/ **84**/20
Cuba /'kju:bə/ **53**
cube /kju:b/ **47**/21
cucumber /'kju:kʌmbə(r)/ **23**/10
cue /kju:/ **79**/5
cuff /kʌf/ **11**/17
Cumbria /'kʌmbrɪə/ **56**
cup /kʌp/ **16**/14, **42**/16, **58**/16
cupboard /'kʌbəd/ **20**/20
curb /kɜ:rb/ **59**/9
curly /'kɜ:lɪ/ **5**/10
curtains /'kɜ:tnz/ **16**/20
curve /kɜ:v/ **47**/27
curve to right /ˌkɜ:rv tʊ 'raɪt/ **61**/8
cushion /'kʊʃn/ **16**/18
customer /'kʌstəmə(r)/ **29**/1
customs /'kʌstəms/ **67**/19
customs officer /'kʌstəmz ˌɒfɪsə(r)/ **67**/20
cut (verb) /kʌt/ **86**/17
cut /kʌt/ **6**/18
cutting board /'kʌtɪŋ bɔ:rd/ **20**/18
cycle (verb) /'saɪkl/ **80**/4
cycle and pedestrian route /ˌsaɪkl ənd pə'destrɪən ru:t/ **61**/9
cycling /'saɪklɪŋ/ **80**/3
cyclist /'saɪklɪst/ **60**/20
cylinder /'sɪlɪndə(r)/ **47**/24
cylinder head /'sɪlɪndə(r) hed/ **64**/17
cymbals /'sɪmblz/ **75**/21
Cyprus /'saɪprəs/ **54**
Czech Republic /ˌtʃek rɪ'pʌblɪk/ **54**

daffodil /'dæfədɪl/ **25**/14
daily routine /ˌdeɪlɪ ru:'ti:n/ **41**/**42**
daisy /'deɪzɪ/ **25**/23
Dakota /də'kəʊtə/ **55**
Dallas /'dæləs/ **55**
dam /dæm/ **73**/14
dance (verb) /dɑ:ns; *US* dæns/ **85**/7
dark /dɑ:k/ **5**/8, **9**/12, **51**/14
dartboard /'dɑ:tbɔ:d/ **79**/2
darts /dɑ:ts/ **79**/1
dashboard /'dæʃbɔ:d/ **64**/20
date /deɪt/ **33**
daughter /'dɔ:tə(r)/ **1**/17
day /deɪ/ **37**
Dayton /'deɪtn/ **55**
December /dɪ'sembə(r)/ **52**
deck /dek/ **69**/4
deep /di:p/ **87**/19
deer /dɪə(r)/ **90**/1
degrees /dɪ'gri:z/ **52**/1, 2, 8
Delaware /'deləweə(r)/ **55**
delicatessen /ˌdelɪkə'tesn/ **27**
delivery /dɪ'lɪvərɪ/ **31**/12, 15
Denbighshire /'denbiʃə(r)/ **56**
Denmark /'denmɑ:k/ **54**
dental assistant /'dentl əˌsɪstənt/ **8**/6
dental nurse /'dentl ˌnɜ:s/ **8**/6
dentist /'dentɪst/ **8**/1
dentist's chair /'dentɪsts ˌtʃeə(r)/ **8**/4
Denver /'denvər/ **55**
department store /dɪ'pɑ:tmənt stɔ:(r)/ **59**/18
departures board /dɪ'pɑ:tʃəz bɔ:d/ **66**/17
departures lounge /dɪ'pɑ:tʃəz ˌlaʊndʒ/ **67**/12
deposit slip /dɪ'pɒzɪt slɪp/ **34**/18
depth /depθ/ **48**/1
Derby /'dɑ:bɪ/ **56**
Derbyshire /'dɑ:bɪʃə(r)/ **56**
Des Moines /də 'mɔɪn/ **55**
describe (verb) /dɪ'skraɪb/ **9**
description /dɪ'skrɪpʃn/ **5**
desert /'dezət/ **73**/15
desk /desk/ **44**/6
despatch-rider /dɪ'spætʃ raɪdə(r)/ **31**/16
dessert /dɪ'zɜ:t/ **28, 28**/6
detached house /dɪˌtætʃt 'haʊs/ **14**/1
detergent /dɪtɜ:dʒənt/ **19**/1
Detroit /dɪ'trɔɪt/ **55**
Devon /'devən/ **56**
diagonal /daɪ'ægənl/ **47**/12
dial /'daɪəl/ **38**/26
diameter /daɪ'æmɪtə(r)/ **47**/5
diamond /'daɪəmənd/ **74**/33
diary /'daɪərɪ/ **44**/21
dice /daɪs/ **74**/28
Dictaphone /'dɪktəfəʊn/ **43**/2
dictate (verb) /dɪk'teɪt/ **43**/1
dictating machine /dɪk'teɪtɪŋ məˌʃi:n/ **43**/2
difficult /'dɪfɪkəlt/ **87**/12
dig (verb) /dɪg/ **83**/7
dime /daɪm/ **35**/4
dining-room /'daɪnɪŋru:m, rʊm/ **15**
dinner /'dɪnə(r)/ **42**/22
dirty /'dɜ:tɪ/ **88**/20
disc jockey /'dɪsk dʒɒkɪ/ **39**/3
dish /dɪʃ/ **15**/6
dish towel /'dɪʃ taʊəl/ **20**/7
dishwashing liquid /'dɪʃwɒʃɪŋ ˌlɪkwɪd/ **20**/5
disk drive /'dɪsk draɪv/ **44**/24
disk jockey /'dɪsk dʒɒkɪ/ **39**/3
district /'dɪstrɪkt/ **56**
District of Columbia /ˌdɪstrɪkt əv kə'lʌmbɪə/ **55**
dive (verb) /daɪv/ **77**/29
diver /'daɪvə(r)/ **77**/30
divided by /dɪ'vaɪdɪd baɪ/ **48**/14
Djibouti /dʒɪ'bu:tɪ/ **54**
do a handstand (verb) /ˌdu: ə 'hændstænd/ **82**/25
do not enter /ˌdu: nɒt 'entə(r)/ **61**/3
dock /dɒk/ **70**/1
doctor /'dɒktə(r)/ **7**/19
doctor's office /'dɒktərz ˌɒfɪs/ **7**
doctor's surgery /'dɒktəz ˌsɜ:dʒərɪ/ **7**
dog /dɒg/ **89**/22
dollar /'dɒlər/ **35**/12, 13
dollar bill /ˌdɒlər 'bɪl/ **35**/7
dolphin /'dɒlfɪn/ **90**/29
Dominican Republic /dəˌmɪnɪkən rɪ'pʌblɪk/ **53**
Donegal /'dɒnɪgɔ:l/ **56**
donkey /'dɒŋkɪ/ **89**/11
doormat /dɔ:mæt/ **18**/21
doorstep /'dɔ:step/ **13**/6
dormer /'dɔ:mə(r)/ **14**/15
Dorset /'dɔ:sɪt/ **56**
double room /ˌdʌbl 'ru:m, 'rʊm/ **71**/7
double yellow lines /ˌdʌbl ˌjeləʊ 'laɪnz/ **60**/22
(double-)bass /ˌdʌbl'beɪs/ **75**/5
double-decker bus /ˌdʌblˌdekə 'bʌs/ **60**/25
doubles match /'dʌblz mætʃ/ **81**/8
Douglas /'dʌgləs/ **56**
Dover /'dəʊvə(r)/ **56**
Down /daʊn/ **56**
down /daʊn/ **57**/13
downstairs /ˌdaʊn'steəz/ **18**/23, **41**/3
dozen /'dʌzn/ **27**/13
dragonfly /'drægənflaɪ/ **92**/5
drainpipe /'dreɪnpaɪp/ **14**/21
drapes /dreɪps/ **16**/20
draughts /drɑ:fts/ **74**/26

drawer /drɔː(r)/ **15**/19, **58**/3
drawing /ˈdrɔːɪŋ/ **74**/2
dress /dres/ **12**/19
dresser /ˈdresər/ **18**/1
dressing gown /ˈdresɪŋ gaʊn/ **11**/13
dressing table /ˈdresɪŋ teɪbl/ **18**/1
dressing up /ˌdresɪŋ ˈʌp/ **12**
dried flowers /draɪd ˈflaʊəz/ **25**/9, **58**/7
drill /drɪl/ **8**/2, **21**/10, 18
drink (verb) /drɪŋk/ **42**/16
drive (verb) /draɪv/ **42**/19
drive /draɪv/ **22**/26
driveway /ˈdraɪvweɪ/ **22**/26
dropper /ˈdrɒpə(r)/ **46**/11
drum /drʌm/ **76**/10
drummer /ˈdrʌmə(r)/ **76**/11
drumsticks /ˈdrʌmstɪks/ **75**/19
dry (verb) /draɪ/ **84**/14
dry /draɪ/ **88**/9
Dublin /ˈdʌblɪn/ **56**
duck /dʌk/ **93**/28
dull /dʌl/ **51**/14
Dumbarton and Clydebank /dʌmˈbɑːtən ənd ˈklaɪdbæŋk/ **56**
Dumfries and Galloway /dʌmˌfriːs ənd ˈgæləweɪ/ **56**
dump truck /ˈdʌmp trʌk/ **61**/14
dumper (truck) /ˈdʌmpə ˌtrʌk/ **61**/14
Dundee /dʌnˈdiː/ **56**
Dungannon /dʌŋˈgænən/ **56**
Durham /ˈdʌrəm/ **56**
dust cloth /ˈdʌst klɔːθ/ **19**/14
dustbin /dʌstbɪn/ **22**/20
duster /ˈdʌstə(r)/ **19**/14
dustpan /ˈdʌstpæn/ **19**/4
duty-free shop /djuːtɪˈfriː ˌʃɒp/ **67**/10

eagle /ˈiːgl/ **93**/8
ear /ɪə(r)/ **3**/3
earring /ˈɪərɪŋ/ **12**/27
Earth /ɜːθ/ **50**/21
easel /ˈiːzl/ **49**/13
east /iːst/ **56**
East China Sea /ˌiːst ˌtʃaɪnə ˈsiː/ **54**/34
East Dunbartonshire /ˌiːst dʌnˈbɑːtənʃə(r)/ **56**
East Sea /ˌiːst ˈsiː/ **54**/36
East Timor /ˌiːst ˈtiːmɔː/ **54**
easy /ˈiːzɪ/ **87**/11
eat (verb) /iːt/ **41**/9, **42**/17, 22
Ecuador /ˈekwədɔː(r)/ **53**
edge /edʒ/ **48**/4
Edinburgh /ˈedɪnbərə/ **56**
eel /iːl/ **91**/11
egg /eg/ **27**/13, 14
eggplant /ˈegplænt/ **23**/20
Egypt /ˈiːdʒɪpt/ **54**
eight /eɪt/ **33**/8
eighteen /ˌeɪˈtiːn/ **33**/18
eighth /eɪtθ/ **33**
eighty /ˈeɪtɪ/ **33**/80
El Paso /el ˈpæsəʊ/ **55**
El Salvador /el ˈsælvədɔː(r)/ **53**
elbow /ˈelbəʊ/ **3**/8
elderly /ˈeldəˡɪ/ **5**/6
electric drill /ɪˌlektrɪk ˈdrɪl/ **21**/10
(electric) guitar /ɪˌlektrɪk gɪˈtɑː(r)/ **76**/8
electric razor /ɪˌlektrɪk ˈreɪzə(r)/ **17**/22
electric teakettle /ɪˌlektrɪk ˈtiːketl/ **20**/19
electrician /ɪˌlekˈtrɪʃn/ **40**/7
electrode /ɪˈlektrəʊd/ **46**/6
electronics store /ɪlekˈtrɒnɪks stɔːr/ **30**
elephant /ˈelɪfənt/ **90**/24
eleven /ɪˈlevn/ **33**/11
eleventh /ɪˈlevnθ/ **33**
embankment /ɪmˈbæŋkmənt/ **62**/3
embroidery /ɪmˈbrɔɪdərɪ/ **74**/18
emergency services /ɪˈmɜːdʒənsɪ ˌsɜːvɪsɪz/ **38**
empty /ˈemptɪ/ **88**/12
engine /ˈendʒɪn/ **64**/15, **65**/28, **66**/3
England /ˈɪŋglənd/ **56**
English Channel /ˌɪŋglɪʃ ˈtʃænl/ **56**
entrance /ˈentrəns/ **66**/21
envelope /ˈenvələʊp/ **26**/3, **32**/6
environment /ɪnˈvaɪərənmənt/ **73**
equals /ˈiːkwəlz/ **48**/15
equator /ɪˈkweɪtə(r)/ **53**/**54**
Equatorial Guinea /ekwəˌtɔːrɪəl ˈgɪnɪ/ **54**
eraser /ɪˈreɪzər/ **49**/26
Eritrea /ˌerɪˈtreɪə/ **54**
Essex /ˈesɪks/ **56**
estate /ɪsˈteɪt/ **63**/14
Estonia /eˈstəʊnɪə/ **54**
Ethiopia /ˌiːθɪˈəʊpɪə/ **54**
Eugene /jʊˈdʒiːn/ **55**
Europe /ˈjʊərəp/ **53**/4
evening /ˈiːvnɪŋ/ **37**/17
examination couch /ɪgˌzæmɪˈneɪʃn kaʊtʃ/ **7**/22
examination table /ɪgˌzæmɪˈneɪʃn teɪbl/ **7**/22
examining table /ɪgˈzæmɪnɪŋ teɪbl/ **7**/22
exchange rate /ɪksˈtʃeɪndʒ reɪt/ **34**/8
exercise book /ˈeksəsaɪz bʊk/ **49**/4
exhaust-pipe /ɪgˈzɔːstpaɪp/ **64**/6
exit ramp /ˈeksɪt ræmp/ **62**/12
exit sign /ˈeksɪt saɪŋ/ **66**/5
expensive /ɪkˈspensɪv/ **87**/8
Express Mail /ɪkˈspres meɪl/ **32**/25
eye /aɪ/ **4**/25, **6**/13
eye drops /ˈaɪ drɒps/ **8**/21
eye test /ˈaɪ test/ **8**/14
eyebrow /ˈaɪbraʊ/ **4**/26
eyeglass case /ˈaɪglæs ˌkeɪs/ **8**/19
eyelash /ˈaɪlæʃ/ **4**/28
eyelid /ˈaɪlɪd/ **4**/27
eyepiece /ˈaɪpiːs/ **46**/22

face /feɪs/ **4**/17
face mask /ˈfeɪs mæsk/ **78**/5
factory /ˈfæktərɪ/ **59**/23
Faeroe Islands /ˈfeərəʊ ˌaɪləndz/ **54**
Fahrenheit /ˈfærənhaɪt/ **52**/1
fair /feə(r)/ **5**/9
fairway /ˈfeəweɪ/ **79**/13
Falkirk /ˈfɔːlkɜːk/ **56**
Falkland Islands /ˈfɔːklənd ˌaɪləndz/ **53**
fall (verb) /fɔːl/ **57**/8, **82**/5
fall /fɔːl/ **52**/11
fall over (verb) /fɔːl ˈəʊvə(r)/ **6**/11
family relationships /ˌfæməlɪ rɪˈleɪʃnʃɪps/ **1**/**2**
farm /fɑːm/ **73**/20
farmer /ˈfɑːmə(r)/ **39**/9
farmhouse /ˈfɑːmhaʊs/ **73**/21
fast /fɑːst; *US* fæst/ **87**/23
fast lane /ˈfɑːst leɪn; *US* ˈfæst/ **62**/7, 17
fat /fæt/ **5**/21
father /ˈfɑːðə(r)/ **1**/6
father-in-law /ˈfɑːðər ɪn lɔː/ **1**/7
faucet /ˈfɔːsɪt/ **19**/19, 20
fax (verb) /fæks/ **43**/10
fax /fæks/ **43**/10
feather /ˈfeðə(r)/ **93**/5
February /ˈfebrʊərɪ; *US* ˈfebrʊerɪ/ **52**
fence /fens/ **22**/15
fender /ˈfendər/ **65**/22
Fermanagh /fəˈmænə/ **56**
fern /fɜːn/ **25**/5
ferry /ˈferɪ/ **70**/9
field /fiːld/ **73**/24, **80**/16, **81**/22
field hockey /ˈfiːld hɒkɪ/ **78**/16
fielder /ˈfiːldə(r)/ **81**/21
Fife /faɪf/ **56**
fifteen /ˌfɪfˈtiːn/ **33**/15
fifth /fɪfθ/ **33**
fifty /ˈfɪftɪ/ **33**/50
Fiji /ˈfiːˌdʒiː/ **54**
file (verb) /faɪl/ **43**/9
file /faɪl/ **21**/13, **44**/14
file cabinet /ˈfaɪl ˌkæbɪnɪt/ **44**/15
filing cabinet /ˈfaɪlɪŋ ˌkæbɪnɪt/ **44**/15
fill (verb) /fɪl/ **83**/9
fill in (verb) /fɪl ˈɪn/ **43**/5
fill out (verb) /fɪl ˈaʊt/ **43**/5
filling /ˈfɪlɪŋ/ **8**/9
filling-station /ˈfɪlɪŋsteɪʃn/ **64**/1
film /fɪlm/ **29**/11
film star /ˈfɪlm stɑː(r)/ **76**/24
filter paper /ˈfɪltə peɪpə(r)/ **45**/11
fin /fɪn/ **91**/3
finger /ˈfɪŋgə(r)/ **3**/20
finish (verb) /ˈfɪnɪʃ/ **42**/18
Finland /ˈfɪnlənd/ **54**
fire /ˈfaɪə(r)/ **16**/4, **38**/8
fire brigade /ˈfaɪə brɪˌgeɪd/ **38**
fire department /ˈfaɪər dɪˌpɑːrtmənt/ **38**
fire extinguisher /ˈfaɪər ɪkˌstɪŋgwɪʃə(r)/ **38**/9
fire fighter /ˈfaɪər faɪtər/ **38**/10
fire-engine /ˈfaɪərendʒɪn/ **38**/4
fireman /ˈfaɪəmən/ **38**/10
fireplace /ˈfaɪəpleɪs/ **16**/3, **58**/6, 7
first /fɜːst/ **33**
first class mail /ˌfɜːrst klæs ˈmeɪl/ **32**/14
first floor /ˌfɜːst ˈflɔː(r)/ **13**/13, 14
first quarter /ˌfɜːrst ˈkwɔːrtər/ **50**/2
first-class post /ˌfɜːstklɑːs ˈpəʊst/ **32**/11
fish /fɪʃ/ **91**
fisherman /ˈfɪʃəmən/ **39**/10
fishing /ˈfɪʃɪŋ/ **72**/13
fishing boat /ˈfɪʃɪŋ bəʊt/ **69**/14
fishing-rod /ˈfɪʃɪŋrɒd/ **72**/15
fist /fɪst/ **3**/10
five /faɪv/ **33**/5
fizzy drink /ˌfɪzɪ ˈdrɪŋk/ **27**/26
flag /flæg/ **59**/19
flame /fleɪm/ **45**/3
flamingo /fləˈmɪŋgəʊ/ **93**/25
flannel /ˈflænl/ **17**/13
flap /flæp/ **32**/7
flash (gun) /ˈflæʃ gʌn/ **29**/18
flashlight /ˈflæʃlaɪt/ **19**/17
flat bottom flask /ˌflæt bɒtəm ˈflɑːsk; *US* flæsk/ **45**/9
flex /fleks/ **19**/11
flight attendant /flaɪt əˈtendənt/ **67**/14
Flintshire /ˈflɪntʃə(r)/ **56**
flipper /ˈflɪpə(r)/ **90**/28
floor /flɔː(r)/ **13**/11, 13, 14, **49**/9

floppy disk /ˌflɒpɪ ˈdɪsk/ **44**/23
Florida /ˈflɒrɪdə/ **55**
florist /ˈflɒrɪst/ **25**
flower /ˈflaʊə(r)/ **57**/12
flower-bed /ˈflaʊəbed/ **22**/24
flowerpot /ˈflaʊəpɒt/ **22**/10
flute /fluːt/ **75**/12
fly /flaɪ/ **92**/1
flyover /ˈflaɪəʊvə(r)/ **62**/10
foal /fəʊl/ **89**/14
focusing control /ˈfəʊkəsɪŋ kənˌtrəʊl/ **46**/18
focusing knob /ˈfəʊkəsɪŋ nɒb/ **46**/18
foggy /ˈfɒgɪ/ **51**/7
fold (verb) /fəʊld/ **86**/19
food processor /ˈfuːd ˌprəʊsesə(r); *US* ˈfuːd ˌprɒsesər/ **20**/25
foot /fʊt/ **3**/13
football /ˈfʊtbɔːl/ **78**/11, 12, **81**
footbrake /ˈfʊtbreɪk/ **64**/27
footbridge /ˈfʊtbrɪdʒ/ **62**/22
forehead /ˈfɒrɪd, *also* ˈfɔːhed; *US* ˈfɔːrɪd/ **4**/18
foreign currency /ˌfɒrən ˈkʌrənsɪ/ **34**/13
forest /ˈfɒrɪst; *US* ˈfɔːrɪst/ **73**/5
fork /fɔːk/ **15**/12, **22**/18
fork-lift truck /ˈfɔːklɪft trʌk/ **63**/8
form /fɔːm/ **43**/5
Fort Worth /ˌfɔːrt ˈwɜːrθ/ **55**
forty /ˈfɔːtɪ/ **33**/40
four /fɔː(r)/ **33**/4
fourteen /ˌfɔːˈtiːn/ **33**/14
fourth /fɔːθ/ **33**
fox /fɒks/ **89**/7
fraction /ˈfrækʃn/ **48**/18
frame /freɪm/ **8**/18, **15**/24, **65**/4
France /frɑːns; *US* fræns/ **54**
freesia /ˈfriːzɪə; *US* ˈfriːʒər/ **25**/20
freeway /ˈfriːweɪ/ **62**/11
freezer /ˈfriːzə(r)/ **20**/15
freezing /ˈfriːzɪŋ/ **52**/7
French fries /ˈfrentʃ fraɪz/ **28**/27
French Guiana /ˌfrentʃ gɪˈɑːnə, gɪˈænə/ **53**
French horn /ˌfrentʃ ˈhɔːn/ **75**/6
Friday /ˈfraɪdɪ/ **33**
fridge /frɪdʒ/ **20**/14
friend /frend/ **42**/20
fringe /frɪndʒ/ **5**/14
frog /frɒg/ **92**/25
from /frɒm/ **57**/7
front /frʌnt/ **48**/7
front desk /ˌfrʌnt ˈdesk/ **71**/1
front door /ˌfrʌnt ˈdɔː(r)/ **14**/3
front garden /ˌfrʌnt ˈgɑːdn/ **22**/21
front teeth /ˌfrʌnt tiːθ/ **8**/11
front walk /ˈfrʌnt wɔːk/ **22**/23
front yard /ˌfrʌnt ˈjɑːrd/ **22**/21
frown (verb) /fraʊn/ **84**/19
fruit /fruːt/ **24, 28**/7
fruit cocktail /ˌfruːt ˈkɒkteɪl/ **28**/11
frying-pan /ˈfraɪɪŋ pæn/ **20**/24
fuel gauge /ˈfjuːəl geɪdʒ/ **64**/23
fuel truck /ˈfjuːəl trʌk/ **63**/3
full /fʊl/ **50**/3, **88**/11
full slip /ˈfʊl slɪp/ **11**/5
funnel /ˈfʌnl/ **45**/10, **70**/10
fur /fɜː(r)/ **89**/20
furrow /ˈfʌrəʊ/ **73**/30
fuselage /ˈfjuːzəlɑːʒ/ **68**/17

Gabon /ˈgæbɒn/ **54**
Galapagos Islands /gəˈlæpəgɒs ˌaɪləndz/ **53**
galaxy /ˈgæləksɪ/ **50**/24
gall-bladder /ˈgɔːl blædə(r)/ **4**/5
gallery /ˈgælərɪ/ **76**/22
Galway /ˈgɔːlweɪ/ **56**
Gambia /ˈgæmbɪə/ **54**
garage /ˈgærɑːʒ, ˈgærɪdʒ; *US* gəˈrɑːʒ/ **14**/2
garbage can /ˈgɑːrbɪdʒ ˌkæn/ **22**/20, **59**/14
garden /ˈgɑːdn/ **22**
gardener /ˈgɑːdnə(r)/ **39**/2
garlic /ˈgɑːlɪk/ **23**/2
gas gauge /ˈgæs geɪdʒ/ **64**/23
gas pedal /ˈgæs pedl/ **64**/28
gas pump /ˈgæs pʌmp/ **64**/11
gas station /ˈgæs steɪʃn/ **64**/1
gate /geɪt/ **22**/22, **66**/22, **67**/15
gateau /ˈgætəʊ; *US* gæˈtəʊ/ **28**/13
gauze /gɔːz/ **45**/25
gauze pad /ˈgɔːz pæd/ **7**/9
gear changer /ˈgɪər tʃeɪndʒər/ **65**/13
gear lever /ˈgɪə liːvə(r)/ **64**/21, **65**/13
gearshift /ˈgɪərʃɪft/ **64**/21
Georgia /ˈdʒɔːdʒə/ **54**
Georgia /ˈdʒɔːrdʒə/ **55**
Germany /ˈdʒɜːmənɪ/ **54**
get dressed (verb) /get ˈdrest/ **41**/8
get out (verb) /get ˈaʊt/ **41**/2
get up (verb) /get ˈʌp/ **41**/2
Ghana /ˈgɑːnə/ **54**
gill /gɪl/ **91**/4
ginger /ˈdʒɪndʒə(r)/ **5**/12
giraffe /dʒɪˈrɑːf; *US* dʒəˈræf/ **90**/23
girl /gɜːl/ **5**/3
give (verb) /gɪv/ **85**/9
give way /ˌgɪv ˈweɪ/ **61**/1
Glasgow /ˈglɑːzgəʊ, ˈglæzgəʊ/ **56**
glass /glɑːs; *US* glæs/ **13**/23, **15**/14
glass rod /ˌglɑːs ˈrɒd; *US* ˌglæs-/ **46**/2
glasses /ˈglɑːsɪz; *US* ˈglæsɪz/ **8**/15
glasses case /ˈglɑːsɪz ˌkeɪs; *US* ˈglæsɪz/ **8**/19
globe /gləʊb/ **49**/11
Gloucester /ˈglɒstə(r)/ **56**
Gloucestershire /ˈglɒstəʃə(r)/ **56**
glove /glʌv/ **10**/15
glue /gluː/ **49**/23
go (verb) /gəʊ/ **41**/3, 4, **42**/24, **57**/6
goal /gəʊl/ **81**/23, 28
goal-post /ˈgəʊlpəʊst/ **81**/27
goalkeeper /ˈgəʊlkiːpə(r)/ **81**/30
goat /gəʊt/ **89**/8
goggles /ˈgɒglz/ **45**/1
golf /gɒlf/ **79**/11
good /gʊd/ **88**/5
goose /guːs/ **93**/27
gorilla /gəˈrɪlə/ **90**/14
grade crossing /ˈgreɪd ˌkrɒsɪŋ/ **66**/2
graduated beaker /ˌgrædʒʊeɪtɪd ˈbiːkər/ **45**/24
graduated cylinder /ˌgrædʒʊeɪtɪd ˈsɪlɪndər/ **46**/3
grain /greɪn/ **73**/27
gram /græm/ **48**/24
granddaughter /ˈgrænˌdɔːtə(r)/ **1**/23
grandfather /ˈgrændˌfɑːðə(r)/ **1**/2
grandmother /ˈgrændˌmʌðə(r)/ **1**/1
grandparent /ˈgrændˌpeərənt/ **1**/21
grandson /ˈgrændsʌn/ **1**/22
grape /greɪp/ **24**/10
grapefruit /ˈgreɪpfruːt/ **24**/21
graphic equalizer /ˌgræfɪk ˈiːkwəlaɪzə(r)/ **30**/17
grass /grɑːs; *US* græs/ **22**/3
grass verge /grɑːs ˈvɜːdʒ/ **62**/23
grasshopper /ˈgrɑːshɒpə(r); *US* ˈgræshɒpər/ **92**/17
gray /greɪ/ **9**/15
Great Britain /ˌgreɪt ˈbrɪtn/ **56**
Great Falls /ˌgreɪt ˈfɔːlz/ **55**
Greater London /ˌgreɪtə ˈlʌndən/ **56**
Greater Manchester /ˌ- ˈmæntʃəstə(r)/ **56**
Greece /griːs/ **54**
green /griːn/ **9**/11, 12, **79**/14
green pepper /ˌgriːn ˈpepə(r)/ **23**/3
Greenland /ˈgriːnlənd/ **53**
greetings card /ˈgriːtɪŋz kɑːd/ **32**/4
grey /greɪ/ **9**/15
ground /graʊnd/ **57**/5
ground floor /ˌgraʊnd ˈflɔː(r)/ **13**/14
groundsheet /ˈgraʊnd ʃiːt/ **71**/20
grow (verb) /grəʊ/ **57**/3, 12
guarantee /ˌgærənˈtiː/ **34**/3
guardrail /ˈgɑːrdˌreɪl/ **62**/19
Guatemala /ˌgwɑːtəˈmɑːlə/ **53**
guest /gest/ **71**/3
Guinea /ˈgɪnɪ/ **54**
Guinea-Bissau /ˌgɪnɪ bɪˈsaʊ/ **54**
gulf /gʌlf/ **53**
Gulf of Alaska /ˌgʌlf əv əˈlæskə/ **53**/16
Gulf of Guinea /ˌgʌlf əv ˈgɪnɪ/ **54**/24
Gulf of Mexico /ˌgʌlf əv ˈmeksɪkəʊ/ **53**/18
gum /gʌm/ **8**/7
gutter /ˈgʌtə(r)/ **14**/22, **59**/8
Guyana /gaɪˈænə/ **53**
gym /dʒɪm/ **82**/15
gymnasium /dʒɪmˈneɪzɪəm/ **82**/15
gymnast /ˈdʒɪmnæst/ **80**/2
gymnastics /dʒɪmˈnæstɪks/ **80**/1
gypsy /ˈdʒɪpsɪ/ **12**/5

hair /heə(r)/ **3**/2, **5, 84**/13–16
hair-drier (*or* -dryer) /ˈheədraɪə(r)/ **18**/20
hairbrush /ˈheəbrʌʃ/ **18**/8
hairdresser /ˈheədresə(r)/ **39**/5
Haiti /ˈheɪtɪ/ **53**
half /hɑːf; *US* hæf/ **27**/14, **37**/9, **48**/21, **50**/2, 4
half moon /hɑːf ˈmuːn; *US* hæf/ **50**/2, 4
half slip /ˈhɑːf slɪp; *US* ˈhæf slɪp/ **11**/8
hammer /ˈhæmə(r)/ **21**/16
hamper /ˈhæmpər/ **17**/16
Hampshire /ˈhæmpʃə(r)/ **56**
hamster /ˈhæmstə(r)/ **89**/25
hand /hænd/ **3**/19, **85**/1
hand drill /ˈhænd drɪl/ **21**/18
hand-towel /ˈhændtaʊəl/ **17**/10
handbag /ˈhændbæg/ **10**/10
handkerchief /ˈhæŋkətʃɪf, *also* -tʃiːf/ **10**/21
handle /ˈhændl/ **30**/9
handlebar /ˈhændlbɑː(r)/ **65**/19
handsaw /ˈhændsɔː/ **21**/22
hang-glider /ˈhæŋˌglaɪdə(r)/ **72**/23
hang-gliding /ˈhæŋˌglaɪdɪŋ/ **72**/22
hanger /ˈhæŋər/ **18**/18
happy /ˈhæpɪ/ **88**/1
hard /hɑːd/ **88**/17
hard shoulder /ˌhɑːd ˈʃəʊldə(r)/ **62**/4
harmonica /hɑːˈmɒnɪkə/ **75**/25
harness /ˈhɑːnɪs/ **72**/26
Hartlepool /ˈhɑːtlɪpuːl/ **56**

Index

hat /hæt/ **12**/17
hatchback /ˈhætʃbæk/ **63**/15
hatchet /ˈhætʃɪt/ **21**/17
have (verb) /hæv/ **6**/4–14, **41**/7, 9, **42**/16
Hawaii /həˈwɑɪi:/ **55**
Hawaiian Islands /həˈwaɪən ˌaɪləndz/ **53**
hawk /hɔ:k/ **93**/10
head /hed/ **3**/1, **5**/7
headache /ˈhedeɪk/ **6**/6
headboard /ˈhedbɔ:d/ **18**/13
headlight /ˈhedlaɪt/ **64**/4
headphones /ˈhedfəʊnz/ **30**/12
health care /ˈhelθ keə(r)/ **7**/**8**
health club /ˈhelθ klʌb/ **42**/19
heart /hɑ:t/ **4**/4, **74**/32
heavy /ˈhevɪ/ **88**/14
hedge /hedʒ/ **22**/27
hedgehog /ˈhedʒhɒg/ **89**/5
heel /hi:l/ **3**/15, **11**/20
height /haɪt/ **48**/2
helicopter /ˈhelɪkɒptə(r)/ **68**/9
helmet /ˈhelmɪt/ **12**/2
hen /hen/ **93**/2
Hereford and Worcester /ˌherɪfəd ənd ˈwʊstə(r)/ **56**
herring /ˈherɪŋ/ **91**/6
Hertfordshire /ˈhɑ:tfədʃə(r)/ **56**
hi-fi /ˈhaɪfaɪ/ **30**/13
hi-fi shop /ˈhaɪfaɪ ˌʃɒp/ **30**
high /haɪ/ **87**/17
Highland /ˈhaɪlənd/ **56**
highway /ˈhaɪweɪ/ **62**/24
hiker /ˈhaɪkə(r)/ **71**/24
hiking /ˈhaɪkɪŋ/ **71**/23
hill /hɪl/ **73**/12
hip-bone /ˈhɪpbəʊn/ **4**/15
hippopotamus /ˌhɪpəˈpɒtəməs/ **90**/22
hit (verb) /hɪt/ **78**/28
hobby /ˈhɒbɪ/ **74**
hockey /ˈhɒkɪ/ **78**/16
hockey ball /ˈhɒkɪ bɔ:l/ **78**/19
hockey player /ˈhɒkɪ pleɪə(r)/ **78**/17
hockey stick /ˈhɒkɪ stɪk/ **78**/18
hold (verb) /həʊld/ **86**/15
hole /həʊl/ **79**/16
hole-punch /ˈhəʊlpʌntʃ/ **44**/7
holiday /ˈhɒlɪdeɪ/ **71**/**72**
holiday resort /hɒlɪdeɪ rɪˌzɔ:t/ **72**/2
hollow /ˈhɒləʊ/ **88**/21
Hollywood /ˈhɒlɪwʊd/ **55**
home /həʊm/ **41**/10
Honduras /hɒnˈdjʊərəs; *US* - dʊərəs/ **53**

Honolulu /ˌhɒnəˈlu:lu:/ **55**
hood /hʊd/ **64**/14
hoof /hu:f/ **89**/12
hook /hʊk/ **19**/16
Hoover /ˈhu:və(r)/ **19**/7
horn /hɔ:n/ **90**/20
horse /hɔ:s/ **89**/13
horse-racing /ˈhɔ:sreɪsɪŋ/ **80**/23
horseback riding /ˈhɔ:rsbæk ˌraɪdɪŋ/ **72**/16, **80**/9
hose /həʊz/ **38**/12, **64**/12, **83**/8
hospital room /ˈhɒspɪtl ru:m, rʊm/ **7**
hospital ward /ˈhɒspɪtl wɔ:d/ **7**
hot /hɒt/ **52**/3
hot water faucet /ˈhɒt wɔ:tər ˌfɔ:sɪt/ **19**/20
hot-air balloon /ˌhɒtˈeə bəˌlu:n/ **72**/21
hot(-water) tap /ˌhɒtˈwɔ:tə ˌtæp/ **19**/20
hotel reception /həʊˌtel rɪˈsepʃn/ **71**/1
hour /ˈaʊə(r)/ **37**
hour-hand /ˈaʊəhænd/ **37**/4
Houston /ˈhju:stən/ **55**
hovercraft /ˈhɒvəkrɑ:ft; *US* -kræft/ **70**/8
hub /hʌb/ **65**/12
Hudson /ˈhʌdsn/ **55**
Hudson Bay /ˌhʌdsn ˈbeɪ/ **53**/17
hug (verb) /hʌg/ **85**/3
human body /ˌhju:mən ˈbɒdɪ/ **3**/**4**
hummingbird /ˈhʌmɪŋbɜ:d/ **93**/16
hump /hʌmp/ **90**/11
hundred /ˈhʌndrəd/ **33**/100
Hungary /ˈhʌŋgərɪ; *US* ˈhʌŋgrɪ/ **54**
hungry /ˈhʌŋgrɪ/ **6**/2
hurt (verb) /hɜ:t/ **6**/12
husband /ˈhʌzbənd/ **1**/18
hydrant /haɪdrənt/ **38**/11
hydrofoil /haɪdrəfɔɪl/ **70**/7
hypotenuse /haɪˈpɒtənju:z; *US* haɪˈpɒtnu:s/ **47**/17

ice-cream /ˌaɪsˈkri:m, *esp US* ˈaɪskri:m/ **28**/10
ice-rink /ˈɑɪsrɪŋk/ **77**/5
ice-skating /ˈaɪsskeɪtɪŋ/ **77**/1
Iceland /ˈaɪslənd/ **54**
Idaho /ˈaɪdəhəʊ/ **55**
Idaho Falls /ˌaɪdəhəʊ ˈfɔ:lz/ **55**
ignition /ɪgˈnɪʃn/ **64**/25
Illinois /ˌɪləˈnɔɪ/ **55**
in /ɪn/ **58**/3, 7
in box /ˈɪn bɒks/ **44**/3
in front of /ɪn ˈfrʌnt əv/ **58**/18
in the middle of /ɪn ðə ˈmɪdl əv/ **58**/13
in-tray /ˈɪntreɪ/ **44**/3
India /ˈɪndɪə/ **54**
Indian /ˈɪndɪən/ **53**/12
Indiana /ˌɪndɪˈænə/ **55**
Indianapolis /ˌɪndɪəˈnæpəlɪs/ **55**
indicator /ˈɪndɪkeɪtə(r)/ **64**/3
Indonesia /ˌɪndəˈni:zɪə; *US* ˌɪndəˈni:ʒə/ **54**
inflatable dinghy /ɪnˌfleɪtəbl ˈdɪŋgɪ/ **70**/14
injection /ɪnˈdʒekʃn/ **7**/21
injured /ˈɪndʒəd/ **38**/15
insect /ˈɪnsekt/ **92**
inside /ˈɪnsaɪd/ **58**/3
inside lane /ˈɪnsaɪd leɪn/ **62**/5
instructor /ɪnˈstrʌktə(r)/ **82**/7
internal /ɪnˈtɜ:nl/ **4**/1
international code /ˌɪntəˈnæʃnəl kəʊd/ **38**/18
intersection /ˌɪntərˈsekʃn/ **60**/21, **62**/25
interstate highway /ˌɪntərsteɪt ˈhaɪweɪ/ **62**/11
intestines /ɪnˈtestɪnz/ **4**/9
into /ˈɪntu:/ **57**/4
Inverclyde /ˌɪnvəˈklaɪd/ **56**
Inverness /ˌɪnvəˈnes/ **56**
Iowa /ˈaɪəwə/ **55**
Ipswich /ˈɪpswɪtʃ/ **56**
Iran /ɪˈrɑ:n/ **54**
Iraq /ɪˈrɑ:k/ **54**
iris /ˈaɪərɪs/ **4**/29, **25**/28
Irish Sea /ˌaɪrɪʃ ˈsi:/ **56**
iron (verb) /ˈaɪən; *US* aɪərn/ **83**/1
iron /ˈaɪən; *US* ˈaɪərn/ **19**/13
ironing-board /ˈaɪənɪŋ bɔ:d; *US* ˈaɪərnɪŋ bɔ:rd/ **19**/9
island /ˈaɪlənd/ **55**
Isle of Man /ˌaɪl əv ˈmæn/ **56**
Isle of Wight /ˌaɪl əv ˈwaɪt/ **56**
Isles of Scilly /ˌaɪlz əv ˈsɪlɪ/ **56**
Israel /ˈɪzreɪl/ **54**
Italy /ˈɪtəlɪ/ **54**
Ivory Coast /ˌaɪvərɪ ˈkəʊst/ **54**

jack /dʒæk/ **74**/31
jacket /ˈdʒækɪt/ **10**/8
jacket potato /ˌdʒækɪt pəˈteɪtəʊ/ **28**/25
jackhammer /ˈdʒækhæmər/ **61**/16
Jackson /ˈdʒæksən/ **55**
Jacksonville /ˈdʒæksənvɪl/ **55**
jam /dʒæm/ **27**/5, 17
Jamaica /dʒəˈmeɪkə/ **53**
January /ˈdʒænjʊərɪ; *US* ˈdʒænjʊerɪ/ **52**
Japan /dʒəˈpæn/ **54**
jar /dʒɑ:(r)/ **27**/5
jaw /dʒɔ:/ **3**/4
JCB /ˌdʒeɪ si: ˈbi:/ **61**/18
jeans /dʒi:nz/ **10**/7
jeep /dʒi:p/ **63**/10
jellyfish /ˈdʒelɪfɪʃ/ **91**/15
jet engine /ˌdʒet ˈendʒɪn/ **68**/19
jewellery *(esp US* **jewelry)** /ˈdʒu:əlrɪ/ **12**
job /dʒɒb/ **39**/**40**
jockey /ˈdʒɒkɪ/ **80**/26
jog (verb) /dʒɒg/ **82**/2
jogger /ˈdʒɒgə(r)/ **82**/3
jogging suit /ˈdʒɒgɪŋ ˌsu:t/ **12**/3
joint /dʒɔɪnt/ **27**/7
Jordan /ˈdʒɔ:dn/ **54**
judo /ˈdʒu:dəʊ/ **79**/26
jug /dʒʌg/ **15**/17
July /dʒu:ˈlaɪ/ **52**
jump (verb) /dʒʌmp/ **78**/21
jump rope /ˈdʒʌmp rəʊp/ **82**/26
junction /ˈdʒʌŋkʃn/ **62**/25
June /dʒu:n/ **52**
Jupiter /ˈdʒu:pɪtə(r)/ **50**/19

Kampuchea /ˌkæmpʊˈtʃɪə/ **54**
kangaroo /ˌkæŋgəˈru:/ **90**/8
Kansas /ˈkænzəs/ **55**
Kansas City /ˌkænzəs ˈsɪtɪ/ **55**
Kara Sea /ˌkɑ:rəˈsi:; *US* ˌkærə/ **54**/40
karate /kəˈrɑ:tɪ/ **79**/27
kayak /ˈkaɪæk/ **69**/19
Kazakhstan /ˌkæzækˈstɑ:n/ **54**
keeping fit /ˌki:pɪŋ ˈfɪt/ **82**
keeping in shape /ˌki:pɪŋ ɪn ˈʃeɪp/ **82**
Kent /kent/ **56**
Kentucky /kenˈtʌkɪ/ **55**
Kenya /ˈkenjə/ **54**
kerb /kɜ:b/ **59**/9
Kerry /ˈkerɪ/ **56**
kettle /ˈketl/ **20**/19, **83**/9
kettledrum /ˈketldrʌm/ **75**/17
key /ki:/ **44**/11, **56**, **75**/24
keyboard /ˈki:bɔ:d/ **44**/22
keyboard player /ˈki:bɔ:d ˌpleɪə(r)/ **76**/12
kidney /ˈkɪdnɪ/ **4**/7
Kildare /kɪlˈdeə(r)/ **56**
Kilkenny /kɪlˈkenɪ/ **56**
kilogram /ˈkɪləgræm/ **48**/25
kilometre /ˈkɪləmi:tə(r), kɪˈlɒmɪtə(r)/ **48**
king /kɪŋ/ **74**/33
Kingston upon Hull /ˌkɪŋgstən əpɒn ˈhʌl/ **56**
Kirgyzstan /ˌkɪəgɪˈstɑ:n/ **54**

kiss (verb) /kɪs/ **85**/2
kit /kɪt/ **74**/7
kitchen /ˈkɪtʃɪn/ **20**
kitten /ˈkɪtn/ **89**/21
kiwi fruit /ˈki:wi: fru:t/ **24**/18
knave /neɪv/ **74**/31
knee /ni:/ **3**/18
kneecap /ˈni:kæp/ **4**/16
kneel (verb) /ni:l/ **82**/21
knife /naɪf/ **15**/10
knitting /ˈnɪtɪŋ/ **74**/21
knitting-needle /ˈnɪtɪŋ ni:dl/ **74**/23
knocker /ˈnɒkə(r)/ **13**/4
Kuwait /kʊˈweɪt/ **54**

lab coat /ˈlæb kəʊt/ **46**/1
label /ˈleɪbl/ **32**/3
ladder /ˈlædə(r)/ **38**/5
ladle /ˈleɪdl/ **20**/11
ladybird /ˈleɪdɪbɜ:d/ **92**/14
ladybug /ˈleɪdɪbʌg/ **92**/14
lake /leɪk/ **55**, **73**/4
Lake Erie /ˌleɪk ˈɪərɪ/ **55**
Lake Huron /ˌleɪk ˈhjʊərɒn/ **55**
Lake Michigan /ˌleɪk ˈmɪʃɪgən/ **55**
Lake Ontario /ˌleɪk ɒnˈteərɪəʊ/ **55**
Lake Superior /ˌleɪk su:ˈpɪərɪər/ **55**
lamb /læm/ **89**/10
lamb chop /ˌlæm ˈtʃɒp; *US* ˈlæm tʃɒp/ **28**/19
lamp /læmp/ **15**/22
lamppost /ˈlæmppəʊst/ **60**/7
lampshade /ˈlæmpʃeɪd/ **15**/23
Lanarkshire /ˈlænəkʃə(r)/ **56**
Lancashire /ˈlæŋkəʃə(r)/ **56**
landing /ˈlændɪŋ/ **68**/8
lane /leɪn/ **80**/19
Laois /li:ʃ/ **56**
Laos /ˈlɑ:ɒs/ **54**
Laptev Sea /ˌlæptev ˈsi:/ **54**/39
Laramie /ˈlærəmɪ/ **55**
large /lɑ:dʒ/ **87**/3
Larne /lɑ:n/ **56**
Las Vegas /lɒs ˈveɪgəs/ **55**
last quarter /ˌlɑ:st ˈkwɔ:rtər/ **50**/4
Latvia /ˈlætvɪə/ **54**
laugh (verb) /lɑ:f; *US* læf/ **84**/18
launch pad /ˈlɔ:ntʃ pæd/ **50**/12
laundry basket /ˈlɔ:ndrɪ bɑ:skɪt/ **17**/16
laundry room /ˈlɔ:ndrɪ ru:m, rʊm/ **19**
lawn /lɔ:n/ **22**/3
lawnmower /ˈlɔ:nməʊə(r)/ **22**/5
leaf /li:f/ **25**/11
leave (verb) /li:v/ **41**/10
Lebanon /ˈlebənən; *US* ˈlebənɒn/ **54**
Leeds /li:dz/ **56**
left lane /ˈleft leɪn/ **62**/17
leg /leg/ **3**/12, **6**/12, 13
Leicester /ˈlestə(r)/ **56**
Leicestershire /ˈlestəʃə(r)/ **56**
Leitrim /ˈli:trɪm/ **56**
lemon /ˈlemən/ **24**/6
length /leŋθ/ **48**/6
lens /lenz/ **8**/16, **29**/17
leopard /ˈlepəd/ **90**/18
Lesotho /leˈsu:tu:/ **54**
letter /ˈletə(r)/ **32**/5, **43**/1, 3, 4, 6, 10
letter-box /ˈletəbɒks/ **13**/5, **31**/11, 14, **59**/3
lettuce /ˈletɪs/ **23**/7
level /ˈlevəl/ **21**/7
level crossing /ˌlevl ˈkrɒsɪŋ/ **66**/2
Liberia /laɪˈbɪrɪə/ **54**
library /ˈlaɪbrərɪ; *US* ˈlaɪbrerɪ/ **57**/6, 7
Libya /ˈlɪbɪə/ **54**
license plate /ˈlaɪsns pleɪt/ **64**/5
lid /lɪd/ **15**/5
lie down (verb) /ˌlaɪ ˈdaʊn/ **84**/23
lifeboat /ˈlaɪfbəʊt/ **69**/18
lift (verb) /lɪft/ **86**/13
light (verb) /laɪt/ **86**/23
light /laɪt/ **9**/11, **18**/16, **88**/13
light switch /ˈlaɪt swɪtʃ/ **18**/27
light-bulb /ˈlaɪtbʌlb/ **19**/15
lighthouse /ˈlaɪthaʊs/ **70**/12
lightning /ˈlaɪtnɪŋ/ **51**/11
lily /ˈlɪlɪ/ **25**/26
Limavady /ˌlɪməˈvædɪ/ **56**
lime /laɪm/ **24**/17
Limerick /ˈlɪmərɪk/ **56**
Lincoln /ˈlɪŋkən/ **55**
Lincolnshire /ˈlɪŋkənʃə(r)/ **56**
line /laɪn/ **47**/25, 26, 29, 30, **66**/7, 12, **69**/6
liner /ˈlaɪnə(r)/ **70**/11
linesman /ˈlaɪnzmən/ **81**/25
lion /ˈlaɪən/ **90**/16
lip /lɪp/ **4**/23
lipstick /ˈlɪpstɪk/ **12**/21
Lisburn /ˈlɪzbən/ **56**
listen (verb) /ˈlɪsn/ **41**/12
Lithuania /ˌlɪθju:ˈeɪnɪə/ **54**
litre /ˈli:tə(r)/ **48**/28
litter-bin /ˈlɪtəbɪn/ **59**/14
little /ˈlɪtl/ **87**/4
Little Rock /ˈlɪtl rɒk/ **55**
liver /ˈlɪvə(r)/ **4**/6
Liverpool /ˈlɪvəpu:l/ **56**
living-room /ˈlɪvɪŋ ru:m, rʊm/ **16**
lizard /ˈlɪzəd/ **91**/28
llama /ˈlɑ:mə/ **90**/12
loaf /ləʊf/ **27**/2
lobster /ˈlɒbstə(r)/ **91**/16
lock /lɒk/ **18**/26, **65**/6
log /lɒg/ **16**/5
London /ˈlʌndən/ **56**
Londonderry /ˌlʌndənˈderɪ/ **56**
long /lɒŋ/ **5**/12, 15
Longford /ˈlɒŋfəd/ **56**
look (verb) /lʊk/ **57**/1, 14
loose /lu:s/ **88**/24
lorry /ˈlɒrɪ/ **63**/4
lorry driver /ˈlɒrɪ draɪvə(r)/ **40**/2
Los Angeles /lɒs ˈændʒəlɪz/ **55**
Lothian /ˈləʊðɪən/ **56**
lotion /ˈləʊʃn/ **17**/21
loud /laʊd/ **88**/3
Louisiana /lu:ˌi:zɪˈænə/ **55**
Louisville /ˈlu:ɪvɪl/ **55**
Louth /lu:θ/ **56**
low /ləʊ/ **87**/18
luggage /ˈlʌgɪdʒ/ **67**/17
luggage reclaim /ˈlʌgɪdʒ rɪˌkleɪm/ **67**/16
lunar module /ˌlu:nə ˈmɒdju:l; *US* ˈmɒdʒu:l/ **50**/5
lunar vehicle /ˌlu:nə ˈvɪəkl; *US* ˈvi:hɪkl/ **50**/8
lunch /lʌntʃ/ **42**/17
lung /lʌŋ/ **4**/3
lychee (*also* litchi) /ˌlaɪˈtʃi:, ˈlaɪtʃi:; *US* ˈli:tʃi:/ **24**/15
Macedonia (Former Yugoslav Republic of ~) /ˌmæsɪˈdəʊnjə/ **54**
Madagascar /ˌmædəˈgæskə(r)/ **54**
magazine /mægəˈzi:n; *US* ˈmægəzi:n/ **26**/7
Magherafelt /ˈmækerəfelt/ **56**
magnet /ˈmægnɪt/ **46**/8
magnifying glass /ˈmægnɪfaɪɪŋ glɑ:s; *US* -glæs/ **45**/14
mail /meɪl/ **31**/10, **41**/6
mail truck /ˈmeɪl trʌk/ **31**/7
mailbag /ˈmeɪlbæg/ **31**/9, 13
mailbox /ˈmeɪlbɒks/ **13**/5, **31**/11, 14, **59**/3
mailman /ˈmeɪlmæn/ **31**/8
main course /ˈmeɪn kɔ:s/ **28**
main river /meɪn rɪvə(r)/ **55**
Maine /meɪn/ **55**
make (verb) /meɪk/ **74**/6
make a deposit (verb) /ˌmeɪk ə dɪˈpɒzɪt/ **34**/17
make a note (verb) /ˌmeɪk ə ˈnəʊt/ **43**/8
make-up /ˈmeɪkʌp/ **12**/20
Malawi /məˈlɑ:wɪ/ **54**
Malaysia /məˈleɪzɪə; *US* məˈleɪʒə/ **54**
Mali /ˈmɑ:lɪ/ **54**
mallet /ˈmælɪt/ **21**/2
man /mæn/ **5**/5, 6, **38**/15
Manchester /ˈmæntʃɪstə(r)/ **56**
mane /meɪn/ **89**/16
mango /ˈmæŋgəʊ/ **24**/19
manhole cover /ˈmænhəʊl kʌvə(r)/ **59**/7
mantel /ˈmæntl/ **16**/2, **58**/9, 10
mantelpiece /ˈmæntlpi:s/ **16**/2, **58**/9, 10
map /mæp/ **49**/18
March /mɑ:tʃ/ **52**
margarine /ˌmɑ:dʒəˈri:n; *US* ˈmɑ:rdʒərɪn/ **27**/20, 28
marina /məˈri:nə/ **69**/10
market /ˈmɑ:kɪt/ **23**/**24**, **23**/1
Mars /mɑ:z/ **50**/20
Maryland /ˈmeərɪlənd/ **55**
mask /mɑ:sk; *US* mæsk/ **7**/17
Massachusetts /ˌmæsəˈtʃu:sɪts/ **55**
mast /mɑ:st; *US* mæst/ **69**/2
mat /mæt/ **82**/17
match /mætʃ/ **81**/1, 8, 12
matter /ˈmætə(r)/ **6**
mattress /ˈmætrɪs/ **18**/11
Mauritania /ˌmɒrɪˈteɪnɪə; *US* ˌmɔ:r-/ **54**
Mauritius /məˈrɪʃəs; *US* mɔ:ˈrɪʃəs/ **54**
May /meɪ/ **52**
Mayo /ˈmeɪəʊ/ **56**
meal /mi:l/ **83**/2
measurement /ˈmeʒəmənt/ **48**
measuring beaker /ˈmeʒərɪŋ bi:kə(r)/ **45**/24
measuring cylinder /ˈmeʒərɪŋ sɪlɪndə(r)/ **46**/3
meat /mi:t/ **27**/8
mechanic /mɪˈkænɪk/ **40**/11
median strip /ˈmi:dɪən strɪp/ **62**/18
medicine /ˈmedsn; *US* ˈmedɪsn/ **7**/1
medicine chest /ˈmedɪsn tʃest/ **17**/1
Mediterranean Sea /ˌmedɪtəˌreɪnɪən ˈsi:/ **54**/23
meet (verb) /mi:t/ **42**/20
melon /ˈmelən/ **24**/1, **28**/2
Memphis /ˈmemfɪs/ **55**
menu /ˈmenju:/ **28**/15
Mercury /ˈmɜ:kjʊrɪ/ **50**/23
Merseyside /ˈmɜ:zɪsaɪd/ **56**

Merthyr Tydfil /ˌmɜːθə ˈtɪdvɪl/ **56**
message /ˈmesɪdʒ/ **32**/9
messenger /ˈmesɪndʒər/ **31**/15, 16
messy /ˈmesɪ/ **88**/8
metal detector /ˈmetl dɪˌtektə(r)/ **67**/8
Mexico /ˈmeksɪkəʊ/ **53**
mezzanine /ˈmezəniːn/ **76**/21
Miami /maɪˈæmɪ/ **55**
Michigan /ˈmɪʃɪgən/ **55**
microbalance /ˈmaɪkrəʊbæləns/ **46**/27
microphone /ˈmaɪkrəfəʊn/ **30**/2
microscope /ˈmaɪkrəskəʊp/ **46**/17
midday /ˌmɪdˈdeɪ/ **37**/13
middle lane /ˈmɪdl leɪn/ **62**/6, 16
Middlesbrough /ˈmɪdlzbərə/ **56**
Midlothian /mɪdˈləʊðiən/ **56**
midnight /ˈmɪdnaɪt/ **37**/13
milk /mɪlk/ **27**/24
millilitre /ˈmɪlɪliːtə(r)/ **48**/27
millimetre /ˈmɪlɪmiːtə(r)/ **48**/29
million /ˈmɪljən/ **33**/1000000
Milwaukee /mɪlˈwɔːkɪ/ **55**
mineral water /ˈmɪnərəl wɔːtə(r)/ **27**/25
Minneapolis /ˌmɪnɪˈæpəlɪs/ **55**
Minnesota /ˌmɪnəˈsəʊtə/ **55**
minus /ˈmaɪnəs/ **48**/12, **52**/8
minute /ˈmɪnɪt/ **37**/14
minute-hand /ˈmɪnɪt hænd/ **37**/3
mirror /ˈmɪrə(r)/ **15**/1
miss (verb) /mɪs/ **81**/29
Mississippi /ˌmɪsɪˈsɪpɪ/ **55**
Missouri /mɪˈzʊərɪ/ **55**
misty /ˈmɪstɪ/ **51**/6
mitt /mɪt/ **78**/4
mixer /ˈmɪksə(r)/ **20**/8
mixing bowl /ˈmɪksɪŋ bəʊl/ **20**/3
Mobile /ˈməʊbiːl/ **55**
model /ˈmɒdl/ **74**/6, 8
Moldova /mɒlˈdəʊvə/ **54**
Monaghan /ˈmɒnəhən/ **56**
Monday /ˈmʌndɪ/ **33**
money /ˈmʌnɪ/ **34**/12, **35**/**36**
money order /ˈmʌnɪ ɔːrdər/ **32**/23
Mongolia /mɒŋˈgəʊlɪə/ **54**
monkey /ˈmʌŋkɪ/ **90**/13
Monmouthshire /ˈmɒnməθʃə(r)/ **56**
monster /ˈmɒnstə(r)/ **12**/13
Montana /mɒnˈtænə/ **55**
month /mʌnθ/ **52**
monthly statement /ˌmʌnθlɪ ˈsteɪtmənt/ **34**/5
moon /muːn/ **50**/1, 2, 3, 4
mooring /ˈmɔːrɪŋ/ **69**/15
mop /mɒp/ **19**/8
Moray /ˈmʌri/ **56**
morning /ˈmɔːnɪŋ/ **37**/15
Morocco /məˈrɒkəʊ/ **54**
mortar /ˈmɔːtə(r)/ **45**/8
mosquito /məsˈkiːtəʊ, *Brit also* mɒs-/ **92**/4
moth /mɒθ/ **92**/9
mother /ˈmʌðə(r)/ **1**/5
mother-in-law /ˈmʌðər ɪn lɔː/ **1**/8
motor bike /ˈməʊtə baɪk/ **65**/25
motor boat /ˈməʊtə bəʊt/ **69**/11
motor cycle /ˈməʊtə ˌsaɪkl/ **65**/25
motor-racing /ˈməʊtəˌreɪsɪŋ/ **80**/5
motorway /ˈməʊtəweɪ/ **62**/1
mountain /ˈmaʊntɪn; *US* ˈmaʊntn/ **55**, **73**/1
moustache /məˈstɑːʃ; *US* ˈmʌstæʃ/ **4**/21
mouth /maʊθ/ **3**/29
movie star /ˈmuːvɪ stɑːr/ **76**/24
movie theater /ˈmuːvɪ θɪətər/ **76**
Moyle /mɔɪl/ **56**
Mozambique /ˌməʊzæmˈbiːk/ **54**
mudguard /ˈmʌdgɑːd/ **65**/22
mug /mʌg/ **20**/16, **58**/5
multiplied by /ˈmʌltɪplaɪd baɪ/ **48**/13
mushroom /ˈmʌʃrʊm, ˈmʌʃruːm/ **28**/21
music /ˈmjuːzɪk/ **41**/12, **76**
musical instrument /mjuːzɪkl ˈɪnstrʊmənt/ **75**
musician /mjuːˈzɪʃn/ **76**/2
mussel /ˈmʌsl/ **91**/23
Myanmar /ˌmɪənˈmɑː(r)/ **54**

nail /neɪl/ **3**/17, **21**/23
nail-brush /ˈneɪlbrʌʃ/ **17**/5
Namibia /nəˈmɪbɪə/ **54**
napkin /ˈnæpkɪn/ **15**/7
narrow /ˈnærəʊ/ **87**/16
Nashville /ˈnæʃvɪl/ **55**
navy /ˈneɪvɪ/ **9**/9
near /nɪə(r)/ **58**/6
neat /niːt/ **88**/7
Neath and Port Talbot /ˈniːθ ənd ˌpɔːt ˈtɔːlbət/ **56**
Nebraska /nəˈbræskə/ **55**
neck /nek/ **3**/5
necklace /ˈneklɪs/ **12**/26
needle /ˈniːdl/ **74**/19
negative /ˈnegətɪv/ **29**/10
Nepal /nɪˈpɔːl; *US* nəˈpɑːl/ **54**
nephew /ˈnevjuː; *US* ˈnefjuː/ **1**/15
Neptune /ˈneptjuːn; *US* ˈneptuːn/ **50**/16
nest /nest/ **93**/13
net /net/ **78**/9, **81**/7
Netherlands /ˈneðələndz/ **54**
Nevada /nəˈvɑːdə/ **55**
new /njuː; *US* nuː/ **87**/6
New Caledonia /ˌnuː kæləˈdəʊnjə/ **54**
New Haven /ˌnuː ˈheɪvn/ **55**
New Jersey /ˌnuː ˈdʒɜːrzɪ/ **55**
New Mexico /ˌnuː ˈmeksɪkəʊ/ **55**
new moon /njuː ˈmuːn/ **50**/1
New Orleans /ˌnuː ˈɔːrliːnz/ **55**
New York /ˌnuː ˈjɔːrk/ **55**
New Zealand /ˌnjuː (*US* ˌnuː) ˈziːlənd/ **54**
Newcastle /ˈnjuːkɑːsl/ **56**
Newport /ˈnjuːpɔːt/ **56**
Newry and Mourne /ˌnjʊərɪ ənd ˈmɔːn/ **56**
news-stand /ˈnjuːzstænd/ **59**/15
news-vendor /ˈnjuːzvendə(r)/ **59**/17
newsagent /ˈnjuːzeɪdʒənt/ **26**
newscaster /ˈnuːzkæstər/ **39**/4
newspaper /ˈnjuːzpeɪpə(r); *US* ˈnuːzpeɪpər/ **26**/8, **41**/11, **42**/14, **59**/16
newsreader /ˈnjuːzriːdə(r)/ **39**/4
newsstand /ˈnuːzstænd/ **26**
Newtownabbey /ˌnjuːtnˈæbɪ/ **56**
next to /nekst tʊ/ **58**/17
Niagara Falls /naɪˌægrə ˈfɔːlz/ **55**
Nicaragua /nɪkəˈrægjʊə; *US* ˌnɪkəˈrɑːgwə/ **53**
nickel /ˈnɪkl/ **35**/3
niece /niːs/ **1**/14
Niger /ˈnaɪdʒə(r)/ **54**
Nigeria /naɪˈdʒɪərɪə/ **54**
night /naɪt/ **37**/18
night table /ˈnaɪt teɪbl/ **18**/10
night-dress /ˈnaɪtdres/ **11**/11
nightgown /ˈnaɪtgaʊn/ **11**/11
nine /naɪn/ **33**/9
nineteen /ˌnaɪnˈtiːn/ **33**/19
ninety /ˈnaɪntɪ/ **33**/90
ninth /naɪnθ/ **33**
no entry /ˌnəʊ ˈentrɪ/ **61**/3
no left turn /ˌnəʊ ˌleft ˈtɜːn/ **61**/7
no U-turn /ˌnəʊ ˌjuːˈtɜːn/ **61**/5
noon /nuːn/ **37**/13
Norfolk /ˈnɔːfək/ **56**
north /nɔːθ/ **56**
North Korea /ˌnɔːθ kəˈrɪə/ **54**
North Sea /ˌnɔːθ ˈsiː/ **54**/21
Northamptonshire /nɔːθˈæmptənʃə(r)/ **56**
Northern Ireland /ˌnɔːðən ˈaɪələnd/ **56**
Northumberland /nɔːθˈʌmbələnd/ **56**
Norway /ˈnɔːweɪ/ **54**
Norwegian Sea /nɔːˌwiːdʒən ˈsiː/ **54**/20
Norwich /ˈnɒrɪtʃ/ **56**
nose /nəʊz/ **4**/20, **68**/13
note /nəʊt/ **36**/9
notebook /ˈnəʊtbʊk/ **44**/13, **49**/4
notice /ˈnəʊtɪs/ **57**/9, 10
notice-board /ˈnəʊtɪsbɔːd/ **44**/1
Nottingham /ˈnɒtɪŋəm/ **56**
Nottinghamshire /ˈnɒtɪŋəmʃə(r)/ **56**
November /nəʊˈvembə(r)/ **52**
nozzle /ˈnɒzl/ **64**/13
number /ˈnʌmbə(r)/ **33**
number-plate /ˈnʌmbə pleɪt/ **64**/5
nurse /nɜːs/ **7**/12
nut /nʌt/ **21**/25, **24**/12

o'clock /əˈklɒk/ **37**/1, 13, 15, 16, 17
oar /ɔː(r)/ **69**/8
objective lens /əbˈdʒektɪv lenz/ **46**/21
oboe /ˈəʊbəʊ/ **75**/13
obtuse angle /ɒbˌtjuːs ˈæŋgl; *US* ɒbˌtuːs -/ **47**/18
ocean /ˈəʊʃn/ **53**
ocean liner /ˈəʊʃn laɪnər/ **70**/11
October /ɒkˈtəʊbə(r)/ **52**
octopus /ˈɒktəpəs/ **91**/12
off /ɒf/ **57**/8
Offaly /ˈɒfəlɪ/ **56**
office /ˈɒfɪs; *US* ˈɔːfɪs/ **43**/**44**
Ohio /əʊˈhaɪəʊ/ **55**
(oil-)tanker /ɔɪlˈtæŋkə(r)/ **70**/6
ointment /ˈɔɪntmənt/ **7**/8
Oklahoma /ˌəʊkləˈhəʊmə/ **55**
Oklahoma City /ˌəʊkləˌhəʊmə ˈsɪtɪ/ **55**
old /əʊld/ **5**/6, **50**/4, **87**/5
Omagh /əʊˈmɑː/ **56**
Omaha /ˈəʊməhɑː/ **55**
Oman /əʊˈmɑːn/ **54**
on /ɒn/ **58**/9
on top of /ɒn ˈtɒp əv/ **58**/11
one /wʌn/ **33**/1
one-family house /ˈwʌnˌfæməlɪ ˌhaʊs/ **14**/1
one-way street /ˌwʌnweɪ ˈstriːt/ **61**/10
onion /ˈʌnɪən/ **23**/11
onto /ˈɒntuː/ **57**/5
open (verb) /ˈəʊpən/ **85**/11
open /ˈəʊpən/ **87**/9
operating room /ˈɒpəreɪtɪŋ ruːm, rʊm/ **7**/16
operating theatre /ˈɒpəreɪtɪŋ θɪətə(r)/ **7**/16
operation /ˌɒpəˈreɪʃn/ **7**
optician /ɒpˈtɪʃn/ **8**/13
orange /ˈɒrɪndʒ; *US* ˈɔːrɪndʒ/ **9**/3, **24**/9
orange juice /ˈɒrɪndʒ dʒuːs; *US* ˈɔː-/ **27**/21

orbit /ˈɔːbɪt/ **50**/13
orchestra /ˈɔːkɪstrə/ **76**/1
orchestra pit /ˈɔːkɪstrə pɪt/ **76**/19
orchestra seats /ˈɔːrkɪstrə siːts/ **76**/20
orchid /ˈɔːkɪd/ **25**/18
Oregon /ˈɒrɪgən/ **55**
organ /ˈɔːgən/ **4**/1
Orkney Islands /ˈɔːknɪ aɪləndz/ **56**
Orlando /ɔːˈlændəʊ/ **55**
ornament / ˈɔːnəmənt/ **58**/12
ostrich /ˈɒstrɪtʃ/ **93**/22
out box /ˈaʊt bɒks/ **44**/4
out of /ˈaʊt əv/ **57**/1
out-tray /ˈaʊtreɪ/ **44**/4
outboard motor /ˌaʊtbɔːd ˈməʊtə(r)/ **70**/15
outer space /ˌaʊtə ˈspeɪs/ **50**
outlet /ˈaʊtlet/ **19**/21
outside /ˈaʊtsaɪd/ **58**/1
outside lane /ˈaʊtsaɪd leɪn/ **62**/7
oval /ˈəʊvl/ **47**/8
oven /ˈʌvn/ **20**/22
oven glove /ˈʌvn glʌv/ **20**/21
over /ˈəʊvə(r)/ **57**/14, **58**/10
overpass /ˈəʊvərpæs/ **62**/20
owl /aʊl/ **93**/12
Oxford /ˈɒksfəd/ **56**
Oxfordshire /ˈɒksfədʃə(r)/ **56**
oyster /ˈɔɪstə(r)/ **91**/21

pack /pæk/ **26**/3, 14, **74**/30
package /ˈpækɪdʒ/ **27**/16, **32**/1
packet /ˈpækɪt/ **26**/3, 14, 15, 16, **27**/16
paddle /ˈpædl/ **69**/20, **78**/27
pads /pædz/ **81**/15
pail /peɪl/ **19**/6
paintbox /ˈpeɪntbɒks/ **49**/15
paintbrush /ˈpeɪntbrʌʃ/ **49**/14
painting /ˈpeɪntɪŋ/ **15**/25, **74**/1
pair of /ˈpeər əv/ **8**/15, **49**/19
Pakistan /ˌpɑːkɪˈstɑːn; *US* ˈpækɪstæn/ **54**
palm /pɑːm/ **3**/22, **25**/16
Panama /ˈpænəmɑː/ **53**
panda /ˈpændə/ **90**/7
pants /pænts/ **10**/4, **11**/10
pantyhose /ˈpæntɪhəʊz/ **11**/7
papaya /pəˈpaɪə/ **24**/14
paper /ˈpeɪpə(r)/ **57**/4, 5, 8, **86**/17-19
paper bag /ˌpeɪpə ˈbæg/ **23**/22
paper-clip /ˈpeɪpəklɪp/ **44**/10
Papua New Guinea /ˌpæpʊəˌnjuː (*US* ˌnuː) ˈgɪnɪ/ **54**
parachute /ˈpærəʃuːt/ **72**/19
parachuting /ˈpærəʃuːtɪŋ/ **72**/18
Paraguay /ˈpærəgwaɪ; *US* ˈpærəgweɪ/ **53**
parakeet /ˈpærəkiːt/ **93**/20
parallel /ˈpærəlel/ **47**/30
paramedic /pærəˈmedɪk/ **38**/17
parcel /ˈpɑːsl/ **32**/1
parent /ˈpeərənt/ **1**/20
park /pɑːk/ **60**/2
parking lot /ˈpɑːrkɪŋ lɒt/ **13**/15
parking notice /ˈpɑːkɪŋ nəʊtɪs/ **59**/2
parking sign /ˈpɑːrkɪŋ saɪn/ **59**/2
parrot /ˈpærət/ **93**/19
part /pɑːrt/ **5**/16
parting /ˈpɑːtɪŋ/ **5**/16
party /ˈpɑːtɪ/ **71**/11
passenger /ˈpæsɪndʒə(r)/ **66**/20, **68**/2
passenger car /ˈpæsɪndʒər kɑːr/ **66**/4
passing lane /ˈpæsɪŋ leɪn/ **62**/17
passport /ˈpɑːspɔːt; *US* ˈpæspɔːrt/ **67**/6
passport control /ˌpɑːspɔːt kənˈtrəʊl; *US* ˌpæspɔːrt/ **67**/5
past /pɑːst; *US* pæst/ **37**/6–9, 14, 18
pâté /ˈpæteɪ; *US* pɑːˈteɪ/ **28**/4
path /pɑːθ; *US* pæθ/ **22**/23, **83**/5
patient /ˈpeɪʃnt/ **8**/3
patio /ˈpætɪəʊ/ **22**/11
pattern /ˈpætn/ **9**
patterned /ˈpætnd/ **9**/21
pavement /ˈpeɪvmənt/ **59**/6
paw /pɔː/ **89**/24
pawpaw /ˈpɔːpɔː/ **24**/14
pay (verb) /peɪ/ **35**
pay in (verb) /ˌpeɪˈɪn/ **34**/17
paying-in slip /peɪɪŋˈɪn slɪp/ **34**/18
PC /ˌpiː ˈsiː/ **44**/25
pea /piː/ **28**/24
peach /piːtʃ/ **24**/11
peacock /ˈpiːkɒk/ **93**/24
peak /piːk/ **73**/2
peanut /ˈpiːnʌt/ **24**/5
pear /peə(r)/ **24**/16
pearl /pɜːl/ **91**/22
pedal /ˈpedl/ **65**/9
pedestrian /pəˈdestrɪən/ **60**/8
pedestrian crossing /pəˌdestrɪən ˈkrɒsɪŋ/ **59**/24
pelvis /ˈpelvɪs/ **4**/15
Pembrokeshire /ˈpembrʊkʃə(r)/ **56**
pen /pen/ **49**/22
pence /pens/ **36**/15-18
pence piece /ˌpens ˈpiːs/ **36**/2–7
pencil /ˈpensl/ **49**/20
pencil-sharpener /ˈpenslʃɑːpnə(r)/ **49**/25
penguin /ˈpeŋgwɪn/ **93**/23
penknife /ˈpennaɪf/ **21**/4
Pennsylvania /ˌpensɪlˈveɪnjə/ **55**
penny /ˈpenɪ/ **35**/2, **36**/2
pepper /ˈpepə(r)/ **15**/16
per cent /pəˈsent/ **48**/17
percussion /pəˈkʌʃn/ **75**
perfume /ˈpɜːfjuːm; *US also* pərˈfjuːm/ **67**/11
perpendicular /ˌpɜːpənˈdɪkʊlə(r)/ **47**/29
Persian Gulf /ˌpɜːʃn ˈgʌlf/ **54**
personal computer /ˌpɜːsənl kəmˈpjuːtə(r)/ **44**/25
personal stereo /pɜːsənl ˈsterɪəʊ/ **30**/11
Perth and Kinross /ˈpɜːθ ənd kɪnˈrɒs/ **56**
Peru /pəˈruː/ **53**
pestle /ˈpesl; *US* ˈpestl/ **45**/7
pet /pet/ **89**
petal /ˈpetl/ **25**/4
Petri dish (*US* **petri dish**) /ˈpetrɪ dɪʃ; *US* piːtrɪ dɪʃ/ **46**/9
petrol pump /ˈpetrəl pʌmp/ **64**/11
pharmacist /ˈfɑːməsɪst/ **39**/6
pheasant /ˈfeznt/ **93**/7
Philadelphia /fɪləˈdelfɪə/ **55**
Philippines /ˈfɪlɪpiːnz/ **54**
Phoenix /ˈfiːnɪks/ **55**
phonecard /ˈfəʊnkɑːd/ **38**/24
photo album /ˈfəʊtəʊ ælbəm/ **29**/12
photographer /fəˈtɒgrəfə(r)/ **40**/4
physical /ˈfɪzɪkl/ **5**
piano /pɪˈænəʊ/ **76**/3
piccolo /ˈpɪkələʊ/ **75**/10
pick up (verb) /pɪk ˈʌp/ **41**/6
pick-up truck /ˈpɪkʌp trʌk/ **63**/7
picnic /ˈpɪknɪk/ **71**/17
picture /ˈpɪktʃə(r)/ **49**/17, **58**/10
pie /paɪ/ **27**/11
piece /piːs/ **27**/10, 12, **49**/24, **86**/17-19
pier /pɪə(r)/ **60**/16
pigeon /ˈpɪdʒɪn/ **93**/14
pile /paɪl/ **26**/8
pill /pɪl/ **7**/7
pillar /ˈpɪlə(r)/ **14**/4
pillar-box /ˈpɪləbɒks/ **59**/3
pillow /ˈpɪləʊ/ **18**/12
pillowcase /ˈpɪləʊkeɪs/ **18**/7
pilot /ˈpaɪlət/ **68**/11
pin /pɪn/ **12**/22, **74**/16
pincer /ˈpɪnsə(r)/ **91**/19
pine cone /ˈpaɪn kəʊn/ **25**/22
pine tree /ˈpaɪn triː/ **25**/1
pineapple /ˈpaɪnæpl/ **24**/8
ping-pong /ˈpɪŋpɒŋ/ **78**/26
pink /pɪŋk/ **9**/2
pins /pɪnz/ **79**/10
pint /paɪnt/ **27**/24
pipette /pɪˈpet/ **46**/12
pitch /pɪtʃ/ **81**/16
pitcher /ˈpɪtʃər/ **15**/17
Pittsburgh /ˈpɪtsbɜːrg/ **55**
plaice /pleɪs/ **91**/10
plaid /plæd/ **9**/20
plain /pleɪn/ **9**/16
plait /plæt/ **5**/17
plane /pleɪn/ **21**/8, **68**/12
planet /ˈplænɪt/ **50**
plant /plɑːnt; *US* plænt/ **16**/19, **58**/11
plaster cast /ˌplɑːstə ˈkɑːst/ **7**/13
plate /pleɪt/ **15**/9, **58**/13, 15, 17
plateau /ˈplætəʊ; *US* plætəʊ/ **73**/18
platform /ˈplætfɔːm/ **66**/6
platform number /ˈplætfɔːm nʌmbə(r)/ **66**/18
play (verb) /pleɪ/ **42**/21
player /ˈpleɪə(r)/ **78**/17
playing-card /ˈpleɪɪŋkɑːd/ **74**/30
pliers /ˈplaɪəz/ **21**/6
plough (*US* **plow**) /plaʊ/ **73**/29
plug /plʌg/ **17**/7, **19**/12
plum /plʌm/ **24**/20
plumber /ˈplʌmə(r)/ **40**/10
plunger /ˈplʌndʒə(r)/ **45**/15
plus /plʌs/ **48**/11
Pluto /ˈpluːtəʊ/ **50**/15
Plymouth /ˈplɪməθ/ **56**
pm (*US* P.M.) /piːˈem/ **37**/16, 17, 18
pneumatic drill /njuːˌmætɪk ˈdrɪl; *US* nuːˌmætɪk ˈdrɪl/ **61**/16
pocket /ˈpɒkɪt/ **11**/18, **79**/7
pocketknife /ˈpɒkɪtnaɪf/ **21**/4
point /pɔɪnt/ **48**/16
Poland /ˈpəʊlənd/ **54**
polar bear /ˈpəʊlə beə(r)/ **90**/6
polaroid camera /ˌpəʊlərɔɪd ˈkæmərə/ **29**/23
pole /pəʊl/ **77**/8
police /pəˈliːs/ **38**
police car /pəˈliːs kɑː(r)/ **38**/2
police officer /pəˈliːs ɒfɪsə(r); *US* ɔːfɪsər/ **38**/3, **59**/5
police station /pəˈliːs steɪʃn/ **38**/1
polka-dot /ˈpɒlkədɒt; *US* ˈpəʊkədɒt/ **9**/18

pond /pɒnd/ **73**/23
pony /'pəʊnɪ/ **89**/15
pony tail /'pəʊnɪ teɪl/ **5**/13
pony-trekking /'pəʊnɪtrekɪŋ/ **72**/16
Poole /pu:l/ **56**
pop group /'pɒp gru:p/ **76**/7
porch /pɔ:tʃ/ **14**/16
port /pɔ:t/ **69/70**
porter /'pɔ:tə(r)/ **71**/2
portion /'pɔ:ʃn/ **27**/10
Portland /'pɔ:rtlənd/ **55**
Portsmouth /'pɔ:tsməθ/ **56**
Portugal /'pɔ:tʃʊgl/ **54**
post /pəʊst/ **31**/10, **41**/6
post office /'pəʊst ɒfɪs; *US* ɔ:-/ **31**/1
postal clerk /'pəʊstl klɜ:rk/ **31**/4
postal code /'pəʊstl kəʊd/ **32**/13
postal order /'pəʊstl ɔ:də(r)/ **32**/22
postal services /'pəʊstl ˌsɜ:vɪsɪz/ **31/32**
postbag /'pəʊstbæg/ **31**/13
postbox /'pəʊstbɒks/ **31**/11
postcard /'pəʊstkɑ:d/ **32**/8
postcode /'pəʊstkəʊd/ **32**/13
poster /'pəʊstə(r)/ **18**/15
postman /'pəʊstmən/ **31**/8
postmark /'pəʊstmɑ:k/ **32**/12
pot /pɒt/ **20**/26, **27**/5, 19
pot holder /'pɒt həʊldər/ **20**/21
potato /pə'teɪtəʊ/ **23**/9
potato chips /pə'teɪtəʊ tʃɪps/ **26**/16, 19
pottery /'pɒtərɪ/ **74**/3
pouch /paʊtʃ/ **90**/9
pound /paʊnd/ **36**/17, 18
pound coin /ˌpaʊnd 'kɔɪn/ **36**/8
pound note /ˌpaʊnd 'nəʊt/ **36**/10–13
pour (verb) /pɔ:(r)/ **83**/11
power saw /'paʊə sɔ:/ **21**/9
Powys /'pəʊɪs/ **56**
pram /præm/ **60**/3
praying mantis /ˌpreɪɪŋ 'mæntɪs/ **92**/19
preposition /ˌprepə'zɪʃn/ **57/58**
prescription /prɪ'skrɪpʃn/ **7**/5
present /'preznt/ **85**/9, 10, 11
Princeton /'prɪnstən/ **55**
print (verb) /prɪnt/ **43**/11
print /prɪnt/ **9**/21, **29**/13, 14
printer /'prɪntə(r)/ **44**/19
printout /'prɪntaʊt/ **44**/18
prism /'prɪzm/ **45**/12
promenade /ˌprɒmə'nɑ:d; *US* 'neɪd/ **72**/5
propeller /prə'pelə(r); *US* prəʊ-/ **68**/15
protractor /prə'træktə(r); *US* prəʊ-/ **49**/7
Providence /'prɒvɪdəns/ **55**
Puerto Rico /ˌpwɜ:təʊ 'ri:kəʊ/ **53**
pull (verb) /pʊl/ **86**/22
pump /pʌmp/ **65**/3
punch (verb) /pʌntʃ/ **79**/22
punnet /'pʌnɪt/ **24**/2
pupil /'pju:pl/ **4**/30, **49**/2
puppy /'pʌpɪ/ **89**/23
purple /'pɜ:pl/ **9**/10
purse /pɜ:s/ **10**/10, **11**/22
push (verb) /pʊʃ/ **86**/21
pushchair /'pʊʃtʃeə(r)/ **60**/4
put down (verb) /ˌpʊt 'daʊn/ **86**/16
pyjamas (*US* pajamas) /pə'dʒɑ:məz; *US* pə'dʒæməz/ **11**/14
pyramid /'pɪrəmɪd/ **47**/23

Qatar /'kʌtɑ:(r)/ **54**
quarter /'kwɔ:tə(r)/ **35**/5, **37**/8, 11, **48**/19
queen /kwi:n/ **74**/32
queue /kju:/ **66**/12
quiet /'kwaɪət/ **88**/4

rabbit /'ræbɪt/ **89**/26
race (verb) /reɪs/ **80**/24
race car /'reɪs kɑ:r/ **80**/7
race car driver /reɪs kɑ:r draɪvər/ **12**/1, **80**/8
racecourse /'reɪskɔ:s/ **80**/28
racehorse /'reɪshɔ:s/ **80**/25
racetrack /'reɪstræk/ **80**/6, 28
racing car /'reɪsɪŋ kɑ:(r)/ **80**/7
racing driver /'reɪsɪŋ draɪvə(r)/ **12**/1, **80**/8
rack /ræk/ **45**/6
racket (*also* racquet) /'rækɪt/ **78**/23
radiator /'reɪdɪeɪtə(r)/ **15**/4
radiator grille /'reɪdɪeɪtə grɪl/ **64**/18
radio /'reɪdɪəʊ/ **30**/15
radio cassette recorder /reɪdɪəʊ kə'set rɪˌkɔ:də(r)/ **30**/8
radish /'rædɪʃ/ **23**/6
radius /'reɪdɪəs/ **47**/3
railings /'reɪlɪŋz/ **60**/9
railroad /'reɪlrəʊd/ **66**
railway /'reɪlweɪ/ **66**
rain (verb) /reɪn/ **51**/2
rainbow /'reɪnbəʊ/ **51**/12
raincoat /'reɪnkəʊt/ **10**/22
rainy /'reɪnɪ/ **51**/2
rake /reɪk/ **22**/7
ranch house /'ræntʃ haʊs/ **14**/19
raspberry /'rɑ:zbrɪ; *US* 'ræzberɪ/ **28**/10
razor /'reɪzə(r)/ **17**/23
razor-blade /'reɪzəbleɪd/ **17**/24
read (verb) /ri:d/ **42**/14, **85**/12
Reading /'redɪŋ/ **56**
rear-light /ˌrɪə'laɪt/ **64**/8
receipt /rɪ'si:t/ **29**/2, **35**/14
receiver /rɪ'si:və(r)/ **38**/23
reception /rɪ'sepʃn/ **71**/1
receptionist /rɪ'sepʃnɪst/ **71**/4
record /'rekɔ:d/ **30**/5
recorder /rɪ'kɔ:də(r)/ **75**/11
rectangle /'rektæŋgl/ **47**/11
red /red/ **5**/12, **9**/1
Red Sea /ˌred 'si:/ **54**/25
Redcar and Cleveland /'redkɑ:r ənd 'kli:vlənd/ **56**
reel /ri:l/ **26**/1, **29**/11, **74**/11
referee /ˌrefə'ri:/ **79**/25
reflector /rɪ'flektə(r)/ **65**/14
refrigerator /rɪ'frɪdʒəreɪtər/ **20**/14
registered post /ˌredʒɪstəd 'pəʊst/ **32**/20
reins /reɪnz/ **80**/14
remote control /rɪˌməʊt kən'trəʊl/ **16**/9
Renfrewshire /'renfruʃə(r)/ **56**
Reno /'ri:nəʊ/ **55**
reptile /'reptaɪl/ **91**
Republic of Ireland /rɪˌpʌblɪk əv 'aɪələnd/ **56**
reservoir /'rezəvwɑ:(r)/ **73**/13
restaurant /'restrɒnt; *US* 'restərənt/ **28**
return address /rɪ'tɜ:rn æˌdres/ **32**/19
Réunion /rɪ'ju:njən/ **54**
rhinoceros /raɪ'nɒsərəs/ **90**/21
Rhode Island /ˌrəʊd 'aɪlənd/ **55**
Rhondda Cynon Taff /ˌrɒndə ˌkʌnən 'tæf/ **56**

rib /rɪb/ **4**/13
ribbon /'rɪbən/ **58**/2, **74**/14
Richmond /'rɪtʃmənd/ **55**
ride (verb) /raɪd/ **80**/10
rider /'raɪdə(r)/ **80**/11
riding /'raɪdɪŋ/ **80**/9
right angle /'raɪt æŋgl/ **47**/15
right lane /'raɪt leɪn/ **62**/15
ring /rɪŋ/ **12**/24, **79**/19
ring binder /'rɪŋ baɪndə(r)/ **44**/16
ring stand /rɪŋ stænd/ **45**/20
rink /rɪŋk/ **77**/5
Rio Grande /ˌri:əʊ 'grænd/ **55**
river /'rɪvə(r)/ **60**/17
roach /rəʊtʃ/ **92**/16
road /rəʊd/ **61/62**, **62**/24
road sign /'rəʊd saɪn/ **59**/1, **61/62**
road work /'rəʊd wɜ:rk/ **61**/13
roadworks /'rəʊdwɜ:ks/ **61**/13
roast /'rəʊst/ **27**/7
roast beef /ˌrəʊst 'bi:f/ **28**/16
roast chicken /ˌrəʊst 'tʃɪkɪn/ **27**/9
robe /rəʊb/ **11**/13
Rochester /'rɒtʃɪstər/ **55**
rock /rɒk/ **70**/13, **73**/9
rocket /'rɒkɪt/ **50**/10
Rocky Mountains /ˌrɒkɪ 'maʊntnz/ **55**
roll /rəʊl/ **26**/1, 6, 15, **27**/4, **29**/11
rolling-pin /'rəʊlɪŋpɪn/ **20**/12
Romania /ru:'meɪnɪə/ **54**
roof /ru:f/ **13**/2, **14**/14, 23
room key /'ru:m ˌki:, 'rʊm/ **71**/5
rooster /'ru:stər/ **93**/4
root /ru:t/ **25**/3
rope /rəʊp/ **79**/20, **82**/12
Roscommon /rɒs'kɒmən/ **56**
rose /rəʊz/ **25**/17
rotary /'rəʊtərɪ/ **60**/26
rotor /'rəʊtə(r)/ **68**/11
rough /rʌf/ **88**/15
round /raʊnd/ **58**/2
round bottom flask /ˌraʊnd ˌbɒtəm 'flɑ:sk; *US* 'flæsk/ **45**/22
roundabout /'raʊndəbaʊt/ **60**/26
row /rəʊ/ **26**/7
rowboat /'rəʊbəʊt/ **69**/7
rowing-boat /'rəʊɪŋbəʊt/ **69**/7
rubber /'rʌbə(r)/ **49**/26
rubber raft /'rʌbər ræft/ **70**/14
rubber tubing /ˌrʌbə 'tju:bɪŋ; *US* ˌrʌbər 'tu:bɪŋ/ **45**/4
rucksack /'rʌksæk/ **66**/16, **71**/25
rug /rʌg/ **16**/6
rugby /'rʌgbɪ/ **78**/14
ruler /'ru:lə(r)/ **49**/21
run (verb) /rʌn/ **80**/21
runner bean /'rʌnə bi:n/ **28**/23
runway /'rʌnweɪ/ **68**/7
Russia /'rʌʃə/ **54**
Russian Federation /ˌrʌʃn fedə'reɪʃn/ **54**
Rwanda /rʊ'ændə/ **54**

Sacramento /ˌsækrə'mentəʊ/ **55**
sad /sæd/ **88**/2
saddle /'sædl/ **65**/2, **80**/12
safari /sə'fɑ:rɪ/ **72**/17
sail /seɪl/ **69**/3
sailboard /'seɪlbɔ:d/ **77**/20
sailboat /'seɪlbəʊt/ **69**/12

sailing /ˈseɪlɪŋ/ **72**/10
sailing-ship /ˈseɪlɪŋ ʃɪp/ **69**/1
sailor /ˈseɪlə(r)/ **39**/11
Saint George's Channel /snt ˌdʒɔːdʒɪz ˈtʃænl/ **56**
salad /ˈsæləd/ **28**/22
salesperson /ˈseɪlzpɜːrsn/ **29**/6
salmon /ˈsæmən/ **91**/9
saloon /səˈluːn/ **63**/12
salt /sɔːlt/ **15**/15
Salt Lake City /ˌsɔːlt ˌleɪk ˈsɪtɪ/ **55**
San Antonio /ˌsæn ænˈtəʊnɪəʊ/ **55**
San Diego /ˌsæn dɪˈegəʊ/ **55**
San Francisco /ˌsæn frænˈsɪskəʊ/ **55**
San Jose /ˌsæn həʊˈzeɪ/ **55**
sand /sænd/ **73**/16
sandal /ˈsændl/ **12**/8
sand-dune /ˈsænddjuːn; *US* duːn/ **73**/17
sandpaper /ˈsændpeɪpə(r)/ **21**/3
sandwich /ˈsænwɪdʒ; *US* -wɪtʃ/ **27**/3
Santa Fe /ˌsæntəˈfeɪ/ **55**
sash window /ˈsæʃ ˌwɪndəʊ/ **13**/8
satellite /ˈsætəlaɪt/ **50**/9
Saturday /ˈsætədɪ/ **33**
Saturn /ˈsætɜːn/ **50**/18
saucepan /ˈsɔːspən; *US* ˈsɔːspæn/ **20**/26
saucer /ˈsɔːsə(r)/ **16**/13
Saudi Arabia /ˌsaʊdɪ əˈreɪbɪə/ **54**
Savannah /səˈvænə/ **55**
saw /sɔː/ **21**/9, 12, 20
saxophone /ˈsæksəfəʊn/ **75**/16
scale /skeɪl/ **17**/14, **31**/2, **46**/23, **53–56**
scales /skeɪlz/ **17**/14, **31**/2, **46**/23, **91**/7
scar /skɑː(r)/ **6**/21
scarf /skɑːf/ **10**/14, **12**/6
scenery /ˈsiːnərɪ/ **76**/14
school bag /ˈskuːl bæg/ **49**/8
school uniform /ˌskuːl ˈjuːnɪfɔːm/ **10**/1
science laboratory /ˈsaɪəns ləˌbɒrətrɪ; *US* ˈlæbrətɔːrɪ/ **45**/**46**
scissors /ˈsɪzəz/ **49**/12
scooter /ˈskuːtə(r)/ **65**/21
score (verb) /skɔː(r)/ **81**/26
scorpion /ˈskɔːpɪən/ **92**/23
Scotch tape /ˈskɒtʃ teɪp/ **26**/1
Scotland /ˈskɒtlənd/ **56**
Scottish Borders /ˌskɒtɪʃ ˈbɔːdəz/ **56**
scourer /ˈskaʊərə(r)/ **20**/6
scouring pad /ˈskaʊərɪŋ pæd/ **20**/6
scratch /skrætʃ/ **6**/17
screen /skriːn/ **44**/26, **76**/23
screw /skruː/ **21**/22
screwdriver /ˈskruːdraɪvə(r)/ **21**/21
scrub brush /ˈskrʌb brʌʃ/ **19**/18
scrubbing-brush /ˈskrʌbɪŋbrʌʃ/ **19**/18
scuba-diving /ˈskuːbədaɪvɪŋ/ **77**/21
sea /siː/ **53**, **73**/8
Sea of Japan /ˌsiː əv dʒəˈpæn/ **54**/36
Sea of Okhotsk /ˌsiː əv əʊˈkɒtsk/ **54**/37
sea wall /ˌsiːˈwɔːl/ **72**/4
seafront /ˈsiːfrʌnt/ **72**/5
(sea)gull /ˈsiːgʌl/ **93**/30
seal /siːl/ **90**/27
seaside /ˈsiːsaɪd/ **72**/1
season /ˈsiːzn/ **52**
seat /siːt/ **57**/3, **65**/2, 23, **67**/13
Seattle /sɪˈætl/ **55**
second /ˈsekənd/ **33**
second floor /ˌsekənd ˈflɔːr/ **13**/13
second-class post /ˌsekəndklɑːs ˈpəʊst/ **32**/15
second-hand /ˈsekəndhænd/ **37**/5
secretary /ˈsekrətrɪ; *US* ˈsekrəterɪ/ **44**/20
sector /ˈsekə(r)/ **47**/6
security /sɪˈkjʊərətɪ/ **67**/7
sedan /sɪˈdæn/ **63**/12
Sellotape /ˈseləteɪp/ **26**/1
semi-detached house /ˌsemɪdɪˌtætʃt ˈhaʊs/ **14**/6
send (verb) /send/ **43**/10
sender /ˈsendə(r)/ **32**/18
Senegal /ˌsenɪˈgɔːl/ **54**
September /sepˈtembə(r)/ **52**
Serbia and Montenegro /ˌsɜːbiə ən mɒntɪˈniːgrəʊ/ **54**
serve (verb) /sɜːv/ **81**/2
server /ˈsɜːvə(r)/ **81**/3
service area /ˈsɜːrvɪs eərɪə/ **61**/11
service line /ˈsɜːvɪs laɪn/ **81**/5
service station /ˈsɜːvɪs steɪʃn/ **61**/11
set /set/ **26**/5
set square /ˈset skweə(r)/ **49**/6
seven /ˈsevn/ **33**/7
seventeen /ˌsevnˈtiːn/ **33**/17
seventh /ˈsevnθ/ **33**
seventy /ˈsevntɪ/ **33**/70
sew (verb) /səʊ/ **83**/4
sewing /ˈsəʊɪŋ/ **74**/9
sewing-machine /ˈsəʊɪŋməˌʃiːn/ **74**/10
shade /ʃeɪd/ **17**/19
shake (verb) /ʃeɪk/ **85**/1
shaker /ˈʃeɪkə(r)/ **74**/27
shallow /ˈʃæləʊ/ **87**/20
shampoo /ʃæmˈpuː/ **17**/26
shape /ʃeɪp/ **47**
shark /ʃɑːk/ **91**/1
shaving cream /ˈʃeɪvɪŋ kriːm/ **17**/25
shaving-foam /ˈʃeɪvɪŋfəʊm/ **17**/25
shears /ʃɪəʒ/ **22**/8
sheep /ʃiːp/ **89**/9
sheet /ʃiːt/ **18**/6, **31**/18
sheet music /ˈʃiːt mjuːzɪk/ **76**/6
Sheffield /ˈʃefiːld/ **56**
shelf /ʃelf/ **20**/23
shell /ʃel/ **91**/26
Shetland Islands /ˈʃetlənd ˌaɪləndz/ **56**
ship /ʃɪp/ **70**/5
shirt /ʃɜːt/ **10**/19
shock absorber /ˈʃɒk əbˌzɔːbə(r)/ **65**/29
shoe /ʃuː/ **10**/23
shoelace /ˈʃuːleɪs/ **11**/23
shoot (verb) /ʃuːt/ **78**/10
shop /ʃɒp/ **59**/12
shop assistant /ˈʃɒp əˌsɪstənt/ **29**/6
short /ʃɔːt/ **5**/8, 9, 10, 11, 19
shorts /ʃɔːts/ **12**/12
shoulder /ˈʃəʊldə(r)/ **3**/6, **62**/14, 23
shower /ˈʃaʊə(r)/ **17**/20, **41**/7
shrimp /ʃrɪmp/ **91**/17
Shropshire /ˈʃrɒpʃə(r)/ **56**
shutter /ˈʃʌtə(r)/ **14**/5
shuttlecock /ˈʃʌtlkɒk/ **78**/25
side /saɪd/ **47**/10, **48**/9
side mirror /ˈsaɪd mɪrər/ **64**/2
side street /ˈsaɪd striːt/ **60**/5
sideboard /ˈsaɪdbɔːd/ **15**/18
sideline /ˈsaɪdlaɪn/ **81**/6
sidewalk /ˈsaɪdwɔːk/ **59**/6
Sierra Leone /sɪˌerə lɪˈəʊn/ **54**
Sierra Nevada /sɪˌerə nəˈvɑːdə/ **55**
sieve /sɪv/ **20**/2
sightseeing /ˈsaɪtsiːɪŋ/ **71**/9
sign (verb) /saɪn/ **43**/6
sign /saɪn/ **57**/9, 10
signal tower /ˈsɪgnəl taʊər/ **66**/1
signal-box /ˈsɪgnəl bɒks/ **66**/1
signature /ˈsɪgnətʃə(r)/ **43**/7
signpost /ˈsaɪnpəʊst/ **60**/23
sing (verb) /sɪŋ/ **85**/6
Singapore /ˌsɪŋəˈpɔː(r)/ **54**
singer /ˈsɪŋə(r)/ **76**/9
single lens reflex camera /ˌsɪŋgl lenz ˈriːfleks ˌkæmərə/ **29**/16
single room /ˌsiŋgl ˈruːm, ˈrʊm/ **71**/6
singles match /ˈsɪŋglz mætʃ/ **81**/1
sink /sɪŋk/ **17**/6, **19**/2
Sioux Falls /ˌsuː ˈfɔːlz/ **55**
sister /ˈsɪstə(r)/ **1**/11
sister-in-law /ˈsɪstər ɪn lɔː/ **1**/13
sit (verb) /sɪt/ **84**/21
six /sɪks/ **33**/6
sixteen /ˌsɪksˈtiːn/ **33**/16
sixth /sɪksθ/ **33**
sixty /ˈsɪkstɪ/ **33**/60
skate (verb) /skeɪt/ **77**/2
skater /ˈskeɪtə(r)/ **77**/3
skeleton /ˈskelɪtn/ **4**/10
ski (verb) /skiː/ **77**/7
ski /skiː/ **77**/9
skiing /ˈskiːɪŋ/ **77**/6
skip (verb) /skɪp/ **82**/27
skipping-rope /ˈskɪpɪŋrəʊp/ **82**/26
skirt /skɜːt/ **10**/11
skull /skʌl/ **4**/11
sky /skaɪ/ **60**/13
skyline /ˈskaɪlaɪn/ **60**/14
skyscraper /ˈskaɪskreɪpər/ **60**/12
slate /sleɪt/ **13**/2, 20
sleep (verb) /sliːp/ **84**/24
sleeping-bag /ˈsliːpɪŋ bæg/ **71**/21
sleeve /sliːv/ **11**/16
slice /slaɪs/ **27**/8
slide /slaɪd/ **29**/9, **46**/20
slide projector /ˈslaɪd prəˌdʒektə(r)/ **29**/8
Sligo /ˈslaɪgəʊ/ **56**
sling /slɪŋ/ **7**/11
slip-road /ˈslɪprəʊd/ **62**/2
slipper /ˈslɪpə(r)/ **11**/12
slot /slɒt/ **38**/25
Slovakia /sləʊˈvækɪə/ **54**
Slovenia /sləʊˈviːnɪə/ **54**
slow /sləʊ/ **87**/24
slow lane /ˈsləʊ leɪn/ **62**/5, 15
SLR camera /ˌes el ˈɑː ˌkæmərə/ **29**/16
slug /slʌg/ **92**/21
small /smɔːl/ **87**/4
smile (verb) /smaɪl/ **84**/17
smoke /sməʊk/ **38**/7
smoked salmon /ˌsməʊkt ˈsæmən/ **28**/3
smokestack /ˈsməʊkstæk/ **70**/10
smooth /smuːð/ **88**/16
snail /sneɪl/ **92**/22
snake /sneɪk/ **91**/27
sneaker /sniːkər/ **12**/4
snooker /ˈsnuːkə(r)/ **79**/4
snorkel /ˈsnɔːkl/ **77**/24
snorkelling (*US* **snorkeling**) /ˈsnɔːklɪŋ/ **77**/23
snout /snaʊt/ **91**/5
snow (verb) /snəʊ/ **51**/3

Index

snow /snəʊ/ **51**/4
snowy /ˈsnəʊɪ/ **51**/3
soap /səʊp/ **17**/8
soccer /ˈsɒkər/ **81**
sock /sɒk/ **11**/4
socket /ˈsɒkɪt/ **19**/21
Socotra /səˈkəʊtrə/ **54**
soda /ˈsəʊdə/ **27**/26
sofa /ˈsəʊfə/ **16**/17
soft /sɒft/ **88**/18
soil /sɔɪl/ **61**/19, **83**/7
solar system /ˈsəʊlə sɪstəm/ **50**
soldier /ˈsəʊldʒə(r)/ **39**/12
solid /ˈsɒlɪd/ **9**/16, **88**/22
solid figure /sɒlɪd ˈfɪgə(r); *US* ˈfɪgjər/ **47**/20
Solomon Islands /ˈsɒləmən ˌaɪləndz/ **54**
Somalia /səˈmɑːlɪə/ **54**
Somerset /ˈsʌməset/ **56**
son /sʌn/ **1**/16
sore /sɔː(r)/ **6**/8
sound system /ˈsaʊnd ˌsɪstəm/ **30**/13
soup /suːp/ **28**/5
south /saʊθ/ **56**
South Africa /ˌsaʊθ ˈæfrɪkə/ **54**
South China Sea /ˌsaʊθ ˌtʃaɪnə ˈsiː/ **54**/33
South Georgia /ˌsaʊθ ˈdʒɔːrdʒə/ **53**
South Korea /ˌsaʊθ kəˈrɪə/ **54**
Southampton /saʊθˈæmptən/ **56**
space /speɪs/ **50**
space shuttle /ˈspeɪs ʃʌtl/ **50**/11
spacesuit /ˈspeɪssuːt/ **50**/7
spade /speɪd/ **22**/19, **74**/34
Spain /speɪn/ **54**
spanner /ˈspænə(r)/ **21**/27
sparrow /ˈspærəʊ/ **93**/15
spatula /ˈspætʃʊlə/ **46**/10
speak (verb) /spiːk/ **85**/5
speaker /ˈspiːkə(r)/ **30**/10
Special Delivery /speʃl dɪˈlɪvərɪ/ **32**/24
spectator /spekˈteɪtə(r); *US* ˈspek-/ **80**/18
speed limit /ˈspiːd lɪmɪt/ **61**/6
speedometer /spiːˈdɒmɪtə(r)/ **64**/24
spider /ˈspaɪdə(r)/ **92**/11
spine /spaɪn/ **4**/14
spiral /ˈspaɪərəl/ **47**/28
spirit-level /ˈspɪrɪtlevl/ **21**/7
spoke /spəʊk/ **65**/7
sponge /spʌndʒ/ **17**/12
spool /spuːl/ **74**/11
spoon /spuːn/ **15**/11
sport /spɔːt/ **77–81**
sports car /ˈspɔːts kɑː(r)/ **63**/11
sports centre /ˈspɔːts sentə(r)/ **42**/19
sprain (verb) /spreɪn/ **6**/14
spring /sprɪŋ/ **52**/9
spring balance /ˌsprɪŋ ˈbæləns/ **46**/24
square /skweə(r)/ **47**/9
squash /skwɒʃ/ **42**/21, **78**/22
squid /skwɪd/ **91**/14
squirrel /ˈskwɪrəl/ **89**/6
Sri Lanka /ˌʃriː ˈlæŋkə/ **54**
St Lawrence /seɪnt ˈlɒrəns/ **55**
St Louis /seɪnt ˈluːɪs/ **55**
St Paul /seɪnt ˈpɔːl/ **55**
stack /stæk/ **24**/22
Staffordshire /ˈstæfədʃə(r)/ **56**
stage /steɪdʒ/ **46**/19, **76**/15
stair /steə(r)/ **18**/22
staircase /ˈsteəkeɪs/ **18**/25
stall /stɔːl/ **23**/1
stalls /stɔːlz/ **76**/20
stamp /stæmp/ **31**/19
stamp album /ˈstæmp ælbəm/ **74**/5
stamp collecting /ˈstæmp kəˌlektɪŋ/ **74**/4
stamp machine /ˈstæmp məˌʃiːn/ **31**/17
stand (verb) /stænd/ **84**/22
stand /stænd/ **23**/1, **81**/24
staple (verb) /ˈsteɪpl/ **43**/4
stapler /ˈsteɪplə(r)/ **44**/12
star /stɑː(r)/ **50**/26
starfish /ˈstɑːfɪʃ/ **91**/20
start (verb) /stɑːt/ **42**/15
starter /ˈstɑːtə(r)/ **28**
starting-block /ˈstɑːtɪŋ blɒk/ **80**/22
starting-gate /ˈstɑːtɪŋ geɪt/ **80**/27
state line /ˌsteɪt ˈlaɪn/ **55**
station /ˈsteɪʃn/ **66**
station wagon /ˈsteɪʃn ˌwægən/ **63**/14
stationery /ˈsteɪʃənrɪ; *US*–nerɪ/ **26**
steak /steɪk/ **28**/18
steering-wheel /ˈstɪərɪŋ wiːl; *US also* hwiːl/ **64**/22
stem /stem/ **25**/19
step /step/ **18**/22, **57**/11, 13
stereo /ˈsterɪəʊ/ **30**/13
stereo system /ˈsterɪəʊ ˌsɪstəm/ **30**/13
stern /stɜːn/ **69**/17
stethoscope /ˈsteθəskəʊp/ **7**/20
steward /ˈstjʊəd/ **67**/13
stick /stɪk/ **78**/18
(sticking-)plaster /ˈstɪkɪŋplɑːstə(r)/ **7**/3
sting /stɪŋ/ **92**/24
stir (verb) /stɜː(r)/ **83**/12
Stirling /ˈstɜːlɪŋ/ **56**
stirrup /ˈstɪrəp/ **80**/13
stockings /ˈstɒkɪŋz/ **11**/6
Stockton-on-Tees /ˌstɒktən ɒn ˈtiːz/ **56**
Stoke-on-Trent /ˌstəʊk ɒn ˈtrent/ **56**
stomach /ˈstʌmək/ **3**/25, **4**/8
stomach-ache /ˈstʌməkeɪk/ **6**/5
stone /stəʊn/ **13**/17
stone wall /ˌstəʊn ˈwɔːl/ **14**/18
stool /stuːl/ **45**/19
stop /stɒp/ **61**/2
stop clock /ˈstɒp klɒk/ **46**/16
stopper /ˈstɒpə(r)/ **17**/7, **46**/4
store /stɔːr/ **29, 59**/12
stormy /ˈstɔːmɪ/ **51**/9
Strabane /strəˈbæn/ **56**
straight /streɪt/ **5**/8, 9, **47**/26, **87**/1
strainer /ˈstreɪnər/ **20**/2
Strait of Dover /ˌstreɪt əv ˈdəʊvə(r)/ **56**
strap /stræp/ **29**/22
Stratford-upon-Avon /ˌstrætfəd əpɒn ˈeɪvən/ **56**
strawberry /ˈstrɔːbrɪ; *US* ˈstrɔːberɪ/ **24**/2
stream /striːm/ **73**/7
street /striːt/ **59**/10
street corner /ˌstriːt ˈkɔːnə(r)/ **59**/11
street sign /ˈstriːt saɪn/ **60**/10
stretch (verb) /stretʃ/ **82**/19
stretcher /ˈstretʃə(r)/ **38**/16
string /strɪŋ/ **26**/2
string bean /ˌstrɪŋ ˈbiːn/ **28**/23
strings /strɪŋz/ **75**
striped /straɪpt/ **9**/17
stroller /ˈstrəʊlər/ **60**/4
strong /strɒŋ/ **87**/22
student /ˈstuːdnt/ **49**/2
stuffed olives /ˌstʌft ˈɒlɪvz/ **27**/23
stumps /stʌmps/ **81**/19
suburbs /sʌˈbɜːbz/ **60**
subway /sʌbweɪ/ **66**
Sudan /suːˈdɑːn; *US* suːˈdæn/ **54**
Suffolk /ˈsʌfək/ **56**
suit /suːt/ **10**/18
suitcase /ˈsuːtkeɪs/ **66**/14, **86**/13–16
summer /ˈsʌmə(r)/ **52**/10
Sun /sʌn/ **50**/14
sun-glasses /ˈsʌnglɑːsɪz; *US* -glæsɪz/ **12**/18
sunbather /ˈsʌnbeɪðə(r)/ **72**/8
sunbed /ˈsʌnbed/ **72**/7
sunburn /ˈsʌnbɜːn/ **6**/16
Sunday /ˈsʌndɪ/ **33**
sunny /ˈsʌnɪ/ **51**/1
sunshade /ˈsʌnʃeɪd/ **72**/9
surf (verb) /sɜːf/ **77**/15
surfboard /ˈsɜːfbɔːd/ **77**/17
surfer /ˈsɜːfə(r)/ **77**/16
surfing /ˈsɜːfɪŋ/ **77**/13
surgeon /ˈsɜːdʒən/ **7**/18
Surinam /ˌsʊərɪˈnæm/ **53**
Surrey /ˈsʌrɪ/ **56**
Sussex /ˈsʌsɪks/ **56**
swallow /ˈswɒləʊ/ **93**/21
swan /swɒn/ **93**/31
Swansea /ˈswɒnzɪ/ **56**
Swaziland /ˈswɑːzɪlænd/ **54**
sweater /ˈswetə(r)/ **10**/6
sweatshirt /ˈswetʃɜːt/ **12**/14
Sweden /ˈswiːdn/ **54**
sweep (verb) /swiːp/ **83**/5
sweet corn /ˈswiːt kɔːn/ **28**/20
sweets /swiːts/ **26**/10, 14, 15, 18
swim (verb) /swɪm/ **77**/26
swimmer /ˈswɪmə(r)/ **77**/27
swimming /ˈswɪmɪŋ/ **77**/25
swimming-pool /ˈswɪmɪŋ puːl/ **77**/28
swimming-trunks /ˈswɪmɪŋ trʌŋks/ **11**/1
swimsuit /ˈswɪmsuːt/ **11**/2
swing (verb) /swɪŋ/ **82**/11
swing /swɪŋ/ **22**/2
Switzerland /ˈswɪtsəlænd/ **54**
synthesizer /ˈsɪnθəsaɪzə(r)/ **76**/13
Syracuse /ˈsɪrəkjuːs/ **55**
Syria /ˈsɪrɪə/ **54**
syringe /sɪrɪndʒ/ **45**/16

T-shirt /ˈtiːʃɜːt/ **10**/5
table /ˈteɪbl/ **57**/8, **58**/4, 5, 6, **79**/6
table tennis /ˈteɪbl tenɪs/ **78**/26
table-cloth /ˈteɪblklɒθ/ **15**/8
tablet /ˈtæblɪt/ **7**/7
tackle (verb) /ˈtækl/ **78**/15
tail /teɪl/ **68**/18, **89**/17, **91**/2
taillight /ˈteɪllaɪt/ **64**/8
Taiwan /taɪˈwɑːn/ **54**
Tajikistan /tæˈdʒiːkɪstɑːn/ **54**
take (verb) /teɪk/ **41**/7, **85**/10
take-off /ˈteɪkɒf/ **68**/6
talc /tælk/ **17**/28
talcum powder /ˈtælkəm paʊdə(r)/ **17**/28
talk (verb) /tɔːk/ **85**/5
tall /tɔːl/ **5**/18
tambourine /ˌtæmbəˈriːn/ **75**/18
Tampa /ˈtæmpə/ **55**

tank top /ˈtæŋk tɒp/ **12**/10
tanker /ˈtæŋkə(r)/ **63**/3
Tanzania /ˌtænzəˈnɪə/ **54**
tape /teɪp/ **32**/2
tape deck /ˈteɪp dek/ **30**/18
tape-measure /ˈteɪpˌmeʒə(r)/ **74**/13
tartan /ˈtɑːtn/ **9**/20
Tasman Sea /ˌtæzmən ˈsiː/ **54**/31
taxi /ˈtæksɪ/ **60**/6
tea /tiː/ **83**/12
tea towel /ˈtiː taʊəl/ **20**/7
teacher /ˈtiːtʃə(r)/ **49**/16
teapot /ˈtiːpɒt/ **16**/11, **58**/16, 17, **83**/11
tear (verb) /teə(r)/ **86**/18
teaspoon /ˈtiːspuːn/ **16**/15
teenage /ˈtiːneɪdʒ/ **5**/3
teenager /ˈtiːneɪdʒə(r)/ **5**/3
(tele)phone booth /ˈtelɪfəʊn buːθ/ **38**/22
(tele)phone box /ˈtelɪfəʊn bɒks/ **38**/22
(tele)phone number /ˈtelɪfəʊn nʌmbə(r)/ **38**/21
telescope /ˈtelɪskəʊp/ **29**/5
television /ˈtelɪvɪʒn/ **16**/23, **42**/23, **58**/18
teller /ˈtelər/ **34**/9
temperature /ˈtemprətʃə(r); *US* ˈtempərtʃʊər/ **6**/10, **52**
ten /ten/ **33**/10
Tennessee /ˌtenəˈsiː/ **55**
tennis /ˈtenɪs/ **81**
tennis-court /ˈtenɪsˌkɔːt/ **81**/10
tent /tent/ **71**/19
tentacle /ˈtentəkl/ **91**/13
tenth /tenθ/ **33**
terminal /ˈtɜːmɪnl/ **67**
terraced house /ˈterəst ˌhaʊs/ **13**/1
test-tube /ˈtest tjuːb; *US* ˈtest tuːb/ **45**/2
Texas /ˈteksəs/ **55**
textbook /ˈtekstbʊk/ **49**/3
Thailand /ˈtaɪlænd/ **54**
thatch /θætʃ/ **13**/21
thatched roof /ˌθætʃt ˈruːf/ **14**/14
The Gulf /ðə ˈgʌlf/ **54**/28
theatre (*US* theater) /ˈθɪətə(r)/ **76**
thermometer /θəˈmɒmɪtə(r)/ **45**/21
thick /θɪk/ **87**/13
thimble /ˈθɪmbl/ **74**/17
thin /θɪn/ **5**/20, **87**/14
third /θɜːd/ **33**, **48**/20
thirsty /ˈθɜːstɪ/ **6**/1
thirteen /ˌθɜːˈtiːn/ **33**/13
thirteenth /ˌθɜːˈtiːnθ/ **33**
thirtieth /ˈθɜːtɪəθ/ **33**
thirty /ˈθɜːtɪ/ **33**/30
thirty-first /ˌθɜːtɪˈfɜːst/ **33**
thousand /ˈθaʊzənd/ **33**/1000
thread /θred/ **74**/11, 20
three /θriː/ **33**/3
three quarters /ˌθiː ˈkwɔːtəz/ **48**/22
throat /θrəʊt/ **3**/27, **6**/8
throttle /ˈθrɒtl/ **65**/26
through /θruː/ **57**/3
throw (verb) /θrəʊ/ **57**/4, 5, **78**/13, **82**/9
thumb /θʌm/ **3**/21
thunderstorm /ˈθʌndəstɔːm/ **51**/10
Thursday /ˈθɜːzdɪ/ **33**
ticket counter /ˈtɪkɪt kaʊntər/ **66**/10
ticket office /ˈtɪkɪt ɒfɪs/ **66**/10
ticket taker /ˈtɪkɪt teɪkər/ **66**/19
ticket-collector /ˌtɪkɪtkəˈlektə(r)/ **66**/19
tidy /ˈtaɪdɪ/ **88**/7
tie /taɪ/ **10**/20
tie up (verb) /ˌtaɪ ˈʌp/ **83**/6
tiger /ˈtaɪgə(r)/ **90**/17
tight /taɪt/ **88**/23
tights /taɪts/ **11**/7
tile /taɪl/ **13**/19, **17**/2
(tiled) floor /ˌtaɪld ˈflɔː(r)/ **49**/9
tiled roof /ˌtaɪld ˈruːf/ **14**/23
time /taɪm/ **37**
timer /ˈtaɪmər/ **46**/16
times /taɪmz/ **48**/13
timetable /ˈtaɪmteɪbl/ **66**/15
tin /tɪn/ **27**/6
tin-opener /ˈtɪn əʊpənə(r)/ **20**/10
Tipp-Ex /ˈtɪpeks/ **44**/9
Tipperary /ˌtɪpəˈreərɪ/ **56**
tired /ˈtaɪəd/ **6**/3
tissues /ˈtɪʃuːz/ **18**/9
to /tuː, tʊ/ **37**/10, 11, 12, **57**/6
toast /təʊst/ **28**/4
toaster /ˈtəʊstə(r)/ **20**/17
toe /təʊ/ **3**/14
Togo /ˈtəʊgəʊ/ **54**
toilet /ˈtɔɪlɪt/ **17**/17
toilet paper /ˈtɔɪlɪt ˌpeɪpə(r)/ **17**/18
Toledo /təˈliːdəʊ/ **55**
tomato /təˈmɑːtəʊ; *US* teˈmeɪtəʊ/ **23**/19
tongs /tɒŋz/ **45**/13
tongue /tʌŋ/ **4**/22
tool /tuːl/ **21**
tool-box /ˈtuːlbɒks/ **21**/1
tooth /tuːθ/ **8**/8
toothache /ˈtuːθeɪk/ **6**/4
toothbrush /ˈtuːθbrʌʃ/ **17**/4
toothpaste /ˈtuːθpeɪst/ **17**/3
top box /ˈtɒp bɒks/ **65**/24
top case /ˈtɒp keɪs/ **65**/24
top floor /ˌtɒp ˈflɔː(r)/ **13**/11
Topeka /təˈpiːkə/ **55**
torch /tɔːtʃ/ **19**/17
Torfaen /ˌtɔːˈvaɪn/ **56**
tortoise /ˈtɔːtəs/ **91**/25
total /ˈtəʊtl/ **35**/15
tour guide /ˈtʊə gaɪd; *Brit also* ˈtɔː/ **71**/10
tourist /ˈtʊərɪst; *Brit also* ˈtɔːrɪst/ **71**/12
toward /tɔːrd/ **57**/10
towards /təˈwɔːdz/ **57**/10
towel rack /ˈtaʊəl ræk/ **17**/9
towel-rail /ˈtaʊəlreɪl/ **17**/9
tower block /ˈtaʊə blɒk/ **60**/12
town /taʊn/ **55**/**56**
town house /ˈtaʊn haʊs/ **13**/1
trachea /trəˈkɪə; *US* ˈtreɪkɪə/ **4**/2
track /træk/ **80**/17, **66**/7
track and field /træk ənd fiːld/ **80**/15
track number /ˈtræk ˌnʌmbər/ **66**/18
track suit /ˈtræk suːt/ **12**/3
tractor /ˈtræktə(r)/ **73**/28
traffic /ˈtræfɪk/ **59**/13
traffic circle /ˈtræfɪk sɜːrkl/ **60**/26
traffic-lights /ˈtræfɪklaɪts/ **60**/19
trailer /ˈtreɪlə(r)/ **63**/9, **68**/3, **71**/27
trailer camp /ˈtreɪlər kæmp/ **71**/26
train /treɪn/ **42**/13, **66**/8
trainer /ˈtreɪnə(r)/ **12**/4
tramline /ˈtræmlaɪn/ **81**/6
trampoline /ˈtræmpəliːn/ **82**/6
trampolining /ˌtræmpəˈliːnɪŋ/ **82**/4
transporter /trænˈspɔːtə(r)/ **63**/1
trash can /ˈtræʃ kæn/ **57**/4, **59**/14
travel agent /ˈtrævl eɪdʒənt/ **40**/3
traveller's cheque (*US* traveler's check) /ˈtrævləz tʃek/ **34**/10, 11
tray /treɪ/ **16**/12
tree /triː/ **22**/4, **25**/1, **57**/3
triangle /ˈtraɪæŋgl/ **47**/13, **49**/6
tricycle /ˈtraɪsɪkl/ **65**/17
Trinidad and Tobago /ˌtrɪnɪdæd ənd təˈbeɪgəʊ/ **53**
triple-pack /ˈtrɪplpæk/ **26**/13
tripod /ˈtraɪpɒd/ **29**/4, **45**/26
trolley /ˈtrɒlɪ/ **28**/6, **46**/15, **67**/18, **86**/21
trombone /trɒmˈbəʊn/ **75**/8
tropic of Cancer /ˌtrɒpɪk əv ˈkænsə(r)/ **53**/**54**
tropic of Capricorn /ˌtrɒpɪk əv ˈkæprɪkɔːn/ **53**/**54**
trousers /ˈtraʊzəz/ **10**/4
trout /traʊt/ **28**/17, **91**/8
trowel /ˈtraʊəl/ **22**/12
truck /trʌk/ **63**/4
truck driver /ˈtrʌk draɪvər/ **40**/2
trumpet /ˈtrʌmpɪt/ **75**/7
trunk /trʌŋk/ **25**/2, **64**/9, **90**/26
tub /tʌb/ **27**/20
tuba /ˈtjuːbə; *US* ˈtuːbə/ **75**/9
tube /tjuːb; *US* tuːb/ **17**/3
Tucson /ˈtuːsɒn/ **55**
Tuesday /ˈtjuːzdɪ/ **33**
tulip /ˈtjuːlɪp; *US* ˈtuːlɪp/ **25**/25
Tulsa /ˈtʌlsə/ **55**
tuna /ˈtjuːnə; *US* ˈtuːnə/ **27**/6, 18
Tunisia /tjuːˈnɪzɪə; *US* tuːˈnɪʒə/ **54**
tunnel /ˈtʌnl/ **66**/9
Turkey /ˈtɜːkɪ/ **54**
turkey /ˈtɜːkɪ/ **93**/6
Turkmenistan /tɜːkˈmiːnɪstɑːn/ **54**
turn right /ˌtɜːn ˈraɪt/ **61**/12
turn signal /ˈtɜːrn ˌsɪgnəl/ **64**/3
turnip /ˈtɜːnɪp/ **23**/18
turntable /ˈtɜːnteɪbl/ **30**/14
turquoise /ˈtɜːkwɔɪz/ **9**/8
turtle /ˈtɜːtl/ **91**/24
tusk /tʌsk/ **90**/25
TV /ˌtiː ˈviː/ **16**/23, **42**/23
TV aerial /ˌtiː ˈviː eərɪəl/ **14**/20
twelfth /twelfθ/ **33**
twelve /twelv/ **33**/12
twentieth /ˈtwentɪəθ/ **33**
twenty /ˈtwentɪ/ **33**/20
twenty-first /ˌtwentɪˈfɜːst/ **33**
twenty-one /ˌtwentɪˈwʌn/ **33**/21
twenty-second /ˌtwentɪˈsekənd/ **33**
twenty-third /ˌtwentɪˈθɜːd/ **33**
twin beds /ˌtwɪn ˈbedz/ **71**/8
Twin Falls /ˌtwɪn ˈfɔːlz/ **55**
twin room /ˌtwɪn ˈruːm, ˈrʊm/ **71**/8
twin-pack /ˈtwɪnˌpæk/ **26**/12
two /tuː/ **33**/2
two-family house /ˈtuːˌfæməlɪ ˌhaʊs/ **14**/6
two-way traffic /ˌtuːweɪ ˈtræfɪk/ **61**/4
Tyne and Wear /ˌtaɪn ənd ˈwɪə(r)/ **56**
type (verb) /taɪp/ **43**/3
typewriter /ˈtaɪpraɪtə(r)/ **44**/27
tyre (*US* tire) /ˈtaɪə(r)/ **65**/27

U-tube /ˈjuːtjuːb; *US* ˈjuːtuːb/ **45**/18
Uganda /juːˈgændə/ **54**

Index

UK /juːˈkeɪ/ **56**
Ukraine /juːˈkreɪn/ **54**
umbrella /ʌmˈbrelə/ **10**/16
umpire /ˈʌmpaɪə(r)/ **81**/11, 20
uncle /ˈʌŋkl/ **1**/4
under /ˈʌndə(r)/ **58**/5
underground /ˈʌndəgraʊnd/ **66**
underneath /ʌndəˈniːθ/ **58**/5
underpants /ˈʌndəpænts/ **11**/10
underpass /ˈʌndəpɑːs; *US* -pæs/ **62**/21
underwear /ˈʌndəweə(r)/ **11**/3
unhappy /ʌnˈhæpɪ/ **88**/2
unitary authority /ˌjuːnətri ɔːˈθɒrəti/ **56**
United Arab Emirates /juːˌnaɪtɪd ˌærəb ˈemɪrəts/ **54**
United Kingdom /juːˌnaɪtɪd ˈkɪŋdəm/ **56**
United States of America /juːˌnaɪtɪd ˌsteɪts əʌ əˈmerɪkə/ **55**
untidy /ʌnˈtaɪdɪ/ **88**/8
up /ʌp/ **57**/11
upstairs /ˌʌpˈsteəz/ **18**/24
Uranus /ˈjʊrənəs/ **50**/17
Uruguay /ˈjʊərəgwaɪ; *US* ˈjʊərəgweɪ/ **53**
US /ˌjuː ˈes/ **55**
USA /ˌjuː es ˈeɪ/ **55**
usher /ˈʌʃə(r)/ **76**/25, 26
usherette /ʌʃəˈret/ **76**/26
Utah /ˈjuːtɔː/ **55**
utility room /juːˈtɪlətɪ ˌruːm, ˌrʊm/ **19**
Uzbekistan /ʊzˈbekɪstɑːn/ **54**

vacation /veɪˈkeɪʃn/ **71/72**
vacuum cleaner /ˈvækjuːm ˌkliːnə(r)/ **19**/7
Vale of Glamorgan /ˌveɪl əv gləˈmɔːgən/ **56**
valley /ˈvælɪ/ **73**/3
valve /vælv/ **65**/11
van /væn/ **31**/7, **63**/5
Vanuatu /ˌvænʊˈɑːtuː/ **54**
vase /vɑːz; *US* veɪs, veɪz/ **15**/20
vault (verb) /vɔːlt/ **82**/16
vaulting-horse /ˈvɔːltɪŋhɔːs/ **82**/18
VCR /ˌviː siː ˈɑː(r)/ **16**/24
vegetable /ˈvedʒtəbl/ **23, 28**
vehicle /ˈvɪəkl; *US* ˈviːhɪkl/ **63**
venetian blind /vəˌniːʃn ˈblaɪnd/ **44**/17
Venezuela /ˌvenɪzˈweɪlə/ **53**
Venus /ˈviːnəs/ **50**/22
verb /vɜːb/ **43, 83–86**
Vermont /vərˈmɒnt/ **55**
vest /vest/ **12**/10
vet /vet/ **40**/6
vice (*US* **vise**) /vaɪs/ **21**/11
video cassette recorder /ˌvɪdɪəʊ kəˈset rɪˌkɔːdə(r)/ **16**/24
(video)tape /ˈvɪdɪəʊteɪp/ **30**/4
Vietnam /ˌvjetˈnæm; *US* ˌvjetˈnɑːm/ **54**
viewfinder /ˈvjuːˌfaɪndə(r) /**30**/3
village /ˈvɪlɪdʒ/ **71**/15
viola /vɪˈəʊlə/ **75**/1
violin /ˌvaɪəˈlɪn/ **75**/4
Virginia /vərˌdʒɪnjə/ **55**
vocalist /ˈvəʊkəlɪst/ **76**/9
volleyball /ˈvɒlɪbɔːl/ **78**/20

waist /weɪst/ **3**/24
waiter /ˈweɪtə(r)/ **28**/14
waiting area /ˈweɪtɪŋ eərɪə/ **67**/12
wake up (verb) /ˌweɪk ˈʌp/ **41**/1
Wales /weɪlz/ **56**
walk (verb) /wɔːk/ **57**/2, 9–11, 13, **82**/1
walk /wɔːk/ **83**/5
Walkman /ˈwɔːkmən/ **30**/11
wall /wɔːl/ **15**/2, **22**/25, **57**/12
wall bars /ˈwɔːl bɑːz/ **82**/14
wall unit /ˈwɔːl juːnɪt/ **16**/21
wallet /ˈwɒlɪt/ **11**/21, 22
wardrobe /ˈwɔːdrəʊb/ **18**/17
warehouse /ˈweəhaʊs/ **70**/3
warm /wɔːm/ **52**/4
Warwickshire /ˈwɒrɪkʃə(r)/ **56**
wash (verb) /wɒʃ/ **84**/13
wash-basin /ˈwɒʃbeɪsn/ **17**/6
washcloth /ˈwɔːʃklɔːθ/ **17**/13
washer /ˈwɒʃər; *US* ˈwɔːʃər/ **21**/26
washing-machine /ˈwɒʃɪŋməˌʃiːn; *US* ˈwɔːʃɪŋməˌʃiːn/ **19**/3
washing-up liquid /wɒʃɪŋˈʌp lɪkwɪd/ **20**/5
Washington /ˈwɒʃɪŋtən/ **55**
Washington DC /ˌwɒʃɪŋtən ˌdiː ˈsiː/ **55**
wasp /wɒsp/ **92**/3
waste-paper basket /ˌweɪstˈpeɪpə bɑːskɪt; *US* ˌweɪstˈpeɪpər bæskɪt/ **16**/16
watch (verb) /wɒtʃ/ **42**/23
watch /wɒtʃ/ **12**/15
water /ˈwɔːtə(r)/ **38**/6, **83**/10, 11
water-ski (verb) /ˈwɔːtəskiː/ **77**/11
water-skier /ˈwɔːtəskiːə(r)/ **77**/12
water-skiing /ˈwɔːtəskiːɪŋ/ **77**/10
watercress /ˈwɔːtəkres/ **23**/13
waterfall /ˈwɔːtəfɔːl/ **73**/6
Waterford /ˈwɔːtəfəd/ **56**
watering-can /ˈwɔːtərɪŋkæn/ **22**/6
wave (verb) /weɪv/ **85**/4
wave /weɪv/ **77**/14
wavy /ˈweɪvɪ/ **5**/11
weak /wiːk/ **87**/21
weather /ˈweðə(r)/ **51**
webbed foot /ˌwebd ˈfʊt/ **93**/29
Wednesday /ˈwenzdɪ/ **33**
week /wiːk/ **37**
weight /weɪt/ **46**/13, **48**/23
welder /ˈweldə(r)/ **40**/9
west /west/ **56**
West Indies /ˌwest ˈɪndɪz/ **53**
West Midlands /ˌwest ˈmɪdləndz/ **56**
Western Isles /ˈwestən ˈaɪls/ **56**
wet /wet/ **88**/10
Wexford /ˈweksfəd/ **56**
whale /weɪl; *US also* hweɪl/ **90**/30
wheel /wiːl; *US also* hwiːl/ **65**/20
wheelbarrow /ˈwiːlbærəʊ; *US also* ˈhwiːlbærəʊ/ **22**/17
wheelchair /ˈwiːltʃeə(r); *US also* ˈhwiːltʃeər/ **7**/15
whisker /ˈwɪskər; *US also* ˈhwɪskər/ **89**/19
whistle /ˈwɪsl; *US also* ˈhwɪsl/ **82**/24
white /waɪt; *US also* hwaɪt/ **9**/14
Wichita /ˈwɪtʃɪtɔː/ **55**
wicket /ˈwɪkɪt/ **81**/19
wicket-keeper /ˈwɪkɪtkiːpə(r)/ **81**/13
Wicklow /ˈwɪkləʊ/ **56**
wide /waɪd/ **87**/15
width /wɪdθ, wɪtθ/ **48**/3
wife /waɪf/ **1**/12
Wiltshire /ˈwɪltʃə(r)/ **56**
wind up (verb) /ˌwaɪnd ˈʌp/ **83**/8
window /ˈwɪndəʊ/ **14**/8, **31**/5, **57**/1, **58**/1, **66**/11, **83**/3
window-box /ˈwɪndəʊbɒks/ **13**/3
window-ledge /ˈwɪndəʊledʒ/ **14**/9
window-sill /ˈwɪndəʊsɪl/ **14**/9
windpipe /ˈwɪndpaɪp/ **4**/2
windscreen /ˈwɪndskriːn/ **64**/19
windscreen wiper /ˈwɪndskriːn ˌwaɪpə(r)/ **64**/10
windshield /ˈwɪndʃiːld/ **64**/19
windshield wiper /ˈwɪndʃiːld ˌwaɪpər/ **64**/10
windsurfer /ˈwɪndsɜːfə(r)/ **77**/19
windsurfing /ˈwɪndsɜːfɪŋ/ **77**/18
windy /ˈwɪndɪ/ **51**/5
wing /wɪŋ/ **68**/16, **93**/17
wing mirror /ˈwɪŋ mɪrə(r)/ **64**/2
wings /wɪŋz/ **76**/18
winter /ˈwɪntə(r)/ **52**/12
wire /ˈwaɪə(r)/ **46**/5
wire mesh screen /ˌwaɪər ˈmeʃ skriːn/ **45**/25
Wisconsin /wɪsˈkɒnsɪn/ **55**
witch /wɪtʃ/ **12**/16
withdraw (verb) /wɪðˈdrɔː/ **34**/15
withdrawal slip /wɪðˈdrɔːəl slɪp/ **34**/19
wolf /wʊlf/ **90**/3
woman /ˈwʊmən/ **5**/4
wood /wʊd/ **13**/22, **73**/19
wooden gate /ˌwʊdn ˈgeɪt/ **14**/17
woodwind /ˈwʊdwɪnd/ **75**
wool /wʊl/ **74**/22
work /wɜːk/ **42**/15, 18
work surface /ˈwɜːk ˌsɜːfɪs/ **20**/13
workbench /ˈwɜːkbentʃ/ **21**/5
worm /wɜːm/ **92**/20
wrapping paper /ˈræpɪŋ ˌpeɪpə(r)/ **26**/6
wrench /rentʃ/ **21**/19, 27
wrestle (verb) /ˈresl/ **79**/24
wrestling /ˈreslɪŋ/ **79**/23
Wrexham /ˈreksəm/ **56**
wrist /rɪst/ **3**/23
writing-paper /ˈraɪtɪŋˌpeɪpə(r)/ **26**/4
Wyoming /waɪˈəʊmɪŋ/ **55**

X-ray (*also* **x-ray**) /ˈeksreɪ/ **8**/10
X-ray scanner /ˈeksreɪ ˌskænə(r)/ **67**/9

yacht /jɒt/ **69**/12
year /jɪə(r), *also* jɜː(r)/ **37**
yellow /ˈjeləʊ/ **9**/5
Yellow Sea /ˌjeləʊ ˈsiː/ **54**/35
Yemen Republic /ˌjemən rɪˈpʌblɪk/ **54**
yield /jiːld/ **61**/1
yoghurt /ˈjɒgət/ **27**/19, 27
yogurt /ˈjəʊgərt/ **27**/19, 27
York /jɔːk/ **56**
Yorkshire /ˈjɔːkʃə(r)/ **56**
young /jʌŋ/ **5**/2

Zambia /ˈzæmbɪə/ **54**
zebra /ˈzebrə, ˈziːbrə/ **90**/15
zero /ˈzɪərəʊ/ **52**/8
Zimbabwe /zɪmˈbɑːbwɪ/ **54**
zip /zɪp/ **74**/12
zip code /ˈzɪp kəʊd/ **32**/16
zipper /ˈzɪpər/ **74**/12
zoom lens /ˈzuːm lenz/ **29**/15
zucchini /zʊˈkiːnɪ/ **23**/12

Aberdeen City 56
Aberdeenshire 56
Aberconwy and Colwyn 56
adresa 32/10, 18, 19
Afghánistán 54
Afrika 53/3
akordeon 75/23
aktovka 10/12
Alabama 55
Albánie 54
album 74/5
Albuquerque 55
Aljaška 55
Aljašský záliv 53/6
Alžírsko 54
americké kuželky 79/8
americký 32, 35
americký fotbal 78/1
Amerika 53, 55
ananas 24/8
andulka 93/20
Anglesey 56
Anglie 56
Angola 54
Angus 56
Anchorage 55
Antarktida 53/7
Antrim 56
Appalačské hory 55
Arabské moře 54/29
Ards 56
Argentina 53
Argyll and Bute 56
arch poštovních známek 31/18
architekt 40/1
Arizona 55
Arkansas 55
arkýřové okno 14/11
Armagh 56
Arménie 54
Asie 53/5
Atlanta 55
Atlantik 53/9, 10
atlet 80/20
atletika 80/15
Austin 55
Austrálie 53/6
autobus poschoďový 60/25
autobus dálkový 63/2
autobusový 59/21, 22
autokempink pro přívěsy 71/26
automat na poštovní známky 31/17
automobil 60/24, 64, 80/7
automobilové závody 80/5
automobilový závodník 12/1, 80/8
autonehoda 38/13
avokádo 24/1
Ayrshire 56
Azerbájdžán 54

babička 1/1
badminton 78/24
badmintonový míček 78/25
Bahamy 53
Bahrajn 54
balicí papír 26/6
balíček 26/3, 27/16, 32/1
balkon 13/12, 57/14, 76/21
balon na horký vzduch 72/21
Baltimore 55
Baltské moře 54/22
banán 24/3
Bangladéš 54
banka 34
baňka s kulatým dnem 45/22
baňka s plochým dnem 45/9
bankovka 35/6-11, 36/9-13
bankovní konto 34/7
bankovní výpis 34/5
Barentsovo moře 54/41
barevný fix 26/5
barevná fotografie 29/13
Barma 54
barva 9
barvy 49/15
basa 75/5
baseball 78/1
baseballová rukavice 78/4
basketbal 78/8
baterie 46/4
baterka 19/17
batoh 66/16, 71/25
bažant 93/7
Beaufortovo moře 53/15
Bedfordshire 56
bedýnka na nářadí 21/1
běhat 41/4, 82/2
Belfast 56
Belgie 54
Belize 53
Bělorusko 54
Bengálský záliv 54/30
Benin 54
benzinové čerpadlo 64/11
benzinový 64/11
Beringovo moře 54/38
Berkeley 55
Berkshire 56
berle 7/14
Bermudy 53
beton 13/8
betonový 14/12
bez vzoru 9/16
bezpečnostní odbavení 67/7
běžecká dráha 80/19
běžet 80/21
Bhútán 54
bicí nástroj 75
biftek 28/18
bílý 9/14
Billings 55
Birmingham 55
Bismarck 55
blahopřání 32/4
blatník 65/22
Blaenau Gwent 56
blejzr 10/3
blesk 51/11
blesk fotografický 29/18
blinkr 64/3
blok poštovních známek 31/20
blond 5/15
bluma 24/20
boční stěna 48/9
bochník 27/2
bolet 6/4-6, 8
Bolívie 53
bonbon 26/10, 14, 15, 18
bonboniéra 26/9
bongo 75/20
bonsaj 25/12
borovicový 25/22
Bosna a Hercegovina 54
Boston 55
bota (nad kotníky) 10/13
Botswana 54
bouřka 51/9, 10
bowling 79/8
box 79/17
box (na poštu) 44/3, 4
boxer 12/9
boxerské rukavice 79/21
brada 3/28
brambor 23/19
brambor pečený ve slupce 28/25
brambor vařený 28/26
bramborové lupínky 26/16, 19
branka fotbalová 81/19
branka kriketová 81/28
brankář 81/10
brašna na fotoaparát 29/21
brašna poštovní 31/13
brát 85/10
bratranec 1/9
brázda 73/30
Brazílie 53
Bridgend 56
Bristol 56
Británie 38
Britské ostrovy 56
britský 32, 36
brokolice 23/17
broskev 24/11
brouk 92/13
brož 12/22
Brunei 54
bruslařka 77/3
brusle 77/4
bruslení 77/1
bruslit 77/2
brýle 8/15, 19
brzdová páka 65/16
břeh 60/18

Rejstřík

březen 52
břidlice 13/20
břidlicový 13/2
břicho 3/25, 6/5
buben 76/10
bubeník 76/11
Buckinghamshire 56
budík 18/14
budova 13, 14, 60/1
Buffalo 55
buldozer s rýpadlem 61/18
Bulharsko 54
bungalov 14/19
Bunsenův hořák 45/5
Burkina 54
burský ořech 24/5
Burundi 54
buvol 90/19
býk 89/3
byreta 46/25

Caernarfonshire and Merionethshire 56
Caerphilly 56
Cambridgeshire 56
Cardiff 56
Cardiganshire 56
Carmarthenshire 56
Carolina 55
Carrickfergus 56
Castlereagh 56
CD přehrávač 30/19
cedník 20/9
celer řapíkatý 23/16
celková částka 35/15
cello 75/3
celní prohlídka 67/19
celník 67/20
cent 35/2, 13
centimetr 48/30
cestička 22/23, 83/5
cestovní šek 34/10, 11
cestující 66/20, 68/2
cibule 23/11, 25/13
ciferník 37/2
cihla 13/16
cihlový 13/7
cikánka 12/5
Cincinnati 55
cisternový vůz 63/3
citron 24/6
cívka filmu 29/11
cívka nitě 74/11
cizí měna 34/13
Clackmannanshire 56
Clare 56
Cleveland 55, 56
Coleraine 56
Colorado 55
conga 75/22
Connecticut 55
cop 5/17
Cornwall 56
Craigavon 56
cuketa 23/12
cukrovinky 26
Cumbria 56
cvrček 92/18
cyklista 60/20
cyklistika 80/3

Čad
čaj 83/12
čajová konvice 16/11, 58/16, 17, 83/11
čára 47/25, 60/22
čarodějnice 12/16
čas 37
časopis 26/7, 58/18, 19
čelist 3/4
čelo 4/18
čepice 10/2
černý 9/13
Černé moře 54/26
černobílý 29/14
čerpací stanice 64/1
čerpadlo 64/11
červ 92/20
červen 52/9
červená řepa 23/8
červenec 52
červený 9/1
česat 84/15
Česká republika 54
česnek 23/2
čéška 4/16
Čína 54
činely 75/21
činžovní dům 13/10
číselník 38/26
číslo 33, 34/7, 66/18
číslo pohotovosti 38
číst 42/14, 85/12
čistý 88/19
číšník 28/14
člun 60/11, 69/7, 9, 11, 14, 18
člun nafukovací 70/14
člun na podvodních křídlech 70/7
čočka 80/16, 20, 22
čokoláda 26/11, 17, 86/20
čokoládový dort 28/13
čtrnáct 33/14
čtverec 47/9
čtvrt 37/8, 11
čtvrtdolar 35/5
čtvrtek 33
čtvrtina 48/19, 22
čtvrtý 33
čtyřhra 81/8
čtyři 33/4
čtyřicet 33/40

Dakota 55
dalekohled 29/5
dálkové ovládání 16/9
dálkový autobus 63/2
Dallas 55
dálnice 62/1, 11
dáma (hra) 74/26
dampr 61/14
Dánsko 54
dárek 85/9, 10, 11
dáseň 8/7
datum 33
dávat 85/9
Dayton 55
dcera 1/17
dědeček 1/2
dechový nástroj 75
dej přednost v jízdě 61/1
deka 18/15
dělat stojku 82/25
Delaware 55
děleno 48/14
delfín 90/29
dělicí pás 62/8, 18
délka 48/6
dělník 61/15
den 37
Denbighshire 56
denní režim 41, 42
Denver 55
Derbyshire 56
děrovačka 44/7
Des Moines 55
desátý 33
deset 33/10
desetidolarový 35/9
desetilibrový 36/11
desetipence 36/5
desetník 35/4
desky 44/14
deštník 10/16
detektor kovů 67/8
Detroit 55
devadesát 33/90
devatenáct 33/19
devátý 33
devět 33/9
devizový kurz 34/8
Devon 56
diapozitiv 29/9
diaprojektor 19/8
diář 44/21
diktafon 43/2
diktovat 43/1
dirigent 76/4
disketa 44/23
disketová jednotka 44/24
diskžokej 39/3
District of Columbia (DC) 55
dítě 1/19, 5/1, 2, 85/2, 4
diváci (sportovní) 78/7
divadlo 76
divák 80/18

dívat se 57/1, 14
dívat se na televizi 42/23
dívka 5/3
dlaň 3/22
dláto 21/14
dlaždicová podlaha 49/9
dlouhý 5/12, 15
dno 45/9, 22, 48/ 8
do 57/6, 11
dobrý 88/5
dodávka 31/7, 63/5
dodávka pick-up 63/7
dok 70/1
dolar 35/12, 13
dolarový 35/7
dole 58/14
dolů (ze schodů) 18/23, 41/3
domácí zvíře 89
domek 14/1
Dominikánská republika 53
dopis 32/5, 43/1, 3, 4, 6
dopisní papír 26/4
doplňkové sektory 18/16
doporučený dopis 32/20, 21
dopravní značka 59/1, 61, 62
Dorset 56
doručování 31/15
dospělý 5/4, 5
dostihová dráha 80/28
dostihový kůň 80/25
dostihy 80/23
došek 13/21
doškový 14/14
dovolená 71, 72
dovolená na lodi 72/11
Down 56
drahý 87/8
dráp 90/5
drát 46/5
drát u jízdního kola 65/7
drátěná mřížka 45/25
drsný 88/15
druhý 33
družice 50/9
držadlo 30/9
držet 86/15
dřevěný 14/17
dřevo 13/22
dřez 19/2
duben 52
duha 51/12
duhovka 4/29
dům činžovní, nájemní 13/1
dům řadový 13/1
Dumbarton and Clydebank 56
Dumfries and Galloway 56
duna 73/17
Dundee 56
Dunganon 56
Durham 56
dutý 88/21
dva 33/2
dvacátý 33
dvacet 33/20
dvacet jedna 33/21
dvacetidolarový 35/10
dvacetilibrový 36/12
dvacetipence 36/6
dvanáct 33/12
dvanáctý 33
dveře 14/43
dvojdomek 14/6
dvojitá zatáčka 61/8
dvojité balení 26/12
dvojitý 60/22
dvojlůžko 71/7
dvouhra 81/1
dvoulůžkový 71/8
dvoupence 36/3
dvůr 57/2
dýchací trubice 77/24
džbán 15/17
džem 27/5, 17
Džibuti 54
džíny 10/7
džíp 63/10

East Dunbartonshire 56
East Riding of Yorkshire 56
Edinburgh 56
Egypt 54
Ekvádor 53
El Paso 55
El Salvador 53
elektrická pila 21/9
elektrický 17/22, 21/10
elektrikář 40/7
elektroda 46/6
elektronika 30
Erijské jezero 55
Essex 56
Estonsko 54
Etiopie 54
Eugene 55
Evropa 53/4
expres 32/24, 25

Faerské ostrovy 54
fagot 75/15
Falkirk 56
Falklandy 53
farma 73/20
farmář 39/9
fax 43/10
faxovat 43/10
fazolový lusk 28/23
fialový 9/10
Fidži 54
Fife 56
filatelie 74/4
Filipíny 54
filmová hvězda 76/24
filtrační papír 45/11
Finsko 54
flétna 75/12
flétna zobcová 75/11
Flintshire 56
Florida 55
formulář 43/5
Fort Worth 55
fotbal 81
fotbalový míč 78/12
Foto-Kino 29
fotoalbum 29/12
fotograf 40/4
fotografie 29/13, 14
Francie 54
Francouzská Guyana 54
frézie 25/20
fronta 66/12
fyzický vzhled 5

Gabun 54
Galapágy 53
galaxie 50/24
galerie 76/22
Gambie 54
garáž 14/2
garnát 91/17
gáza 7/9
Georgie 55
Ghana 54
Glasgow 56
globus 49/11
golf 79/11
golfová dráha 79/13
golfová hůl 79/15
gorila 90/14
grafický equalizér 30/17
gram 48/24
gramofon 30/14
gramofonová deska 30/5
grapefruit 24/21
Great Falls 55
green 79/14
grep 24/21
Grónsko 53
Gruzie 54
Guatemala 53
Guinea 54
Guinea-Bissau 54
Guinejský záliv 54/24
guma 49/26
gumová hadice 45/4
Guyana 53
gymnasta 80/2
gymnastika 80/1

háček 19/16
had 91/27
hadice 38/12, 64/12, 83/8
Haiti 53
hala 67/12

Rejstřík

halenka 10/9
Hampshire 56
harmonika (foukací) 75/25
Hartlepool 56
hasák 21/19
hasicí přístroj 38/9
hasič 38/10
hasičská stanice 38
hasičský vůz 38/4
hausbót 69/9
Havajské ostrovy 53
Havaj 55
házet 57/5, 82/9
helikoptéra 68/9
helma 12/2
herec 76/16
herečka 76/17
Hereford and Worcester 56
Hertfordshire 56
hi-fi věž 30/13
Highland 56
hlad 6/2
hladký 88/16
hlasatelka 39/4
hlasitý 88/3
hlava 3/1, 6/6, 64/17
hlávkový salát 23/7
hlavní 28, 55
hledáček 30/3
hlemýžď 92/22
hloubka 48/1
hluboký 87/9
hmyz 92
hnědý 9/4
hnízdo 93/13
hoblík 21/8
hoboj 75/13
hodina 37/1, 6, 7, 14
hodinky 12/15
hodinová ručička 37/4
hodiny 15/26, 58/8
hodit 78/13
hokejista 78/17
hokejka 78/18
hokejový míček 78/19
holicí strojek 17/22, 23
Hollywood 55
holub 93/4
Honduras 53
Honolulu 55
hora 73/1
horko 52/3
horolezec 72/25
horolezectví 72/24
hořák 20/27
Hořejší jezero 55
hořet 86/24
host 71/3
hotelový 71/1
hotelový sluha 71/2
hotovost 34/15, 35
houba 28/21
houba mycí 17/12
houba na mytí nádobí 20/6
houpačka 22/2
houpat se 82/11
housenka 92/8
houska 27/4
housle 75/4
Houston 55
hrábě 22/7
hrací deska 74/25
hráč na klávesové nástroje 76/12
hrad 71/13
hrana 48/4
hranice 53, 56
hranice státu (v USA) 55
hranol 45/12
hranolky 28/27
hrášek 28/24
hrát 42/21
hrb 90/11
hrdlo 3/27
hrnek 20/16, 58/5
hrnčířství 74/3
hroch 90/22
hrozen 24/10
hrudní kost 4/12
hruď 3/26
hruška 24/16
hřeben 17/27
hřebík 21/23
hříbě 89/14
hříva 89/14
hubený 5/20
hubice 64/13
hudba 41/12, 76
hudební nástroj 75
hudebník 76/2
Hudson 55
Hudsonův záliv 53/17
hůlka 77/8
humr 91/16
Huronské jezero 55
husa 93/27
hvězda 50/26
hvězdice 91/20
hydrant 38/11
hýždě 3/11

chalupa 14/13
chapadlo 91/13
Charleston 55
Charlotte 55
Cheshire 56
Chicago 55
Chile 53
chirurg 7/18
chladič kondenzační 45/23
chladič auta 64/18
chladno 52/5
chlapec 5/2
chléb 27/2
chlopeň 32/7
chňapka 20/21
chobot 90/26
chobotnice 91/12
chod 28
chodec 59/24, 60/8
chodidlo 3/13
chodit 82/1
chodník 59/6
Chorvatsko 54
chránič 81/15
chryzantéma 25/15
chřest 23/5
chytač 78/6
chytat 82/10

Idaho 55
Idaho Falls 55
Illinois 55
Indiana 55
Indianapolis 55
Indický oceán 53/2
Indie 54
Indonésie 54
injekce 7/21
instalatér 40/10
invalidní vozík 7/15
Inverclyde 56
Iowa 55
Ipswich 56
Irák 54
Írán 54
iris 25/28
Irská republika 56
Island 54
Itálie 54
izolepa 26/1
Izrael 54

jablečný koláč 28/8
jablko 24/4
Jackson 55
Jacksonville 55
jahoda 24/2
jachta 69/12
jachta kajutová 69/13
Jamajka 53
jamka 79/6
jamkoviště 79/14
Japonské moře 54/36
Japonsko 54
jaro 52/9
jasno 51/13
játra 4/6
jazyk 4/22
Je mlha. 51/7
Je opar (mlžný). 51/6
Je vítr. 51/5
jeden 33/1

jedenáct **33**/11
jedenáctý **33**
jednobarevný **9**/16
jednolůžkový **71**/6
jednooká zrcadlovka **29**/6
jednosměrná ulice **61**/10
jehla **74**/19
jehlan **47**/23
jehličnatý strom(ek) **25**/1
jehně **74/10**
jehněčí **28**/19
jelen **90**/1
Jemenská republika **54**
jeřáb **70**/2
jestřáb **93**/10
ještěrka **91**/28
jet autem **42**/19
jet dostih **80**/24
jeviště **76**/15
jezdec na koni **80**/11
jezdit na kole **80**/4
jezdit na koni **80**/10
jezdit na vodních lyžích **77**/11
jezero **55**, **73**/4
ježek **89**/3
jídelna **15**
jídelní lístek **28**/5
jídlo **83**/2
Jihočínské moře **54**/33
jiný **75**
jít **41**/3, 4, **42**/13, **57**/2, 6, 9-11, 13
jít spát **42**/13
jízda na koni **80**/9
jízda na ponících **72**/16
jízdní kolo **65**/1
jízdní řád **66**/15
jizva **6**/21
jižní **53**/10, 13
Jižní Afrika **54**
Jižní Amerika **53**/2
Jižní Dakota **55**
Jižní Georgie **55**
Jižní Karolína **55**
Jižní Korea **54**
Jižní ledové moře **53**/11
joggistka **82**/3
jogurt **27**/19, 27
Jordánsko **54**
judo **79**/26
Jupiter **50**/19

kabát **10**/17
kabelka **10**/10
kabriolet **63**/13
kadeřnice **39**/5
kachlík **17**/2
kachna **93**/28
kajak **69**/19
kajuta **69**/5
kajutová jachta **69**/13
kaktus **25**/21
kalendář **44**/2
kalhotky **11**/10
kalhoty **10**/4
kalhoty krátké **12**/12
Kalifornie **55**
kalkulačka **49**/5
Kambodža **54**
kamelot **59**/7
kámen **13**/17
kamenný **14**/18
Kamerun **54**
Kanada **53**
kanál **72**/12
kanár **93**/18
Kanárské ostrovy **54**
kancelář **44**
kancelářská sponka **44**/10
Kansas **55**
Kansas City **55**
kapátko **46**/11
kapesník **10**/21
kapesní nůž **21**/4
kapota **64**/14
kapradí **25**/5
kapsa **11**/18, **79**/7
kapsle **7**/6
karafiát **25**/24
karate **79**/27
karavan **63**/9, **71**/27
Karelské moře **54**/40
Karibské moře **53**/19
kárový král **74**/33
karta **74**/30
kartáč na vlasy **18**/8
kartáček na nehty **17**/5
kartáček zubní **17**/4
kartáčovat **84**/16
kartotéka **44**/8
Kaspické moře **54**/27
kašel **6**/9
Katar **54**
káva **42**/16
kavárna **59**/4
kávová konvice **15**/21
Kazachstán **54**
kazeta **30**/6, **58**/3
kazetový přehrávač **30**/18
kbelík **19**/6
kel **90**/25
kelímek jogurtu **27**/19
kelímek na tavení kovu **46**/26
Kent **56**
keř **22**/9, **58**/1
kilogram **48**/25
kilometr **48**
Kingston upon Hull **56**
kino **76**
Kirgizstán **54**
kiwi **24**/18
kladivo **21**/16
klarinet **75**/4
klávesa **75**/24
klávesnice **44**/22
klavír **76**/3
klečet **82**/21
klenba **14**/10
klepadlo **13**/4
klepeto **91**/19
kleště kombinačky **21**/6
kleště laboratorní **45**/13
klíč **44**/11, **71**/5
klíč na matice **21**/27
klika pedálu **65**/5
klobouk **12**/17
klokan **90**/8
klubko **26**/2
kluziště **77**/5
kmen **25**/2
kniha **58**/4, 14, 15, **85**/12
knihovna **57**/6, 7
knihovna (nábytek) **58**/11-14
knír **4**/21
knoflík **74**/15
koberec **16**/7
kobylka luční **92**/17
kočárek **60**/3
kočka **89**/18
kohout **93**/4
kohoutek na studenou vodu **19**/19
kohoutek na teplou vodu **19**/20
kokosový ořech **24**/7
koktejl **28**/11
kolečko **22**/17
kolej **66**/7
koleno **3**/18
kolibřík **93**/16
kolíček na prádlo **19**/10
kolmice **47**/29
kolo **65**/20
kolo jízdní **65**/1
kolovrátek **21**/15
Kolumbie **55**
komár **92**/4
kombajn **73**/25
kombi (menší, třídveřové) **63**/15
kombi (větší, pětidveřové) **63**/14
kombinačky **21**/6
kombiné **11**/5
komín **14**/7
komín kovový **70**/10
komora **19**
kompaktní disk **30**/7
končit **42**/18
konferenční stolek **16**/8
Kongo **54**
kónická baňka **45**/17
kontaktní čočka **8**/20, 22
kontrabas **75**/5
kontrola pasová **67**/5
kontrolní ústřižek **34**/2
kontrolor jízdenek **66**/15
konvice **20**/19, **83**/9

Rejstřík

konvice čajová 16/11, 58/16, 17, 83/11
konvice kávová 15/21
konzerva 27/6
kopec 73/12
kopie 43/11
kopretina 25/23
kopyto 89/12
Korálové moře 54/32
kořen 25/3
kosmonaut 50/6
Kostarika 53
kostka, kostky (hra) 74/28
kostka mýdla 17/8
kostkovaný 9/19
kostra 4/10
koš 16/16, 17/16, 58/2
košíček jahod 24/2
košík 24/22, 25/6
košile 10/19, 83/1
koště 2213
kotě 89/21
kotleta 28/19
kotník 3/16, 6/14
kotouček 26/1
kotva 70/16
kov 67/8
koupelna 17
koupelnový 17/1
kouř 38/7
koza 89/8
krab 91/18
krabice 18/9, 27/1
krabice džusu 27/21
krabice na sušenky 16/10
krabička margarínu 27/20
krajina 71/16
krajnice travnatá 62/23
krajnice zpevněná 62/4
králík 89/26
krát 48/13
krátké kalhoty 12/12
krátký 5/8-11
kráva 89/1
kravata 10/20
krb 16/3, 58/6, 7
krbová římsa 58/10
kreditní karta 34/4
krejčovský metr 74/13
krémový 9/6
kreslení 74/2
krev 6/19
kreveta 91/17
kriket 81
kriketový zápas 81/12
krk 3/5, 6/8
krocan 93/6
krokodýl 91/20
krokodýl (svorka) 46/7
kropicí konev 22/6
kruh 47/1
kruhový objezd 60/26
krunýř 91/26
kružítko 49/19
krychle 47/21
krytý vchod 14/16
křeček 89/25
křeslo 16/22
křeslo zubařské 8/4
křída 49/24
křídlo 68/16, 93/17
křídlový člun 70/7
křivka 47/27
křivý 87/2
křižovatka 60/21, 62/25
křížový kluk 74/31
Kuba 53
kudlanka nábožná 92/19
kudrnatý 5/10
kufr 66/14, 86/13-16
kufr automobilu 64/9
kufr na nosič 65/24
kuchařka 20/4
kuchařská kniha 20/4
kuchyně 20
kuchyňský robot 20/25
kukla 92/7
kukuřice 28/20
kulatý 45/22
kulečník 79/4
kulisa 76/14
kůň 89/13
kupovat 41/11
kur domácí 93/1
kůra 25/8
kurýr 31/15, 16
kuře 27/10, 93/3
kuře pečené 27/9
kus 27/12, 86/17-19
Kuvajt 54
kužel 47/22
kužel (dopravní) 61/17
kuželka 79/10
kuželková dráha 79/9
květák 23/4
květen 52
květina 25/9, 10, 57/12, 58/7
květináč 22/10
květinářství 25
květinový truhlík 13/3
kyčelní kost 4/15
Kypr 54
kyslíková bomba 77/22
kytara (elektrická) 76/8

laboratorní plášť 46/1
laboratorní váhy 46/23
laboratoř 45, 46
labuť 93/31
láhev 27/25
lahůdkářství 27
lama 90/12
lámat 86/20
lampa 15/22
Lanarkshire 56
Lancashire 56
lanko 65/15
lano 69/6, 82/12
Laos 54
Laramie 55
Larne 56
Las Vegas 55
lavička 22/14, 57/3
lebka 4/11
leden 52
lednička 20/14
ledvina 4/7
lehátko 72/7
lehký 88/13
Leicestershire 56
lék 7/1
lékárnice 39/6
lékař 7/19
lékařský předpis 7/5
leopard 90/18
lepicí páska 32/2
lepidlo 49/23
les 73/5
lesík 73/19
lesní roh 75/6
Lesotho 54
letadlo 68/12
létání balonem 72/20
létání na rogalu 72/22
letecká pošta 32/17
letecký dispečer 68/5
letenka 67/2
letiště 67, 68
letištní budova 67
léto 52/10
letovisko72/2
letuška 67/14
leukoplast 7/10
lev 90/16
levný 87/7
levý 62/17
lézt 82/13
ležet 84/23
Libanon 54
líbat 85/2
Libérie 54
libra 36/8, 17, 18
Libye 54
liči 24/15
líčidla 12/20
lidský 3, 4
lilek 23/20
lilie 25/26
Limavady 56
límec 11/15
limeta 24/17
limonáda 27/26
Lincolnshire 56
Lisburn 56

list 25/11
listonoš 31/8
listopad 52
liška 89/7
litr 48/28
Little Rock 55
Litva 54
lodyha 25/19
loď 70/5, 11
loket 3/8
lokomotiva 66/3
Londonderry 56
lopatka (na sázení) 22/12
lopatka na smetí 19/4
Los Angeles 55
losos 28/3, 91/9
Lothian 56
Lotyšsko 54
Louisiana 55
Louisville 55
ložní prádlo 18/2
ložnice 18
lunární modul 50/5
lunární vozidlo 50/8
lupa 45/14
lupenková pila 21/20
lurč 74/24
lůžko 71/7
lyže 77/9
lyžování 77/6
lyžovat 77/7
lžíce 15/11
lžička 16/15

Madagaskar 54
Maďarsko 54
Magherafelt 56
magnet 46/8
Maine 55
maják 70/12
Makedonie 54
Malajsie 54
Malawi 54
Mali 54
malinový 28/10
malování 74/1
Malviny 53
malé dítě 5/1
malý 5/19, 87/4
mandle 28/17
mango 24/19
manžel 1/18
manželka 1/12
manžeta 11/17
mapa 49/18
margarín 27/20, 28
Maroko 54
Mars 50/20
Maryland 55
maska 12
maska chytače 78/5
máslo 27/29
maso 27/8
Massachussetts 55
mast 7/8
materiál 13
matice 21/25
matka 1/5
matrace 18/11
Mauretánie 54
Mauricius 54
mávat 85/4
medúza 91/15
medvěd 90/4
mechanik 40/11
měkký 88/8
mělký 88/20
meloun 24/1, 28/2
Memphis 55
měna 34/13
Merkur 50/23
Merseyside 56
Merthyr Tydfil 56
měřítko 53, 55
měsíc 52
město 55, 59, 60
metr 48
metro 66
Mexický záliv 53/18
Mexiko 53
mezi 58/8
Miami 55
Midlothian 56
míchačka betonu 63/6
míchat 83/12
Michigan 55
Michiganské jezero 55
mikina 12/14
mikrofon 30/20
mikroskop 46/17
mikrováhy 46/27
mililitr 48/27
milimetr 48/29
milion 33
Milwaukee 55
miminko 5/1
mince 35/1, 36/1
mincíř 46/14
minerálka 27/25
Minneapolis 55
Minnesota 55
minout (branku) 81/29
minus 48/12, 52/8
minuta 37/6, 7, 10, 12, 14
minutová ručička 37/3
mířit 79/3
mísa 15/6
mísa na zadělávání 20/3
miska 15/13
Mississippi 55
Missouri 55
mixér 20/8
mléko 27/24
mluvit 85/5
Mobile 55
model 74/8
modelářská stavebnice 74/7
modelářství 74/6
modrý 9/7
modřina 6/15
mokrý 88/10
Moldávie 54
Mongolsko 54
Monmouthshire 56
monokl 6/20
Montana 55
mop 19/8
Moray 56
moře 53, 73/8
Moře Laptěvů 54/39
mořská želva 91/24
most 60/15
motocykl 65/25
motor 64/15, 65/28, 68/19
motorest 61/11
motorový člun 69/11
motýl 92/6
moucha 92/1
Moyle 56
Mozambik 54
mračit se 84/19
mrakodrap 60/12
mravenec 92/15
mrazák 20/15
mrkev 23/14
mrznout 52/7
mřížka drátěná 46/25
mřížka chladiče 64/18
můra 92/9
můstek pro pěší 62/22
mušle 91/23
muž 5/5, 6
Myanmar 54
mýdlo 17/8
mýt 84/13
mýt okno 83/3

na 58/9, 11
naaranžované květiny 25/10
naběračka 20/11
náboj kola 16/12
nad 58/10, 15
nadhazovač v kriketu 81/17
nadhazovat v kriketu 81/18
nadjezd 62/10, 20
nádraží 66
nádrž 73/13
nafukovací člun 70/14
náhorní plošina 73/18
nahoru (do schodů) 18/24
nahoře 58/11, 12
náhrdelník 12/26
nachlazení 6/7

Rejstřík

nájemní dům 13/10
náklad 70/4
nákladní automobil 40/2, 63/4
nalévat 83/11
nálevka 45/10
Namibie 54
námořník 39/11
náplast 7/3
naplňovat 83/9
náprsní taška 11/21
náprstek 74/17
náramek 12/23
nárazník 64/7
narcis 25/14
národní směrové číslo 38/20
nářadí 21
násep 62/3, 13
Nashville 55
násobeno 48/13
nástěnka 44/1
nástroj (hudební) 75
nástup do letadla 68/1
nástupiště 66/6, 18, 21
náušnice 12/27
navíjet 83/8
Neath and Port Talbot 56
Nebraska 55
neděle 33
negativ 29/10
nehet 3/17, 17/5
nejvyšší patro 13/11
Německo 54
nemocniční 7
Nepál 54
Neptun 50/16
nést 86/14
nešťastný 88/2
neteř 1/14
netopýr 89/4
netvor 12/13
neuklizený 88/8
Nevada 55
New Hampshire 55
New Haven 55
New Jersey 55
New Mexico 55
New Orleans 55
New York 55
Newport 56
Newry and Mourne 56
Newtownabbey 56
Niagara Falls 55
Niger 54
Nigérie 54
Nikaragua 53
niklák 35/3
nit 74/20
nízký 87/18
Nizozemsko 54
noc 37/18
noční košile 11/11
noční stolek 18/10
noha 3/12, 6/12, 13
noha s plovací blánou 93/29
Norfolk 56
Norské moře 54/20
Norsko 54
North Down 56
Northamptonshire 56
Northumberland 56
nos 4/20
nos (letadla) 68/13
nosič 71/2
nosič holí (golfových) 79/12
nosítka 38/16
nosník 8/17
nosorožec 90/21
Nottinghamshire 56
noty 76/6
Nová Kaledonie 54
novinový stánek 59/15
noviny 26/8, 41/11, 42/14, 59/16
nový 87/6
nový měsíc 50/1
Nový Zéland 54
nožní brzda 64/27
nůž 15/10
nůžky 49/12
nůžky na živý plot 22/8

o 58/4
obálka 26/3, 32/6
obdélník 47/11
obecenstvo 76/28
obědvat 42/17
oběžná dráha 50/13
obchod 59/12
obchodní dům 59/18
obilné pole 73/26
obilné vločky 27/1
objektiv 29/17, 46/21
objem 48/26
objímat 85/3
oblačno 51/8
oblast 56
oblek 10/18
oblékat se 41/8
obličej 4/17
obloha 60/13
oblouk 14/10, 47/7
obočí 4/26
obratník Kozoroha 53/54
obratník Raka 53/54
obraz 15/25, 49/17, 58/10
obrazovka 44/26
obroučky 8/18
obrubník 59/9
obtížný 87/12
obvaz 7/2
obvaz sádrový 7/13
obvod kruhu 47/2
obytné stavení farmáře 73/21
obytný přívěs 63/9, 71/27
obývací pokoj 16
obzor 60/14
ocas 68/18
ocasní ploutev 91/2
oceán 53
oční kapky 8/21
oční vyšetření 8/14
odbavení 67/1
odbavovací přepážka 67/4
oděv 9-11
odcházet 41/10
odjezd 66/17
odletová hala 67/12
odměrná kádinka 45/24
odměrný válec 46/3
odpadkový koš 57/4, 59/14
odpálit 78/28
odpoledne 37/16
odrazové sklo 65/14
ofina 5/13
oheň 16/4
Ohio 55
ohnivzdorný kastrol 20/1
ohon 89/17
ohon (z vlasů) 5/13
Ochotské moře 54/37
ochranné brýle 45/1
okapová roura 14/21
okapový žlab 14/22
okenice 14/5
okenní římsa 14/9
okenní žaluzie 44/17
Oklahoma 55
Oklahoma City 55
okno 13/8, 9, 14/8, 11, 57/1, 58/1, 83/3
oko 4/25
okolo 58/2
okulár 46/22
okurka 23/10
okvětní lístek 25/4
okýnko 31/5, 66/11
oliheň 91/14
oliva 27/23
Omagh 56
Omaha 55
Omán 54
omezení rychlosti 61/6
opánek 12/8
opékač topinek 20/17
operace 7
operační sál 7/16
opice 90/13
opravný lak 44/9
optik 8/13
oranžový 9/3
ordinace 7
Oregon 55
orel 93/8
orgán 4/1
orchestr 76/1

orchestřiště 76/19
orchidej 25/18
Orkneje 56
Orlando 55
ořech 24/12
ořezávátko 49/25
osel 89/11
osm 33/8
osmdesát 33/80
osmnáct 33/18
osmý 33
osobní počítač 44/25
osobní linková loď 70/11
ostrov 55
ostrov Man 56
ostrov Wight 56
ostrý úhel 47/19
osuška 17/11
otec 1/6
otevřený 87/9
otěže 80/14
otvírač na konzervy 20/10
otvor na mince 38/25
ovál 47/8
ovce 89/9
ovoce 24, 28/7
ovocný 28/11
Oxfordshire 56
ozdobný předmět 58/12

pacient 8/3
Pacifik 53/13, 14
padák 72/19
padat 82/5
padesát 33/50, 36/16
padesátidolarový 35/11
padesátilibrový 36/13
padesátipence 36/7
pádlo 69/20
Pákistán 54
palec (ruky) 3/21
palice 21/2
palička 75/19
palivoměr 64/23
pálka na stolní tenis 78/27
pálkař (v baseballu) 78/3
pálkař (v kriketu) 81/14
pálkařská přilba 78/2
palma 25/16
paluba 69/4
palubní karta 67/3
Panama 53
panda 90/7
pánev 14/15
pánev (kuchyňská) 20/24
pantofel 11/12
papája 24/14
papír 17/18, 45/11, 57/4, 5, 8, 86/17-19
papír balicí 26/6
papír na vyhození 16/16
papírnické potřeby 26
papírový kapesník 18/9
papírový sáček 23/22
papoušek 93/19
paprika 23/3
paprsek 65/7
Papua-Nová Guinea 54
paragon 29/2, 35/14
Paraguay 53
parašutismus 72/18
parfém 67/11
park 60/2
parkovací značka 59/2
parkoviště 13/15
paroh 90/2
pas 67/6
pás 3/24
pásek 12/11
páska (závěsná) 7/11
pasový 67/5
paštika 28/4
pata 3/15
pátek 33
páteř 4/14
patnáct 33/15
patro 13/11, 13
pátý 33
páv 93/24
pavouk 92/11
pavučina 92/12
paže 3/7
pečeně 27/7
pečené kuře 27/9
pedál kola 65/9
pedál plynu 64/28
pekař 39/7
Pembrokeshire 56
pěna na holení 17/25
pence 36/2, 14-17
peněženka 11/22
peněžní automat 34/16
peněžní poukázka 32/22, 23
peníze 34/12, 35, 36
peníze nazpět 35/16
Pensylvánie 55
pepř 15/16
perla 91/22
pero (kuličkové) 49/22
pero (ptačí) 93/5
Perský záliv 54/28
Perth and Kinross 56
Peru 53
pes 89/22
pěst 3/10
pěší turista 71/24
pěší turistika 71/23
pěšinka 5/16
pět 33/5
pěticent 35/3
pětidolarová bankovka 35/8
pětilibrový 36/10
pětipence 36/4
Petriho miska 46/9
pevný 88/23
Philadelphia 55
Phoenix 55
piknik 71/17
pikola 75/10
pikové eso 74/34
pila 21/9, 20
pilník 21/13
pilot 68/11
pilotní kabina 68/14
pinta 27/24
pipeta 46/12
písek 73/16
pískat 82/23
píst 45/15
píšťalka 82/24
pít 42/16
Pittsburgh 55
placení v hotovosti 35
plachetnice 69/1
plachta 69/3
plachtění 72/10
plakat 84/20
plakát 18/15
plamen 45/3
plameňák 93/25
planeta 50
plášť do deště 10/22
plášť do laboratoře 46/1
plátek 27/8
platýz 91/10
plavání 77/25
plavat 77/26
plavba výletní 72/6
plavec 77/27
plavecký bazén 77/28
plavky (dámské) 11/2
plavky (pánské) 11/1
plaz 91
pláž 72/3, 73/10
plechovka 27/26
pleš 5/7
pletací jehlice 74/23
pletení 74/21
plivátko 8/5
plíce 4/3
plněné pečivo 27/11, 12
plněný 27/23
plnovous 4/24
plný 88/11, 22
plochý 45/9
plomba 8/9
plot 22/15
plot železný 60/9
plot živý 22/27
ploutev 90/28, 91/3
pluh 73/29
plus 48/11
Pluto 50/15
plyn (u motorového vozidla) 64/28, 65/26

Rejstřík

pneumatická sbíječka 61/16
pneumatika 65/27
poblíž 58/6
pobřeží 72/1
Pobřeží slonoviny 54
pobřežní zeď 72/4
počasí 51
pod 58/5, 16
podávající hráč 81/3
podávat (v tenisu) 81/2
podávat si ruce 85/1
podél 57/12
podepisovat 43/6
podjezd 62/21
podlaha 49/9
podlážka 71/20
podložka 21/26
podnos 16/12
podpatek 11/20
podpis 43/7
podprsenka 11/9
podšálek 16/13
podzim 52/11
pohárek (na vrhání kostek) 74/27
pohlednice 32/8
pohoří 55
pohotovostní služba 38
pohovka 16/17
pokládat 86/16
pokladna 29/3
pokladna (nádražní) 66/10
pokladník 34/9
poklička 15/5
poklop kanálové šachty 59/7
pokoj 71/5-8
pokoj nemocniční 7
polární medvěd 90/6
polaroid 29/23
polař 81/21
polař u branky (v kriketu) 81/13
pole 73/24, 81/22
poledne 37/13
poleno 16/5
polévka 28/5
police 20/23
policejní auto 38/2
policejní stanice 38/1
policie 38
policista 59/5
policistka 38/3
polobotka 10/23
poloměr 47/3
polovina 48/21
Polsko 54
polštář 16/18, 18/12
pomalý 62/5, 15, 87/24
pomeranč 24/9
pomerančový 27/21
pomezní rozhodčí 81/25
pondělí 33
poník 72/16, 89/15
ponožka 11/4
popelnice 22/20
poranit (si) 6/12
porce 27/10
Portland 55
Portoriko 53
Portugalsko 54
pořadač 44/16
poschoďový autobus 60/25
posílat 43/10
poslední čtvrt měsíce 50/4
poslouchat 41/12
postel 18/3, 41/2
postranní čára 81/6
postranní ulice 60/5
postranní zákulisí 76/18
pošmourno 51/14
pošta 31/10, 41/6
pošta 1. a 2. třídy 32/11, 14, 15
poštovní brašna 31/13
poštovní dodávka 31/7
poštovní razítko 32/12
poštovní schránka 31/11, 14, 59/3
poštovní služby 31/32
poštovní směrovací číslo 32/13, 16
poštovní úřad 31/1
poštovní úřednice 31/4
poštovní vak 31/9
poštovní známka 31/19
potápění s akvalungem 77/21
potápění s dýchací trubicí 77/23
potok 73/7
poupě 25/27
poušť 73/15
pouzdro na brýle 8/19
povlak na polštář 18/7
Powys 56
pozemní hokej 78/16
poznamenávat si 43/8
poznámkový blok 44/13
pozoun 75/8
požár 38/8
práce 42/15, 18
práce na silnici 61/13
pracovní plocha 20/13
pracovní stůl 21/5
pracovnice cestovní kanceláře 40/3
pracovník záchranné služby 38/17
pračka 19/3
prádelní šňůra 19/22
prádelník 18/19
prádlo 17/16
práh 13/6
prachovka 19/14
prapor 59/19
prarodič 1/21
pravítko 49/21
pravý 62/15
pravý úhel 47/15
prázdný 88/12
Princeton 55
prkno na surfing 77/17
prkno na windsurfing 77/20
prkýnko 20/18
probudit se 41/1
procento 48/17
prodavač 29/6
prodejna 30
prodejna bezcelního zboží 67/10
programátor 40/5
prohlídka památek 71/9
promenáda 72/5
promítací plátno 76/23
propínací svetr 12/7
proplácení cestovního šeku 34/10
proplácení šeku 34/14
prosinec 52
prostěradlo 18/6
prostor mezi brankami (kriketu) 81/16
prostředek na mytí nádobí 20/5
protikladný 87/88
proudový 68/19
proužkovaný 9/17
provázek 26/2
provazy (v ringu) 79/20
Providence 55
provoz 59/13
provoz oběma směry 61/4
prst 3/20
prst (u nohy) 3/14
prsten 12/24
pršet 51/2
průdušnice 4/2
pruh (jízdní) 62/5, 6, 7, 15, 16, 17
průměr 47/5
průvodkyně 71/10
první 13/13, 33
první čtvrt měsíce 50/2
před 58/18
předklonit se 82/22
předkrm 28
předložka (koberec) 16/6
předložka (gramatická) 57, 58
předměstí 60
přední 8/11
přední sklo (u auta) 64/19
přední stěna 48/7
přední světlo 64/4
předpis (lékařský) 7/5
přehazovačka 65/13
přehoz 18/4
přehrada 73/14
přechod 59/24
překládat papír 86/19
přepážka 31/3
přepážka odbavovací 67/4
přepona 47/17
přes 57/2, 14
přeskakovat 82/16
příborník 15/18
příbuzenské vztahy 1/2
přídavné jméno 87/88

příď 69/16
přicházet 57/7
příjezdová cesta 22/16
přikázaný směr doprava 61/12
přikrývka 18/5
přilba 12/2
přímka 47/26
připevnit sešívačkou 43/4
přistání 68/8
přístav 69/70
přistávací dráha 68/7
přístaviště 69/10
přístavní molo 60/16
přístrojová deska 64/20
přístřešek u autobusové zastávky 59/21
přítel 42/20
přívěs obytný 63/9, 71/27
přívěsný lodní motor 70/15
přízemí 13/14
přízemí (v hledišti) 76/20
psací stroj 44/27
psací stůl 44/6
psát na psacím stroji 43/3
pstruh 28/17, 91/8
pštros 93/22
pták 93
půda 83/7
půl 37/9
půlnoc 37/13
půltucet 27/14
pudr (talkový) 17/28
pumpička 65/3
punčochové kalhoty 11/7
punčochy 11/6
puntíkovaný 9/18
pytel 83/6
pytlík bonbónů 26/14
pyžamo 11/14

racek 93/30
radiátor 15/4
rádio 30/15
radiomagnetofon 30/8
ragby 78/14
rajče 23/19
rajská polévka 28/5
raketa 50/10
raketa (sportovní) 78/23
raketoplán 50/11
Rakousko 54
rám 15/24, 65/4
rameno 3/6
ramínko na šaty 18/18
ráno 37/15
recepce 71/1
recepční 71/4
Redcar and Cleveland 56
registratura 44/15
reklama 59/20
rendlík 20/26
Renfrewshire 56
Reno 55
rentgen 8/10
rentgenový snímač 67/9
reproduktor 30/10
restaurace 28
ret 4/23
Réunion 54
Rhondda Cynon Taff 56
Rhode Island 55
ribstol 82/14
Richmond 55
ring 79/19
Rio Grande 55
rodiče 1/20
rodina 1
rodinný domek 14/1
rogalo 72/23
roh 48/5, 59/11, 79/18
roh (zvířecí) 90/20
rohožka 18/21
Rochester 55
rok 37
role (papíru) 26/6
roleta 17/19
rolička bonbónů 26/15
rostbíf 28/16
rostlina 16/19, 58/11
rotor 68/10
roura 14/21
rouška 7/17
rovná se 48/15
rovník 53
Rovníková Guinea 54
rovnoběžka 47/30
rovný 5/8, 9, 87/1
rozbalovat dárek 85/11
rozhodčí 79/25
rozhodčí tenisu, kriketu 81/11, 20
rozjezdová dráha 68/7
rozlišovací číslo 38/18
rozměry 48
roztok na čištění 8/22
rožeň 22/16
rtěnka 12/21
ruční pilka 21/12
ruční vrtačka 21/18
ručník 17/9, 10
Rudé moře 54/25
ruka 3/19, 85/1
rukáv 11/16
rukavice 10/15
Rumunsko 54
Ruská federace 54
Rusko 54
růst 57/3, 12
růže 25/17
růžičková kapusta 23/15
růžový 9/2
Rwanda 54
ryba 91
rybář 39/10
rybář (sportovní) 72/14
rybaření 72/13
rybářský člun 69/14
rybářský prut 72/15
rybník 73/23
rýč 22/19
rychlý 62/7, 17, 87/23
rypec 91/5
ryšavý 5/12
rýt 83/7
rýžák 19/18

řada 26/7
řadicí páka 64/21
řadový dům 13/1
řapíkatý celer 23/16
řasa oční 4/28
Řecko 54
ředkvička 23/6
řeka 55, 60/17
řeka sv. Vavřince 55
řemen 29/22
řeřicha 23/13
řetěz 65/8
řetězové kolo 65/10
řetízek 12/25
řezník 39/8
říční člun 69/9
řídicí letištní věž 68/4
řidič 40/2
řídítka 65/19
říjen 52
římsa nad krbem 16/2
říznutí 6/18

Sacramento 55
sáček 24/12, 26/10, 16
sada 26/5
sada karet 74/30
sádrový obvaz 7/13
safari 72/17
Saint Louis 55
Saint Paul 55
sako 10/8
salát 28/22
Salt Lake City 55
San Antonio 55
San Diego 55
San Francisco 55
San Jose 55
sandál 12/8
sanitka 38/14
Santa Fe 55
saponát 19/1
satelit 50/9
Saturn 50/18
Saúdská Arábie 54
Savannah 55
saxofon 75/16
sběrač míčků 81/9
sbírání známek 74/4

Rejstřík

sbírat (ze země) 41/6
Scilly 56
Scottish Borders 56
sdělení 32/9
Seattle 55
sedadlo 67/13
sedan 63/12
sedět 84/21
sedlo (kola, jezdecké) 65/2, 80/12
sedlo skútru 65/23
sedm 33/7
sedmdesát 33/70
sedmnáct 33/17
sedmý 33
sekačka trávy 22/5
sekera 21/17
sekretář 44/20
seknout 79/28
sektorová stěna 16/21
semafor 60/19
sendvič 27/3
Senegal 54
servírovací stolek 28/6
servisová čára 81/5
sestra 1/11
sestřenice 1/9
sešit 49/4
sešívačka 44/12
setkávat se 42/20
severní 53/9, 14
Severní Amerika 53/1
Severní Dakota 55
Severní Irsko 56
Severní Karolína 55
Severní Korea 54
Severní ledový oceán 53/8
Severní moře 54/21
Shetlandy 56
Shropshire 56
schod 18/22, 57/11, 13
schodiště 18/25
schránka na dopisy 31/14
schůzka 43/8
Sierra Leone 54
Sierra Nevada 55
silnice 61/62, 62/24
silný 87/22
silueta (proti obloze) 60/14
Singapur 54
Sioux Falls 55
síto 20/2
síť 81/7
síťka 78/9
skafandr 50/7
skákání na trampolíně 82/4
skákat (přes švihadlo) 82/27
Skalisté hory 55
skála 70/13, 73/9
skelný papír 21/3
skladiště 70/3
skleněná tyčinka 46/2
sklenice 15/14
sklenice džemu 27/5
sklíčko 46/20
sklo 13/23
sklo (u auta) 64/10, 19
skočit po hlavě 77/29
skokan do vody 77/30
skórování 81/23
skotská kostka 9/20
Skotsko 56
skrz 57/3
skříňka 17/1, 20/20
skupina turistů 71/10
skupina pop music 76/7
skútr 65/21
slabý 87/21
sleď 91/6
slepice 93/2
slimák 92/21
slipy 11/10
slon 90/24
sloup 14/4
Slovensko 54
slovesa z kancelářské praxe 43
sloveso 83-86
Slovinsko 54
složit (v ragby) 78/15
sluchátka 30/12
sluchátko (telefonní) 38/24
Slunce 50/14
sluneční brýle 12/18
sluneční soustava 50
slunečník 72/9
slunící se člověk 72/8
sluníčko sedmitečné 92/14
smát se 84/18
(směrem) k 57/10
(směrem) od 57/9
směrové číslo země 38/19
smetáček 19/5
smetana 28/12
smutný 88/2
smyčcový nástroj 75
smyčec 75/2
snadný 87/11
sněžit 51/3
snídat 41/9
sníh 51/4
sobota 33
Socotra 55
Somálsko 54
Somerset 56
souhvězdí 50/25
sova 93/12
spací pytel 71/21
spálenina (ze slunce) 6/16
spát 84/24
spěšná zásilka 32/24, 25
spirála 47/28
spodní prádlo 11/3
spodnička 11/8
Spojené arabské emiráty 54
Spojené státy americké 55
spojka (u auta) 64/26
spona 11/19
sport 77-81
sportovní auto 63/11
sportovní kočárek (skládací) 60/4
sportovní středisko 42/19
sprcha 17/20
sprchovat se 41/7
squash 42/21, 78/22
srdce 44/4
srdcová dáma 74/32
Srí Lanka 54
srpen 52
srst 89/20
Staffordshire 56
stan 71/19
stánek na trhu 23/1
stanování 71/18
start (letadla) 68/6
startovací blok 80/22
startovací box 80/27
startovací plošina 50/12
starší 5/6
starý 5/6, 87/5
stát 53, 55
stát (sloveso) 84/22
stativ 29/4
státní hranice 53, 56
státní poznávací značka 64/5
stav bankovního konta 34/6
stavební dělník 61/15
stavební materiál 13
stavědlo 66/1
steak 28/18
stěna 15/2
stěrač 64/10
stetoskop 7/20
stezka pro pěší a cyklisty 61/9
stěžeň 69/2
stínítko 15/23
Stirling 56
sto 33/100
Stockton-on-Tees 56
stodola 73/22
stoh košíků 24/22
stoh novin 26/8
stojan 45/6
stojan (malířský) 49/13
stojan s úchytkou 45/20
stojka 82/25
stolek 58/5, 6
stolek (mikroskopu) 46/19
století 37
stolička 45/19
stolička (zub) 8/12
stolní tenis 78/26
stonek 25/19
stopky 46/16
Strabane 56

strana 47/10
strom 57/3
strom(ek) 22/4
strop 16/1
stružka 59/8
strýc 1/4
střed 47/4
středa 33
střední 62/6, 16
Středoafrická republika 54
Středozemní moře 54/23
střecha 13/2, 14/14, 23
střevo 4/9
stříhat 86/17
stříkačka 45/16
střílet 78/10
stuha 58/2, 74/14
stupeň 52/1, 2, 8
stupeň Celsia 52/2
stůj! 61/2
stůl 57/8, 58/4, 79/6
Súdán 54
Suffolk 56
suchý 88/9
sukně 10/11
sůl 15/15
surfař 77/16
surfing 77/13
surfovat 77/15
Surinam 54
Surrey 56
Sussex 56
sušenka 16/10, 27/15, 16
sušené květiny 25/9, 10, 58/7
sušit 84/14
suterénní 13/9
svářeč 40/9
svazek květin 25/9
Svazijsko 54
svěrák 21/11
svět 53/54
světadíl 53
světle zelený 9/11
světlo 18/16
světlý 5/9
svetr 10/6
svíčka 15/3, 58/8, 9, 86/23, 24
Svítí slunce. 51/1
svodidlo 62/9, 19
svorka 46/7
Swansea 56
syn 1/16
synovec 1/15
syntezátor 76/13
sýr 27/22
Syracuse 55
Sýrie 54

šachy 74/29
šála 10/14
Šalamounovy ostrovy 54
šálek 16/14, 58/16
šampon 17/26
šátek 12/6
šatník 18/17
šaty 12/6
šedý 9/15
šedesát 33/60
šek 34/ 10, 11, 14, 43/4
šeková karta 34/3
šeková knížka 34/1
šest 33/6
šestnáct 33/16
šestý 33
šicí stroj 74/10
šipky 79/1
široký 87/15
šířka 48/3
šiška 25/22
šít 83/4
šití 74/9
školní taška 49/8
školní uniforma 10/1
škorpion 92/23
škrábanec 6/17
šlehačka 28/12
šňůra (elektrická) 19/11
šortky 12/12
špachtle 46/10
Španělsko 54
špatný 88/6
špendlík 74/16
šperk 12
špinavý 88/20
šroub 21/24
šroubovák 21/21
šťastný 88/1
štěně 89/23
štětec 49/14
štítek 32/3
šupina 91/7
šváb 92/16
švagr 1/10
švagrová 1/13
švédská bedna 82/18
Švédsko 54
švihadlo 82/18
Švýcarsko 54

tableta 7/7
táboření 71/18
tabule 49/1
tabule s názvem ulice 60/10
tabule s odjezdy 66/17
tabulka čokolády 26/11, 86/20
tác 16/12
Tádžikistán 54
tágo 79/5
táhnout 86/22
tachometr 64/24
taktovka 76/5
talíř 15/9, 58/13, 15, 17
tamburína 75/18
Tampa 55
tancovat 85/7
tanker 70/6
Tanzanie 54
tartanový 9/20
Tasmanovo moře 54/31
taška 66/13
taška (krytinová) 13/19
taška školní 49/8
tašková střecha 14/23
taxi 60/6
taxík 60/6
teenager 5/3
tele 89/2
telefonní budka 38/22
telefonní číslo 38/21
telefonní karta 38/24
telefonní záznamník 44/5
těleso 47/20
televize 42/23
televizní anténa 14/20
televizor 16/23, 58/18, 19
tělo 3/4
tělocvična 82/15
tenis 81
teniska 12/4
tenisový kurt 81/10
tenký 87/14
Tennessee 55
tepláková souprava 12/3
teplý 52/4
teploměr 45/21
teplota 6/10, 52
terč na šipky 79/2
těrka 45/7
teta 1/3
Texas 55
těžký 88/14
Thajsko 54
Tchaj-wan 54
tchán 1/7
tchyně 1/8
tichý 88/4
tílko 12/10
Tipperary 56
tisíc 33/1000
tiskárna 44/19
tisknout 43/11
tkanička 11/23
tlačit 86/21
tlapa 89/24
tleskat 85/8
tlumič (nárazů) 65/29
tlustý 5/21, 87/13
tmavě zelený 9/12
tmavomodrý 9/9
tmavý 5/8
toaletní papír 17/18
toaletní stolek 18/1
toast 28/4

Rejstřík

Togo 54
Toledo 55
tonometr 7/23
Topeka 55
Torfaen 56
továrna 59/23
trafika 26
trajekt 70/9
traktor 73/28
trampolína 82/6
transfokátor 29/15
transportér 63/1
trať 66/7
travnatá krajnice 62/23
trávník 22/3
trenér 82/7
trh 23/24
trhat 86/18
tribuna 81/24
tričko 10/5
triedr 29/7
Trinidad a Tobago 53
trojité balení 26/13
trojnožka 45/26
trojúhelník 47/13, 49/6
trombon 75/8
trouba 20/22
trs 24/3
trubka 75/7
truhlář 40/8
trup (letadla) 68/17
trychtýř 45/10
tryskový 68/19
třecí miska 45/8
třetí 33
třetina 48/20
třešně 28/1
tři 33/3, 37/12
třicátý 33
třicet 33/30
třída 49
tříkolka 65/17
třináct 33/13
třináctý 33
třmen 80/13
tuba 17/3
tuba (hudební nástroj) 75/9
tucet 27/13
Tucson 55
tučňák 93/23
tuleň 90/27
tulipán 25/25
Tulsa 55
tuňák 27/6, 18
tunel 66/9
Tunisko 54
tupý úhel 47/18
Turecko 54
turista 71/11
turistka 71/12
Turkménistán 54
tužka 49/20
tvar 47
tvarohový dort 28/9
tvář 4/19
tvrdý 88/17
tvrdý kartáč 19/18
Twin Falls 55
tyč 81/27
týden 37
tygr 90/17
tykadlo 92/10
tympán 75/17
Tyne and Wear 56
tyrkysový 9/8

u 58/6
U-trubice 45/18
ubrousek 15/7
ubrus 15/8
učebnice 49/3
učitelka 49/16
udeřit 79/22
údolí 73/3
udržování kondice 82
Uganda 54
úhloměr 49/7
úhlopříčka 47/12
úhoř 91/11
ucho 3/3
ukazatel 60/23
ukládání peněz 34/17
uklizený 88/7
Ukrajina 54
ulice 59/10, 11, 60/5
ulička (v hledišti) 76/27
umělec 39/1
umyvadlo 17/6
unavený 6/3
uniforma 10/1
únor 52
upadnout 6/11
úplněk 50/3
uprostřed 58/13
Uran 50/17
úraz 6
úrovňový železniční přejezd 66/2
Uruguay 53
USA 55
usmívat se 84/17
ústa 3/29
ústřice 91/21
Utah 55
utěrka 20/7
úterý 33
útes 73/11
uvaděč 76/25
uvaděčka 76/26
uvázání lodi 69/15
úvaz 72/26
uvnitř 58/3
Uzbekistán 54
uzený 28/3
úzký 87/16

v 58/3, 7, 12, 14
vagon 66/4
váha 17/14, 31/2
váha (hmotnost) 48/23
vak 90/9
Vale of Glamorgan 56
válec 47/24, 64/17
váleček (na těsto) 20/12
vana 17/15
Vanuatu 54
vánoční stromek 25/1
vařič 71/22
vařit 83/2
vařit se 83/10
vata 7/4
váza 15/20
vážka 92/5
včela 92/2
večer 37/17
večeřet 42/22
vedle 58/17
vejce 27/13, 14
věk 5
velbloud 90/10
velkoměsto 55, 56
velký 5/18, 87/3
Velký Londýn 56
Velký Manchester 56
velryba 90/30
Venezuela 53
venkov 71/16
ventilek 65/11
Venuše 50/22
Vermont 55
veslo 69/8
veslový člun 69/7
vesmír 50
vesnice 71/15
vestavěný blesk 29/20
věšáček 19/16
věšák na ručníky 17/9
veterinářka 40/6
větev 25/7
veverka 89/6
vchod 14/3
víčko oční 4/27
videokamera 30/1
videokazeta 30/4
videorekordér 16/24
vidle 22/18
vidlička 15/12
Vietnam 54
vikýř 14/15
víno 24/10
viola 75/1
violoncello 75/3
Virginie 55
vjezd 22/26

vjezd na dálnici 62/2
vjezd zakázán 61/3
vkladní lístek 34/18
vlak 42/13, 66/8
vlasy 3/2, 5, 18/20, 84/13-16
vlaštovka 93/21
vlk 90/3
vlna (materiál) 74/22
vlna (vodní) 77/14
vlnitý 5/11
vnější pruh (jízdní) 62/7
Vnější Hebridy 56
vnitřní orgány 4/1
vnitřní pruh (jízdní) 62/5
vnučka 1/23
vnuk 1/22
voda 38/6, 83/10, 11
voda po holení 17/21
vodní lyžař 77/12
vodní lyžování 77/10
vodnice 23/18
vodopád 73/6
vodováha 21/7
voják 39/12
volant 64/22
volejbal 78/20
volný 88/24
vosa 92/3
vousy 89/19
vozidlo 63
vozík 46/15, 67/18, 68/3, 86/22
vrabec 93/15
vrána 93/11
vrátit se 41/5
vrátka 14/17, 22/22
vrchol (hory) 73/2
vrchol (trojúhelníka) 47/14
vrtačka 8/2, 21/10, 18
vrtule 68/15
vrtule (nosná) 68/10
vrtulník 68/9
vrut 21/22
vstávat 41/2
vstřelit gól 81/26
vstup 66/21
vteřinová ručička 37/5
vyběrní lístek 34/19
vybírání schránky 31/6
vybírat hotovost 34/15
výdej zavazadel 67/16
výdejna jízdenek 66/10
vydlážděná plocha za domem 22/11
výfuk 64/6
vyhazovat 57/4
východ (k letadlům) 67/15
východ (označení) 66/5
Východočínské moře 54/34
výjezd z dálnice 62/12
výklopný vůz 61/14
výletní plavba 72/6
výměna peněz 34/12
vypínač (světla) 18/27
výprava (divadelní) 76/14
vyplnit formulář 43/5
vysavač 19/7
výseč 47/6
vyskočit 78/21
vysokozdvižný vozík 63/8
vysoký 5/18, 87/17
vysoušeč vlasů 18/20
vysunovací okno 13/18
vyšetřovací lůžko 7/22
vyšívání 74/18
výška 48/2
výšková budova 60/12
vytáhnout se 82/19
výtisk 44/18
vývěsní tabule 57/9, 10
vyvrtnout (si) 6/14
vzduchový filtr 64/16
vznášedlo 70/8
vzor 9
vzorovaný 9/21

Wales 56
walkman 30/11
Warwickshire 56
Washington 55
Washington DC 55
West Midlands 56
Wichita 55
Wiltshire 56
windsurfař 77/19
windsurfing 77/18
Wisconsin 55
Wrexham 56
Wyoming 55

York 56
Yorkshire 56

z 57/1, 7
za 37/10, 12, 58/19
začínat 42/15
záda 3/9
zadek 3/11
zadní sklo u auta 64/10
zadní stěna 48/10
zadní světlo 64/8
záď 69/17
záhlaví postele 18/13
zahrada 22
zahrada před domem 22/21
zahrada za domem 22/1
zahradník 39/2
záchod 17/17
záchranná služba 38
záchranný člun 69/18
zákaz odbočení vlevo 61/7
zákaz otáčení 61/5
zákazník 29/1
základna 47/16
základní čára (tenisového hřiště) 81/4
zaklonit se 82/20
zákulisí postranní 76/18
zákusek 28
záliba 74
záliv 53
Zambie 54
zámek (u dveří) 18/26, 65/6
zámek (budova) 71/14
zaměstnání 39, 40
zametat 83/5
zaostřovací šroub 46/18
Západní Virginie 55
zapalování 64/25
zapalovat 86/23
zápas 79/23
zápasit 79/24
zápěstí 3/23
zařazovat 43/9
září 52
zastávka 59/22
zástrčka 19/12
zásuvka 15/19, 58/3
zásuvka (elektrická) 19/21
zatáčka 61/8
zátka 17/7, 46/4
zavazadla 67/17
zavazovat 83/6
závaží 46/13
závěs 16/20
závodní automobil 80/7
závodní dráha 80/6, 17
závora 66/22
zavřený 87/10
zdravotní péče 7/8
zdravotní sestra 7/12
ze 57/8, 13
zebra 90/15
zedník 40/12
zeď 13/7, 14/12, 18, 22/25, 57/12
zelený 23/3
zelenina 23, 28
zelí 23/21
zem 57/5
Země 50/21
zemědělec 39/9
zemina 61/19
zesilovač 30/16
zima 52/6, 12
Zimbabwe 54
zip 74/12
zkumavka 45/2
zlomek 48/18
zlomit (si) 6/13
zmrzlina 28/10
značka dopravní 59/1
značka parkovací 59/2
známka 74/4, 5
zobák 93/9, 26
zoom 29/15

Rejstřík

zornice **4**/30
zpáteční adresa **32**/18, 19
zpětné zrcátko vnější **64**/2
zpěvák **76**/9
zpevněná krajnice **62**/4, 14
zpívat **85**/6
zraněný **38**/15
zrcadlo **15**/1
zrní **73**/27
zrzavý **5**/12
zub **6**/4, **8**/8, 11
zubař **8**/1
zubařské křeslo **8**/4
zubní kartáček **17**/4
zubní pasta **17**/3
zubní sestra **8**/6
zubní vrtačka **8**/2
zvedat **86**/13
zvíře **89**/**90**
zvonek **65**/18

žába **92**/25
žábra **91**/14
žák **49**/2
žaludek **4**/8
žárovka **19**/15
žebro **4**/13
žebřík **38**/5
žehlicí prkno **19**/9
žehlička **19**/13
žehlit **83**/1
železnice **66**
železniční přejezd **66**/2
železný plot **60**/9
želva **91**/25
želva mořská **91**/24
žena **5**/4
žesťový nástroj **75**
židle **49**/10
žihadlo **92**/24
žiletka **17**/24
žíněnka **82**/17
žínka **17**/13
žirafa **90**/23
živočich **92**
životní prostředí **73**
živý plot **22**/27
žízeň **6**/1
žížala **92**/20
žlučník **4**/5
žlutý **9**/5, **60**/22
Žluté moře **54**/35
žokej **80**/26
žralok **91**/1
župan **11**/13

People and Health Pages 1-8

1 Who's who?

Read the sentences about this family and then write the names in the family tree.

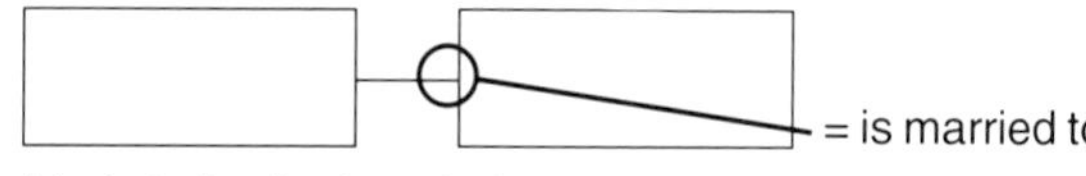

Peter is married to Ann and they have a daughter called Laura.
Peter's parents are Jack and Rosy.
Ann's sister, Sarah, has a son called Leo.

Linda is Ann's sister-in-law.
Alan's mother-in-law is called Joan.
Jamie is Leo's cousin.
Bill has got two grandsons and one granddaughter.

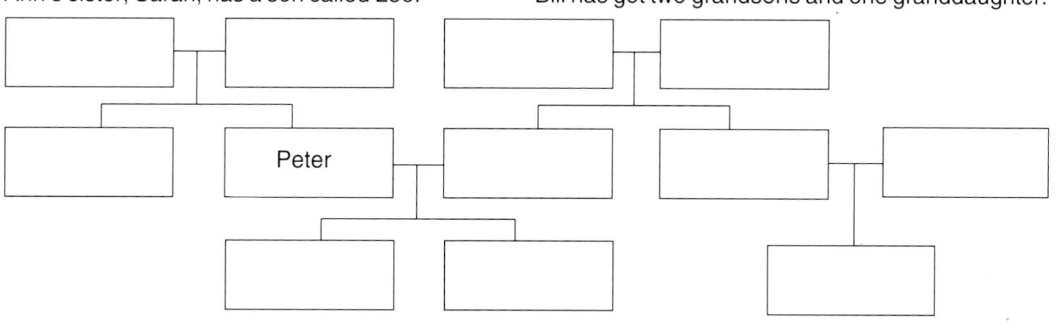

2 The Human Body

There are sixteen parts of the body hidden in this square. Can you find them all?

thumb

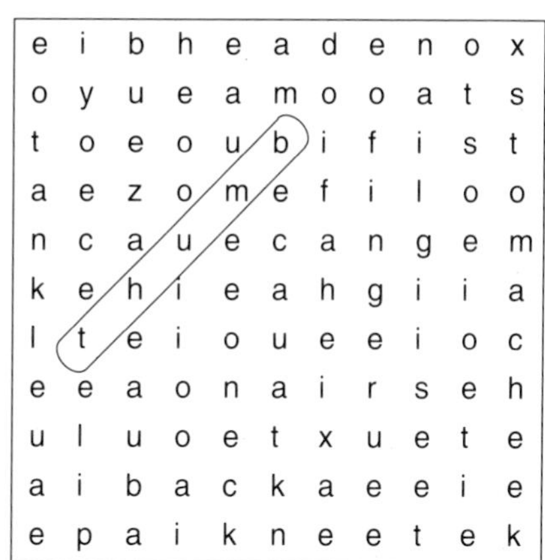

3 What's the matter?

Match what the patient says to the doctor's advice.

Patient

a I have dreadful earache.
b I've got a sore throat and a temperature.
c I've fallen over and hurt my arm.
d I've got a small scratch on my leg.
e I've got terrible toothache.

a *3* b___ c___ d___ e___

Doctor

1 Take two of these tablets and go straight to bed.
2 You probably need a filling.
3 Put two drops in each ear twice a day.
4 We'll need to put it in a sling.
5 Put some of this ointment on it and then cover it with a plaster.

Exercises page 127

Clothes Pages 9-12

1 Test your memory!

Look carefully at page 10.

Fill in the missing words in the sentences below. Use words from the box.

a The woman is wearing a ________ blouse and a ________ blue jacket.

b The boy is wearing a ________ blazer and ________ trousers.

c The man is wearing a red and white ________ tie and he is carrying a raincoat.

d The girl is wearing a ________ coat and a ________ scarf.

polka-dot	tartan	pink	grey	striped	plain	patterned

■ *Language note*

The man in the picture is **wearing** a suit and he is **carrying** a raincoat.

2 What other things are people carrying in the picture? Write some sentences.

____

____

____

____

____

3 Match each of these words with the right part of the body.

trainer	head
belt	hand
watch	neck
glove	waist
tights	foot
helmet	legs
tie	wrist

4 Find the words from the mixed-up letters. They are all things that people wear or carry. When you have finished, read down the box to find the mystery word.

1 FRIEHCEKHDAN
2 FRASC
3 LABRUMEL
4 ERUPS
5 RECIFEABS
6 RENGIRA
7 LACKENCE
8 NABAHGD
9 GIRN
10 LOSECAHE
11 LAWLET
12 GESSNALUSS

	Letters given in the grid
1	h a n d k e r c h i e f
2	f
3	b
4	p
5	a
6	n
7	k
8	a
9	i
10	s
11	l
12	a

At Home Pages 15-22 and 58

1 Find the word in each group that is different from the others.

a mug cup freezer saucer teapot

b scales aftershave soap shampoo toothpaste

c wardrobe sideboard vase wall unit chest of drawers

d duster brush scourer oven mop

e rake watering-can shears lawnmower bush

2 Write in the words.

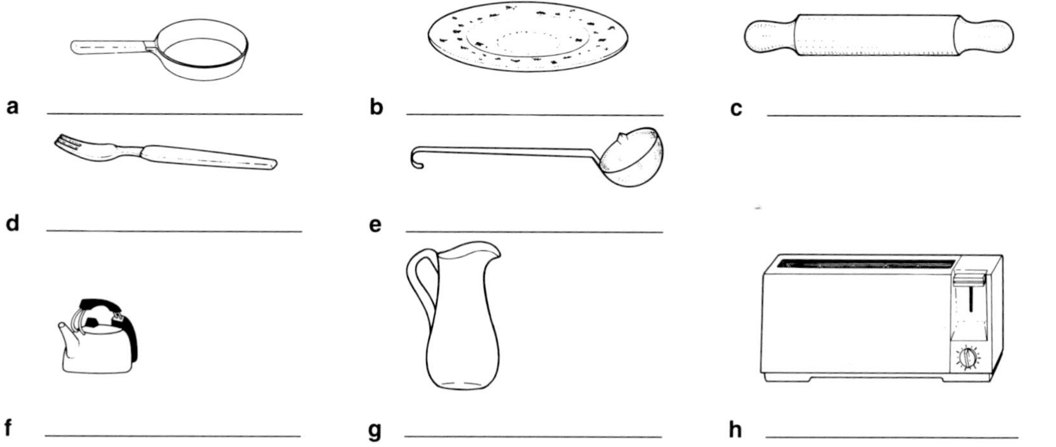

a ______________ **b** ______________ **c** ______________

d ______________ **e** ______________

f ______________ **g** ______________ **h** ______________

3 Test your memory!

Look at page 18 for two minutes, then read these sentences about the picture. Decide if they are true or false.

a The box of tissues is in the bedside cabinet.
b There's a poster over the bed.
c There's a hair-drier on the dressing table.
d The dressing table is in front of the chest of drawers.
e The blanket is under the bedspread.
f There's a coat-hanger betweeen the light and the alarm clock.

If the sentences are false, write them correctly.

____

____

____

____

Exercises page 129

Shopping and Food Pages 23-28

1 Match a word in A with the right word in B.

A	B
a tube of	chocolate
a loaf of	cereal
a bar of	toothpaste
a bottle of	margarine
a jar of	jam
a packet of	bread
a tub of	biscuits
a box of	mineral water

2 Complete these dialogues using words from the box. Use each word only once.

1 a Can I help you?
  b Yes, please. How much are the ______________?
  a They're 70p a bunch.
  b And the strawberries?
  a 85p a ______________.

2 a I'd like some ______________ for my wife's birthday.
  b Certainly, sir. Any particular kind?
  a Well, yes, she likes these blue ones.
  b Oh, you mean ______________.

3 a I'm looking for a ______________ of chocolates. Have you got any?
  b They're up on the top ______________.
  a They're a present for somebody so I'll need a roll of ______________ and a ______________ of Sellotape too, please.

4 a Are you ready to order? Here comes the ______________.
  b No, I haven't decided yet. Are you going to have a ______________?
  a Yes, I think I'll have the melon.

flowers	bananas	starter	shelf	punnet	waiter	wrapping paper	irises	box	reel

3 Where do each of the conversations in exercise 2 take place?

1 ______________ 3 ______________

2 ______________ 4 ______________

Dates and Times Pages 33 and 37

1 Look at the clocks, then find two ways of saying each time, using the expressions in the box.

1 c, ________ 2 ________

00:00

3 ________ 4 ________

14:45

5 ________ 6 ________

a	midnight
b	ten to five
c	eleven fifty-five
d	four fifty
e	a quarter to three in the afternoon
f	six thirty pm
g	seven minutes past four
h	two forty-five pm
i	half past six in the evening
j	twelve o'clock at night
k	five to twelve
l	four o seven

2 Dates

John always forgets important dates so he writes them down at the beginning of the year in a special page in his diary.

Look at the page, then answer the questions by writing the dates **in words**.

Important dates 1998

16/4 Mum's birthday

1/5 holiday (3 weeks)

3/8 Aunt Edna arrives from Australia

12/9 our wedding anniversary

22/11 – 30/11 exams!

a When is John's mother's birthday?

____

b When does John's holiday begin?

____

c On what date does Aunt Edna arrive?

____

d When is John's wedding anniversary?

____

e On what date do his exams finish?

____

Exercises page 131

At Work Pages 39-40 and 43-44

1 What do we call someone who...

...reads the news aloud on the radio or TV?

____

...arranges people's holidays for them?

____

...works with wood?

____

... makes bread and cakes?

____

...treats sick animals?

____

...repairs cars?

____

2 Read these job advertisements and decide what job is being offered in each one.

a Ladies' and gentlemen's ***** needed for modern salon. Experience of cutting all types of hair necessary.

b ***** for long-distance deliveries. Must have licence.

c WANTED! Qualified ***** for small chemist's. Duties to include dispensing prescriptions plus general shop work.

d EXPERIENCE IN RADIO? Love all kinds of music? 'Joy FM' is looking for a *****.

a ____________________

b ____________________

c ____________________

d ____________________

3 Office wordsearch

There are thirteen words connected with the office in this square. Can you find them all?

e a n d i s k a i l s
i o c h e q u e o e i
u b o i e s y f u t w
f c t t a i k d n t a
t i e y u n r i g e a
e u l p e e r a c r i
i e i e l p u r d x x
n g r p i u o y a e u
e c a o o i e f m i o
s t e o x p u u o y e
s n o t e b o o k a e

cheque

____

Describing Things Pages 47-49 and 87-88

1 Write the names of these shapes.

a ______ b ______

c ______ d ______

e ______ f ______

■ *Language note*

We say: This page is **rectangular**.
(Not: **a rectangle.**)
Rectangular is an adjective.

Noun	*Adjective*
rectangle	rectangular
triangle	triangular
circle	circular
oval	oval
square	square
cylinder	cylindrical

2 Match these questions and answers by writing the correct number next to the questions.

Question		*Answer*
a What shape is it?		1 It's used for measuring things and for drawing straight lines.
b How much does it weigh?		2 This one is made of plastic but they are also made of wood.
c How big is it?		3 It's rectangular.
d What's it made of?		4 About 10g.
e What's it used for?		5 It's about 15 cm long, 3 cm wide and 0.2 cm thick.

What is it? It's on page 49 of this dictionary. ______

3 Find the opposites of these adjectives and write them in the puzzle.

1 crooked
2 thin
3 light
4 tight
5 empty
6 hollow
7 dry

Now read down the box to find another adjective!

3 heavy

Exercises page 133

The Weather Pages 51-52 and 56

1 Look at the weather map of the British Isles below. Find a symbol for each of the words in the box and draw it.

sun	cloud	rain
wind	fog	snow

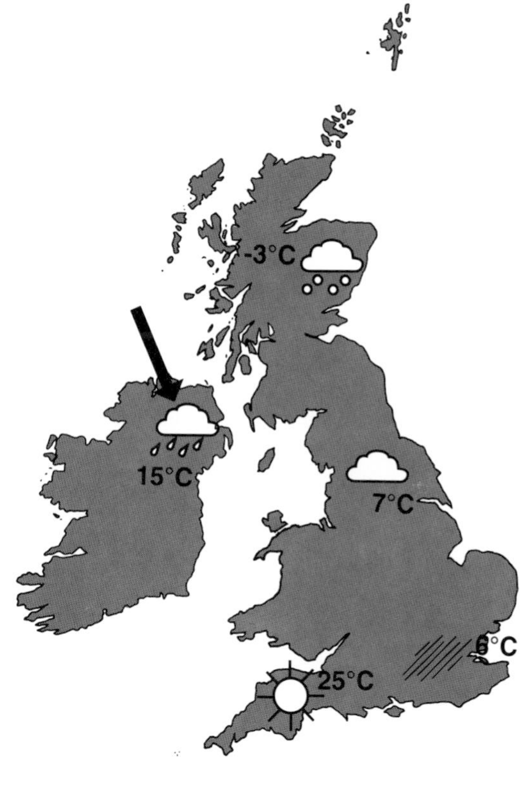

■ *Language note*

The adjective from { **cloud** is **cloudy**.
sun is **sunny**.

Make adjectives from the other words in the box. (If you are not sure about the spelling, check on page 51.)

wind ______________

snow ______________

fog ______________

rain ______________

2 Look at the weather map and write in the missing information below.

Tomorrow's Weather

The South-East will start the day quite (1) ______________ and (2) ______________, but in the South-West it's going to be rather (3) ______________ and (4) ______________. Further north it will be (5) ______________ all day with a maximum (6) ______________ of 7°C.

Over in Northern Ireland it will be (7) ______________ with some (8) ______________ during the morning and it will be very (9) ______________ on the coast. Up in Scotland the temperature will fall to (10) ______________ 3°C and there may be some (11) ______________.

The City Pages 57 and 59-60

1 Letter-box or mailbox?

These are six things that you can find in a city street. Complete the table by writing the British or American words.

British	*American*
letter-box	
	sidewalk
crossroads	
	traffic circle
	trash can
pedestrian crossing	

2 Look at the pictures and complete the sentences using words from the box.

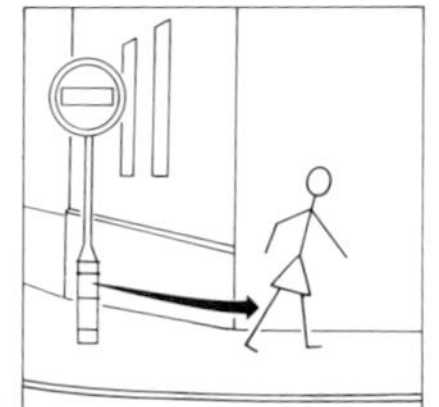

a

b

c

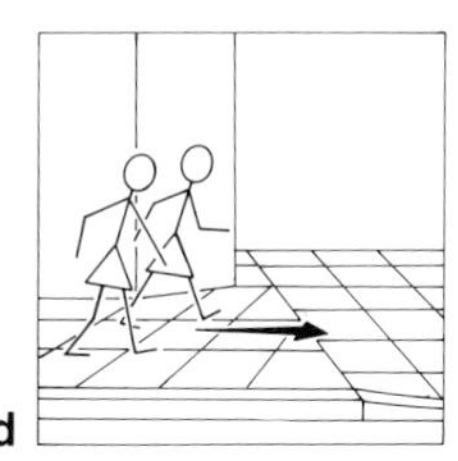

d

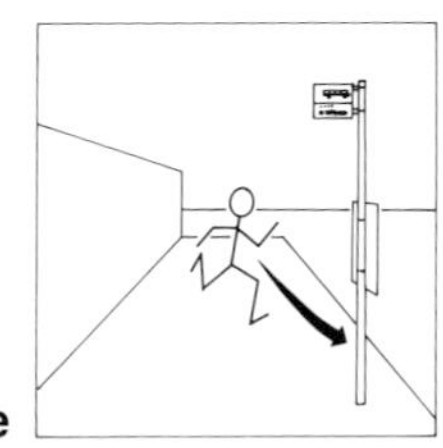

e

bus stop	building	pavement	across	away from
into	road sign	towards	along	road

a She is walking ________________
the ________________ .

b He is going ________________ the
________________ .

c She is going ________________ the
________________ .

d They are walking ________________
the ________________ .

e He is running ________________
the ________________ .

Exercises page 135

Travelling Pages 63-68

1 Label these pictures.

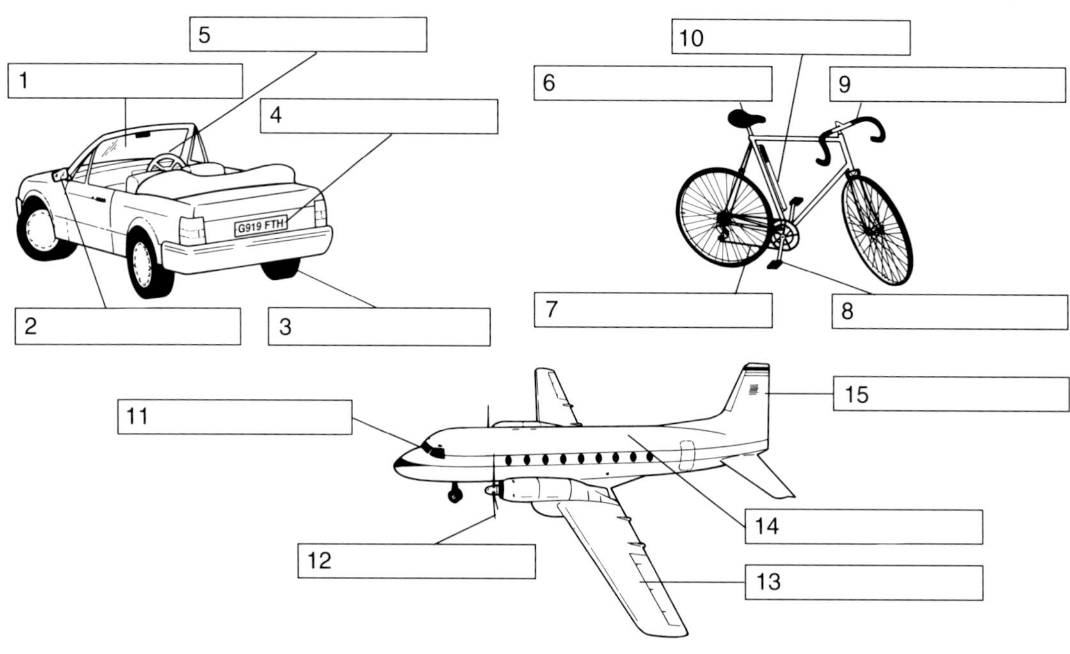

2 Airport crossword

Across

1 ____ pass

5

6 ____ desk
(where you go to collect your *1 across*)

7

8 departure ____

10 You sit on this.

Down

2 ____ ticket

3 The part of the plane where the passengers are.

4 You can find an X-ray scanner here.

9 'Your flight is now boarding at ____ six.'

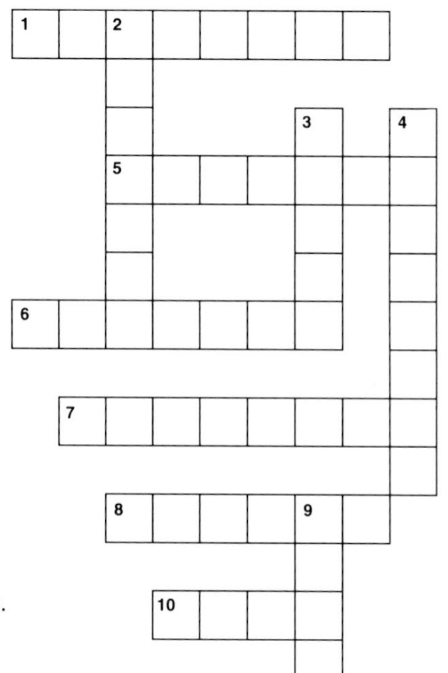

On Holiday Pages 71-73

Read the hotel information, look at the pictures, and fill in the missing words.

Sunnyview Hotel - information

Please leave your [1] ____ ____ at the hotel reception when you go out.

Thank you.

Activities

Dalton Lake is only half a mile from the hotel. There you can go [2] _ _ _ _ _ _ _ _ _ or [3] _ _ _ _ _ _ _ _ _.

Northend-by-the-sea is a pretty holiday resort. Go [4] _ _ _ _ _ _ _ along the cliffs or just sit on the [5] _ _ _ _ _ _ and enjoy the sun!

If you want to do something really exciting, why not try [6] _ _ _ _ _ _ _ _ _ _ _ _ _ or even [7] _ _ _ _ - _ _ _ _ _ _ _ _ _ _?

SIGHTSEEING

Monday: Visit to Longleat, a historic [8] _ _ _ _ _ _ _ _ _ _ _ _ _ _ in Wiltshire.

Wednesday: A tour of the local countryside. A [9] _ _ _ _ _ _ _ _ _ is provided.

Friday: Coach trip to a beautiful [10] _ _ _ _ _ _ _ _ _ _ _ _.

Bring your camera!

1

2

3

4

5

6

7

8

9

10

Exercises page 137

Music and Theatre Pages 75-76

1 **Write the names of these instruments. The words are in the box, but the letters of each word have been mixed up.**

a

b
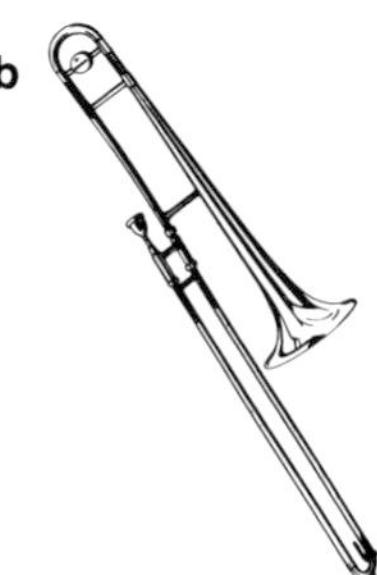

c
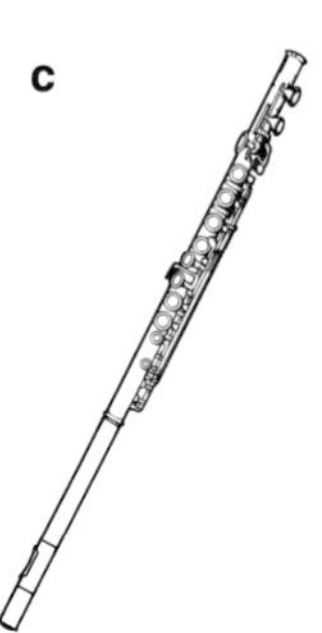

d
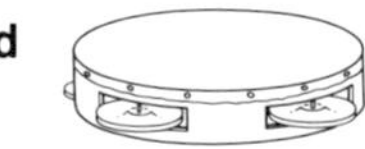

e

f

tufel	olcel
phosanoex	bornmote
beamotunir	slycbam

2 **What's the word?**

a You walk along this to get to your seat in a cinema or a theatre.

— — — — —

b He or she helps you to find your seat.

— — — — —

c Somebody who plays a large percussion instrument.

— — — — — — — —

d Where the orchestra sits.

— — —

e The American word for a 'balcony' in a cinema or a theatre.

— — — — — — — — — —

f Actors and actresses wait here before they go on stage.

— — — — —

g A word that means 'singer'.

— — — — — — — — —

h Things on the stage of a theatre that make it look like a real place.

— — — — — — — —

Now take the first letter of each of the words you found for **a**, **b** and **c**, the second letter of **d** and **e** and the third letter of **f**, **g** and **h**. You will then have the word for a group of people who are watching a film or a play!

____

Sports Pages 77-81

1 **Fill in the table using words from the box.**
Use each word only once.

Sport	Person	Place	Equipment
		court	
	caddy		
cricket			
		track	
			starting-gate

racket athlete jockey club horse-racing stumps starting-block golf field racecourse batsman tennis athletics umpire fairway

2 **Sports Quiz**

a Name three sports in which players **tackle** each other.

____

b What is the other name for **ping-pong**?

____

c Name three objects that you need for playing baseball.

____

d In which sport do players use **sticks**?

____

e Name a sport that takes place under water.

____

f Name three sports that need a **net**.

____

Exercises page 139

Verbs Pages 83-86

---

1 What shall I do now?

Bob never knows what to do. Give him some advice by writing the correct numbers by the letters.

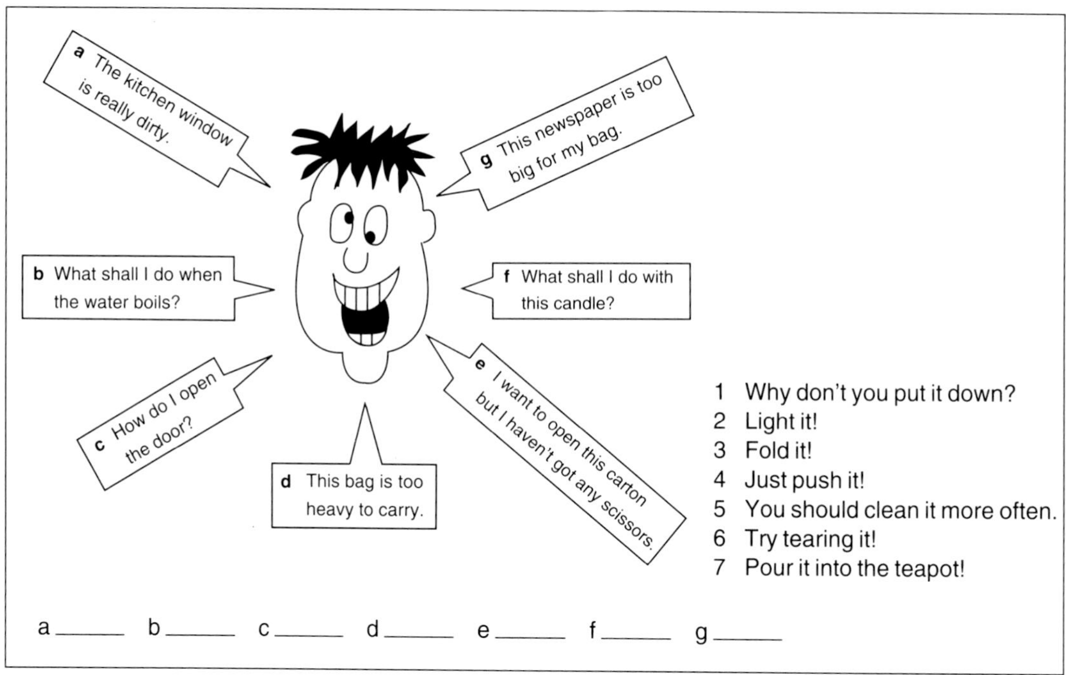

a The kitchen window is really dirty.
b What shall I do when the water boils?
c How do I open the door?
d This bag is too heavy to carry.
e I want to open this carton but I haven't got any scissors.
f What shall I do with this candle?
g This newspaper is too big for my bag.

1 Why don't you put it down?
2 Light it!
3 Fold it!
4 Just push it!
5 You should clean it more often.
6 Try tearing it!
7 Pour it into the teapot!

a _____ b _____ c _____ d _____ e _____ f _____ g _____

---

2 Match these verbs to the right thing or person.

You can...

cook	a friend
brush	a glass
dig	the drive
hug	your hair
shake	dinner
sweep	hands
fill	the soil